Codes of Ethics
for the Helping Professions

Fifth Edition

Prepared by

Gerald Corey
California State University, Fullerton

Marianne Schneider Corey
Private Practice

D1472569

CENGAGE
Learning·

Australia • Brazil • Mexico • Singapore • United Kingdom • United States

CENGAGE
Learning®

Codes of Ethics for the Helping Professions, **Fifth Edition**

Gerald Corey, Marianne Schneider Corey

Product Director: Jon-David Hague

Product Manager: Julie Martinez

Associate Content Developer: Amelia Blevins

Product Assistant: Kyra Kane

Associate Marketing Manager: Shanna Shelton

Content Project Manager: Ruth Sakata Corley

Art Director and Cover Designer: Caryl Gorska

Manufacturing Planner: Judy Inouye

Rights Acquisitions Specialist: Tom McDonough

Production and Composition: Cenveo® Publisher Services

Text Researcher: PreMediaGlobal

Copy Editor: Kay Mikel

Cover Image: Level1studio

For product information and technology assistance, contact us at **Cengage Learning Customer & Sales Support, 1-800-354-9706**. For permission to use material from this text or product, submit all requests online at **www.cengage.com/permissions**. Further permissions questions can be e-mailed to **permissionrequest@cengage.com**.

Library of Congress Control Number: 2013952152

ISBN 13: 978-1-285-77767-2
ISBN 10: 1-285-77767-0

Cengage Learning
200 First Stamford Place, 4th Floor
Stamford, CT 06902
USA

Cengage Learning is a leading provider of customized learning solutions with office locations around the globe, including Singapore, the United Kingdom, Australia, Mexico, Brazil, and Japan. Locate your local office at **www.cengage.com/global**.

Cengage Learning products are represented in Canada by Nelson Education, Ltd.

To learn more about Cengage Learning Solutions, visit **www.cengage.com**.
Purchase any of our products at your local college store or at our preferred online store **www.cengagebrain.com**.

Printed in the United States of America
1 2 3 4 5 6 7 17 16 15 14 13

Contents

National Board for Certified Counselors (NBCC)
Code of Ethics

Preamble

The National Board for Certified Counselors (NBCC) provides national certifications that recognize individuals who have voluntarily met standards for general and specialty areas of counseling practice. Counselors certified by NBCC may also identify with different professional associations and are often licensed by jurisdictions that promulgate standards of behavior. Regardless of any other affiliation, this Code of Ethics is applicable to all NBCC applicants and National Certified Counselors (NCCs).

This Code establishes the minimum ethical behaviors and provides an expectation of and assurance for the ethical practice for all who use the professional services of NCCs. Furthermore, it provides an enforceable set of directives and assures a resource for those served in the case of a perceived violation.

NCCs are required to adhere to all of the directives.

Sanctions of applicants and credential holders under this Code are issued by NBCC only if the provisions of the NBCC Code of Ethics are found to have been violated.

Directives

NCCs take appropriate action to prevent harm.

1. NCCs, recognizing the potential for harm, shall not share information that is obtained through the counseling process without specific written consent by the client or legal guardian except to prevent clear, imminent danger to the client or others or when required to do so by a court order.
2. NCCs shall respect client's privacy and shall solicit only information that contributes to the identified counseling goals.
3. NCCs generally shall not accept goods or services from clients in return for counseling services in recognition of the possible negative effects, including perceived exploitation. NCCs may accept goods, services or other nonmonetary compensation from clients only in cases where no referrals are possible or appropriate and if the arrangement is discussed with the client in advance, is an exchange of a reasonable equivalent value, does not place the counselor in an unfair advantage, is not harmful to the client or their treatment and is documented in the counseling services agreement.
4. NCCs shall not accept gifts from clients except in cases when it is culturally appropriate or therapeutically relevant because of the potential confusion that may arise. NCCs shall consider the value of the gift and the effect on the therapeutic relationship when contemplating acceptance. This consideration shall be documented in the client's record.

5. NCCs shall not engage in harmful multiple relationships with clients. In the event that a harmful multiple relationship develops in an unforeseen manner, the NCC shall discuss the potential effects with the client and shall take reasonable steps to resolve the situation, including the provision of referrals. This discussion shall be documented in the client's record.

6. NCCs shall discuss important considerations to avoid exploitation before entering into a non-counseling relationship with a former client. Important considerations to be discussed include amount of time since counseling service termination, duration of counseling, nature and circumstances of client's counseling, the likelihood that the client will want to resume counseling at some time in the future; circumstances of service termination and possible negative effects or outcomes.

7. NCCs shall not engage in any form of sexual or romantic intimacy with clients or with former clients for two years from the date of counseling service termination.

8. NCCs shall not engage in sexual harassment, which is defined as a single act or multiple occurrences of verbal, nonverbal or physical actions that are known to be unwelcome or that are of the severity to be perceived as harassment by a reasonable person.

9. NCCs shall take proactive measures to avoid interruptions of counseling services due to illness, vacations or unforeseen circumstances. To prevent the harm that may occur if clients are unable to access professional assistance, such measures shall identify other professionals with whom the NCC has a working agreement or local emergency service agencies that can respond to clients in a mental health crisis.

10. NCCs shall create written procedures regarding the handling of client records in the event of their unexpected death or incapacitation. In recognition of the harm that may occur if clients are unable to access professional assistance in these cases, these procedures shall ensure that the confidentiality of client records is maintained and shall include the identification of individual(s) who are familiar with ethical and legal requirements regarding the counseling profession and who shall assist clients in locating other professional mental health providers as well as ensure the appropriate transfer of client records. These written procedures shall be provided to the client, and the NCC shall provide an opportunity for the client to discuss concerns regarding the process as it pertains to the transfer of his or her record.

11. NCCs who act as counselor educators, field placement or clinical supervisors shall not engage in sexual or romantic intimacy with current students or supervisees. They shall not engage in any form of sexual or romantic intimacy with former students or supervisees for two years from the date of last supervision contact.

12. NCCs who provide clinical supervision services shall keep accurate records of supervision goals and progress and consider all information gained in supervision as confidential except to prevent clear, imminent danger to the client or others or when legally required to do so by a court or government agency order. In cases in which the supervisor receives a court or governmental agency order requiring the production of supervision records, the NCC shall make reasonable attempts to promptly notify the supervisee. In cases in which the supervisee is a student of a counselor education program, the supervisor shall release supervision records consistent with the terms of the arrangement with the counselor education program.

13. NCCs who provide clinical supervision services shall intervene in situations where supervisees are impaired or incompetent and thus place client(s) at risk.
14. NCCs who provide clinical supervision services shall not have multiple relationships with supervisees that may interfere with supervisors' professional judgment or exploit supervisees. Supervisors shall not supervise relatives.
15. NCCs who seek consultation (i.e., consultees) shall protect client's confidentiality and unnecessary invasion of privacy by providing only the information relevant to the consultation and in a manner that protects the client's identity.
16. NCCs shall not release the results of tests and assessments to individuals other than the client without prior written consent except as required to prevent clear, imminent danger to the client or others; by written agreement with the client; or when legally required to do so by a court order or governmental agency.
17. NCCs shall protect the welfare of research participants by taking reasonable precautions to prevent negative psychological or physical effects.
18. NCCs shall protect the identities of research participants by appropriately disguising data except when there is a detailed written authorization.
19. NCCs shall recognize the potential harm of informal uses of social media and other related technology with clients, former clients and their families and personal friends. After carefully considering all of the ethical implications, including confidentiality, privacy and multiple relationships, NCCs shall develop written practice procedures in regard to social media and digital technology, and these shall be incorporated with the information provided to clients before or during the initial session. At a minimum, these social media procedures shall specify that personal accounts will be separate and isolated from any used for professional counseling purposes including those used with prospective or current clients. These procedures shall also address "friending" and responding to material posted.
20. NCCs shall not use social media sources (e.g., updates, tweets, blogs, etc.) to provide confidential information regarding client cases that have not been consented to by the client. To facilitate the secure provision of information, NCCs shall inform clients prior to or during the initial session about appropriate ways to communicate with them. Furthermore, NCCs shall advise clients about the potential risks of sending messages through digital technology and social media sources.
21. NCCs who use digital technology (e.g., social media) for professional purposes shall limit information posted to that which does not create multiple relationships or which may threaten client confidentiality.

NCCs provide only those services for which they have education and qualified experience.

22. NCCs shall perform only those professional services for which they are qualified by education and supervised experience.
23. NCCs shall seek professional assistance or withdraw from the practice of counseling if their mental or physical condition makes it unlikely that the counselor will be able to provide appropriate services.
24. NCCs shall seek supervision and consultation with other qualified professionals when unsure about client treatment or professional practice responsibilities.
25. NCCs shall use or interpret only the specific tests and assessments for which they have the required education and supervised experience.

26. NCCs shall demonstrate multicultural competence and shall not use techniques that discriminate against or show hostility towards individuals or groups based on gender, ethnicity, race, national origin, sexual orientation, disability, religion or any other legally prohibited basis. Techniques shall be based on established theory. NCCs shall discuss appropriate considerations and obtain written consent from the client(s) prior to the use of any experimental approach.

NCCs promote the welfare of clients, students, supervisees or the recipients of professional services provided.

27. NCCs shall discuss with prospective clients the appropriateness of counseling services offered and shall not offer services if there is reasonable cause to believe clients will not benefit.
28. NCCs who provide supervision services shall present supervisees with feedback according to a schedule with identified evaluation dates as well as on appropriate occasions throughout the process.
29. NCCs shall promote the welfare of supervisees by discussing ethical practices relating to supervision as well as the legal standards that regulate the practice of counseling.
30. NCCs who provide supervision services shall establish with their supervisees procedures for responding to crisis situations or expressing concerns regarding the supervision process. This information shall be provided in verbal and written formats.
31. NCCs who seek consultation (i.e., consultees) shall promote welfare by selecting appropriate professionals who can specifically respond to the identified issue with the client, supervisee or student.
32. NCCs who provide consultative services (i.e., consultants) shall establish a written plan with the professional seeking assistance. This plan shall include the identification of the primary client concern or issue, consultation goals, potential consequences of actions, evaluation and other future steps. The consultant shall document this information in their professional records. Brief collaborative conversations between an NCC and other professionals are not considered consultations as long as no identifying client information is provided.
33. NCCs shall limit the use of tests and assessments to those that are current, specifically necessary for the provision of quality services, and that have been carefully considered in terms of the instrument's validity, reliability, psychometric limitations and appropriateness for use in a given situation or with a particular client.
34. NCCs shall protect the confidentiality and security of tests or assessments, reports, data and any transmission of information in any form.
35. NCCs shall recognize results that are outside the norms for a given test and assessment, and shall document in the client's record how those results will be appropriately used in the counseling process.
36. NCCs who develop tests or assessments for measuring personal characteristics, development, diagnoses, goal attainment or other similar clinical uses shall provide test users with written information regarding the benefits and limitations of test instruments, including appropriate use, test results and interpretation.

37. NCCs who develop tests and assessments for measuring personal characteristics, development, diagnoses, goal attainment or other similar clinical uses shall identify other potential sources of appropriate information and shall emphasize to test users the importance of basing decisions on multiple sources rather than a single criterion.

NCCs communicate truthfully.

38. NCCs shall accurately represent their current qualifications and credentials in counseling or closely related disciplines. NCCs shall not use doctorate degrees with relation to professional counseling duties unless they are specific to counseling or mental health disciplines.
39. NCCs shall identify only earned degrees in counseling or closely related disciplines when it comes to all counseling work including publications. Listed degrees from programs in the United States must be from colleges and universities that were accredited at the time of graduation by one of the regional accrediting organizations recognized by the Council for Higher Education Accreditation (CHEA).
40. NCCs who have been awarded honorary degrees shall clearly distinguish these from earned degrees.
41. NCCs shall correct known misrepresentations of their qualifications and credentials by others and shall not allow such information to be used in a misleading way.
42. NCCs shall take credit only for work that they have performed, and when quoting the work of others, shall provide appropriate references.
43. NCCs shall provide accurate reports which are based on direct experiences with individual(s) or documentation from other professionals when providing opinions. NCCs shall limit opinions to areas within their expertise.
44. NCCs shall accurately note in the client's or supervisee's records all information necessary for the provision of quality services or as required by laws, regulations or institutional procedures.
45. NCCs who provide supervision services shall present accurate written information to supervisees regarding the NCC's credentials as well as information regarding the process of supervision. This information shall include any conditions of supervision, supervision goals, case management procedures, confidentiality and its limitations, appraisal methods and timing of evaluations.
46. NCCs who provide consultative services (i.e., consultants) shall use accurate information regarding their qualifications in relation to the identified concerns or situations.
47. NCCs who seek case consultation services from another professional shall document consultation in clients' records.
48. NCCs shall accurately report test and assessment results and limit conclusions to those based on evidence, taking into consideration any influences that may affect results such as health, motivation and multicultural factors. NCCs shall generally avoid making decisions based on a single test or assessment result.
49. NCCs shall note in the results and interpretation when tests and assessments are not administered under standard conditions or when unusual behavior or irregularities occur during the testing session.

50. NCCs shall not misrepresent a test or the results and shall provide accurate information in the event that he or she becomes aware of any false statements.
51. NCCs shall report to participants the subject and features of the study after research data is collected, as well as clarify any misconceptions about the research.
52. NCCs shall accurately report results of research, including limitations and variables that may have impacted the outcomes.
53. NCCs shall take reasonable steps to publicly correct errors in their published research if any are discovered.
54. NCCs shall include all electronic communications exchanged with clients and supervisees, including those through digital technology and social media methods, as a part of the record, even when strictly related to clerical issues such as change of contact information or scheduling appointments. All electronic therapeutic communication methods shall use encryption and password security.

NCCs recognize that their behavior reflects on the integrity of the profession as a whole, and thus, they avoid actions which can reasonably be expected to damage trust.

55. NCCs shall retain client records for a minimum of five years unless state or federal laws require additional time. After the required retention period, NCCs shall dispose of records in a manner that protects client confidentiality.
56. NCCs shall act in a professional manner by protecting against unauthorized access to confidential information. This includes data contained in electronic formats. NCCs shall inform any subordinates who have physical or electronic access to information of the importance of maintaining privacy and confidentiality.
57. NCCs shall make all reasonable efforts to inform clients and former clients prior to the court-ordered release of confidential client information. In the event that the client seeks to prevent the release, the NCC shall request that a court withdraw any order to release confidential information due to the potential harm to the client or the counseling relationship. When ordered to disclose confidential client information by a court or governmental agency, NCCs shall release only the required information. Any release of information shall be appropriately documented in accordance with the practice setting.
58. NCCs shall not provide forensic evaluation services concerning current or past clients or client's family members. Also, NCCs shall not provide forensic evaluation services regarding their own family members, friends or professional associates.
59. NCCs who are retiring or departing from an established practice with other mental health professionals shall notify current and former clients as appropriate regarding their pending departure from the practice. Such notifications should include information about record availability and access, and contact information of appropriate referrals within the established practice.
60. NCCs who practice in multiple settings (e.g., agencies and private practice settings) shall not increase their private practices by referring clients from the setting of contact unless by specific prior arrangement with authorized individuals in the agency or group setting. In such situations, clients shall be instructed of their right to request to be referred to another professional in the original setting of contact.

61. NCCs shall not misuse their professional influence or meet their own needs at the expense of clients or their welfare. This shall include the promotion of products developed by the NCC.
62. NCCs shall not solicit testimonials from current clients or their families and close friends. Recognizing the possibility of future requests for services, NCCs shall not solicit testimonials from former clients within two years from the date of service termination.
63. NCCs shall not provide references if they have reasonable belief that the individual counselor is not qualified, is not able to provide competent professional services or presents a risk of harm to others.
64. NCCs who provide supervision services to supervisees who have more than one supervisor (e.g., field placement and university) shall exchange contact information and communicate regularly about the shared supervisee's performance.
65. NCCs who develop tests or assessments for measuring personal characteristics, development, diagnoses, goal attainment or other similar clinical uses shall provide written evidence that technical features (e.g., reliability, validity) are consistent with the identified purposes.
66. NCCs shall limit use of information obtained through digital technology and social media sources (e.g., Facebook, LinkedIn, Twitter, etc.) in accordance with established practice procedures provided to clients at the initiation of services.

NCCs recognize the importance of and encourage active participation of clients, students or supervisees.

67. NCCs conducting counseling with more than one client at a time (e.g., group or family counseling) shall discuss with clients the nature, the rights and responsibilities as well as the possible additional limitations of confidentiality. NCCs shall also describe the steps that they will take in the event that having multiple clients in session creates issues between or concerning clients.
68. NCCs who learn that a client is receiving additional mental health services from other professionals shall discuss with the client the importance of developing clear agreements to avoid client confusion and conflict. Following this discussion, NCCs shall request the client's written consent to inform the other professional(s) of the counseling relationship and to collaborate on the provision of mental health services. This discussion and the client's response to the request shall be documented in the client's record.
69. NCCs shall inform clients of the purposes, goals, procedures, limitations, potential risks and benefits of services and techniques either prior to or during the initial session. NCCs also shall provide information about client's rights and responsibilities including billing arrangements, collection procedures in the event of nonpayment, confidentiality and its limitations, records and service termination policies as appropriate to the counseling setting. This professional information shall be provided to the client in verbal and written forms (i.e., the counseling services agreement). NCCs shall have a reasonable basis for believing that the information provided is understood. NCCs shall document any client concerns related to the information provided in the client's record.

70. NCCs shall respond to client requests for access to or copies of records within a practical timeframe. Additionally, NCCs shall provide an opportunity for the client to discuss the content of the record. If there is a reasonable basis to believe that providing such access will cause harm, the NCC shall discuss the request and possible effects; however, the information ultimately belongs to the client, and thus must be released. Records requests and any discussion regarding the provision shall be documented in the client's record.

71. NCCs who become aware of another mental health professional's unethical behavior shall first attempt to resolve issues through reasonable means except when state regulations require immediate reporting. In the event that it cannot be resolved, the NCC shall report the matter to all appropriate professional regulatory organizations and agencies.

72. NCCs shall obtain a client's consent prior to the provision of services. In private practice or other similar situations, this consent shall be documented in writing in a counseling services agreement. This counseling services agreement shall become a part of the client's record.

73. NCCs shall work collaboratively with clients in the creation of written plans of treatment that offer attainable goals and use appropriate techniques consistent with client's psychological and physical needs and abilities.

74. NCCs shall update the client's record throughout the counseling relationship when changes occur in the treatment plan, including those relating to goals, roles and techniques. The NCC shall obtain the client's written approval on such updates.

75. NCCs shall clearly designate in writing the primary client in the record. NCCs shall also identify in the record individuals who are receiving related professional services in connection with such client relationship. In the event of working with minors or individuals who are unable to give informed consent, NCCs shall discuss relevant considerations regarding the preferences of the individuals receiving services and legal guardian's rights and obligations. This information shall become a part of the client's record.

76. NCCs shall discuss service termination with clients when there is a reasonable belief that the clients are no longer benefiting from or are unlikely to benefit from future services. NCCs shall not abruptly terminate counseling services without good cause or significant justification, and in such cases, shall provide appropriate referrals.

77. NCCs shall provide referrals if the client cannot afford services, at the client's request or as appropriate at the conclusion of a professional counseling service relationship.

78. NCCs who act as university, field placement or clinical supervisors shall ensure that supervisees provide accurate information to clients about the supervisee's professional status (i.e., intern, licensed, etc.)

79. NCCs shall provide complete information regarding the format (electronic or otherwise), administration purpose, and the desired outcome, risks and limitations prior to the use of a test or assessment. NCCs shall have a reasonable basis for believing that the information provided is understood.

80. NCCs shall seek information, such as limitations, regarding a client which may affect the administration or interpretation of results prior to use of a test or assessment. If appropriate, the NCC may provide a referral to another

professional who specializes in the evaluation of individuals with similar conditions. This discussion shall be documented in the client's record.

81. NCCs shall provide critical information to potential research subjects that will assist them in reaching a determination about participation. This information shall include the research's purpose, process, duration, potential consequences, and procedures as well as the participant's right to refuse or withdraw participation.

82. NCCs shall obtain prior consent from all research participants. This consent process shall contain relevant information with regard to the recording of voices or images of participants. In the event of conducting research with individuals who are unable to give informed consent, NCCs shall document considerations between the potential subject's desire to participate and the legal guardian's consent.

83. NCCs shall not employ deceptive techniques in research unless there are no alternatives and there is significant prospective scientific, educational or clinical value. In all cases, NCCs shall review potential techniques and shall not use any that can be reasonably expected to cause harm, as well as provide an explanation to participants during the debriefing.

84. NCCs shall carefully consider ethical implications, including confidentiality and multiple relationships, prior to conducting research with students, supervisees or clients. NCCs shall not convey that participation is required or will otherwise negatively affect academic standing, supervision or counseling services.

NCCs are accountable in their actions and adhere to recognized professional standards and practices.

85. NCCs shall comply with all NBCC policies, procedures and agreements, including all disclosure requirements.

86. NCCs shall adhere to legal standards and state board regulations.

87. NCCs shall not engage in unlawful discrimination.

88. NCCs who make statements in a public manner shall state that their opinions represent their personal views and not another organization unless officially authorized to do otherwise.

89. NCCs providing public presentations by any means, shall ensure that statements are consistent with this Code of Ethics.

90. NCCs who act as university, field placement or clinical supervisors shall require that supervisees provide the supervising NCC's name, credentials and contact information to the supervisee's clients.

91. NCCs shall follow administration and interpretation protocols for tests and assessments, including the use of appropriate software if using electronic measures.

92. NCCs shall comply with identified security protocols when using published tests and assessments.

93. NCCs shall comply with intellectual property laws and other accepted publication guidelines.

94. NCCs shall comply with applicable guidelines when designing, conducting or reporting research, including those of an institutional review board.

95. NCCs shall credit the work of others who have contributed to research or publication either through joint authorship, acknowledgment or other appropriate means.

Code of Professional Ethics
For Rehabilitation Counselors

Adopted in June 2009 by the Commission on Rehabilitation Counselor Certification for its Certified Rehabilitation Counselors. This Code is effective as of January 1, 2010. Developed and Administered by the Commission on Rehabilitation Counselor Certification (CRCC®)

TABLE OF CONTENTS

Preamble

Rehabilitation counselors provide services within the Scope of Practice for Rehabilitation Counseling. They demonstrate beliefs, attitudes, knowledge, and skills, to provide competent counseling services and to work collaboratively with diverse groups of individuals, including clients, as well as with programs, institutions, employers, and service delivery systems and provide both direct (e.g., counseling) and indirect (e.g., case review, feasibility evaluation) services. Regardless of the specific tasks, work settings, or technology used, rehabilitation counselors demonstrate adherence to ethical standards and ensure the standards are vigorously enforced. The Code of Professional Ethics for Rehabilitation Counselors, henceforth referred to as the Code, is designed to provide guidance for the ethical practice of rehabilitation counselors.

The primary obligation of rehabilitation counselors is to clients, defined as individuals with or directly affected by a disability, functional limitation(s), or medical condition and who receive services from rehabilitation counselors. In some settings, clients may be referred to by other terms such as, but not limited to, consumers and service recipients. Rehabilitation counseling services may be provided to individuals other than those with disabilities. Rehabilitation counselors do not have clients in a forensic setting. The subjects of the objective and unbiased evaluations are evaluees. In all instances, the primary obligation remains to clients or evaluees and adherence to the Code is required.

The basic objectives of the Code are to: (1) promote public welfare by specifying ethical behavior expected of rehabilitation counselors; (2) establish principles that define ethical behavior and best practices of rehabilitation counselors; (3) serve as an ethical guide designed to assist rehabilitation counselors in constructing a professional course of action that best serves those utilizing rehabilitation services; and, (4) serve as the basis for the processing of alleged Code violations by certified rehabilitation counselors.

Rehabilitation counselors are committed to facilitating the personal, social, and economic independence of individuals with disabilities. In fulfilling this commitment, rehabilitation counselors recognize diversity and embrace a cultural approach in support of the worth, dignity, potential, and uniqueness of individuals with disabilities within their social and cultural context. They look to professional values as an important way of living out an ethical commitment. The primary values that serve as a foundation for this Code include a commitment to:

- Respecting human rights and dignity;
- Ensuring the integrity of all professional relationships;
- Acting to alleviate personal distress and suffering;
- Enhancing the quality of professional knowledge and its application to increase professional and personal effectiveness;
- Appreciating the diversity of human experience and culture; and,
- Advocating for the fair and adequate provision of services.

These values inform principles. They represent one important way of expressing a general ethical commitment that becomes more precisely defined and action-oriented when expressed as a principle. The fundamental spirit of caring and respect with which the Code is written is based upon six principles of ethical behavior:

Autonomy: To respect the rights of clients to be self-governing within their social and cultural framework.
Beneficence: To do good to others; to promote the well-being of clients.
Fidelity: To be faithful; to keep promises and honor the trust placed in rehabilitation counselors.
Justice: To be fair in the treatment of all clients; to provide appropriate services to all.
Nonmaleficence: To do no harm to others.
Veracity: To be honest.

Although the Code provides guidance for ethical practice, it is impossible to address every possible ethical dilemma that rehabilitation counselors may face. When faced with ethical dilemmas that are difficult to resolve, rehabilitation counselors are expected to engage in a carefully considered ethical decision-making process. Reasonable differences of opinion can and do exist among rehabilitation counselors with respect to the ways in which values, ethical principles, and ethical standards would be applied when they conflict. While there is no specific ethical decision-making model that is most effective, rehabilitation counselors are expected to be familiar with and apply a credible model of decision-making that can bear public scrutiny. Rehabilitation counselors are aware that seeking consultation and/or supervision is an important part of ethical decision-making.

The Enforceable Standards within the Code are the exacting standards intended to provide guidance in specific circumstances and serve as the basis for processing complaints initiated against certified rehabilitation counselors.

Each Enforceable Standard is not meant to be interpreted in isolation. Instead, it is important for rehabilitation counselors to interpret standards in conjunction with other related standards in various sections of the Code. A brief glossary is located after Section L to provide readers with a concise description of some of the terms used in the Code.

Enforceable Standards of Ethical Practice

Section A: The Counseling Relationship

A.1. Welfare of Those Served by Rehabilitation Counselors

a. PRIMARY RESPONSIBILITY
The primary responsibility of rehabilitation counselors is to respect the dignity and to promote the welfare of clients. Clients are defined as individuals with, or directly affected by a disability, functional limitation(s), or medical condition and who receive services from rehabilitation counselors. At times, rehabilitation counseling services may be provided to individuals other than those with a disability. In all instances, the primary obligation of rehabilitation counselors is to promote the welfare of their clients.

b. REHABILITATION AND COUNSELING PLANS
Rehabilitation counselors and clients work jointly in devising and revising integrated, individual, and mutually agreed upon rehabilitation and counseling plans that offer a reasonable promise of success and are consistent with the abilities and circumstances of clients. Rehabilitation counselors and clients regularly review rehabilitation and counseling plans to assess continued viability and effectiveness.

c. EMPLOYMENT NEEDS
Rehabilitation counselors work with clients to consider employment consistent with the overall abilities, functional capabilities and limitations, general temperament, interest and aptitude patterns, social skills, education, general qualifications, transferable skills, and other relevant characteristics and needs of clients. Rehabilitation counselors assist in the placement of clients in available positions that are consistent with the interest, culture, and the welfare of clients and/or employers.

d. AUTONOMY
Rehabilitation counselors respect the rights of clients to make decisions on their own behalf. On decisions that may limit or diminish the autonomy of clients, decision-making on behalf of clients is taken only after careful deliberation. Rehabilitation counselors advocate for the resumption of responsibility by clients as quickly as possible.

A.2. Respecting Diversity

a. RESPECTING CULTURE
Rehabilitation counselors demonstrate respect for the cultural background of clients in developing and implementing rehabilitation and treatment plans, and providing and adapting interventions.

b. NONDISCRIMINATION
Rehabilitation counselors do not condone or engage in discrimination based on age, color, race, national origin, culture, disability, ethnicity, gender, gender identity,

15

religion/spirituality, sexual orientation, marital status/partnership, language preference, socioeconomic status, or any basis proscribed by law.

A.3. Client Rights in the Counseling Relationship

a. PROFESSIONAL DISCLOSURE STATEMENT
Rehabilitation counselors have an obligation to review with clients orally, in writing,
and in a manner that best accommodates any of their limitation, the rights and
responsibilities of both rehabilitation counselors and clients. Disclosure at the outset
of the counseling relationship should minimally include: (1) the qualifications, credentials, and relevant experience of the rehabilitation counselor; (2) purposes, goals, techniques, limitations, and the nature of potential risks, and benefits of services; (3)
frequency and length of services; (4) confidentiality and limitations regarding confidentiality (including how a supervisor and/or treatment team professional is involved);
(5) contingencies for continuation of services upon the incapacitation or death of the
rehabilitation counselor; (6) fees and billing arrangements; (7) record preservation and
release policies; (8) risks associated with electronic communication; and, (9) legal
issues affecting services. Rehabilitation counselors recognize that disclosure of these
issues may need to be reiterated or expanded upon throughout the counseling relationship, and/or disclosure related to other matters may be required depending on the nature of services provided and matters that arise during the rehabilitation counseling
relationship.

b. INFORMED CONSENT
Rehabilitation counselors recognize that clients have the freedom to choose whether
to enter into or remain in a rehabilitation counseling relationship. Rehabilitation
counselors respect the rights of clients to participate in ongoing rehabilitation counseling planning and to make decisions to refuse any services or modality changes,
while also ensuring that clients are advised of the consequences of such refusal. Rehabilitation counselors recognize that clients need information to make an informed decision regarding services and that professional disclosure is required for informed
consent to be an ongoing part of the rehabilitation counseling process. Rehabilitation
counselors appropriately document discussions of disclosure and informed consent
throughout the rehabilitation counseling relationship.

c. DEVELOPMENTAL AND CULTURAL SENSITIVITY
Rehabilitation counselors communicate information in ways that are both developmentally and culturally appropriate. Rehabilitation counselors provide services (e.g.,
arranging for a qualified interpreter or translator) when necessary to ensure comprehension by clients. In collaboration with clients, rehabilitation counselors consider
cultural implications of informed consent procedures and, when possible, rehabilitation counselors adjust their practices accordingly.

d. INABILITY TO GIVE CONSENT
When counseling minors or persons unable to give voluntary consent, rehabilitation
counselors seek the assent of clients and include clients in decision-making as appropriate. Rehabilitation counselors recognize the need to balance the ethical rights of

clients to make choices, the mental or legal capacity of clients to give consent or assent, and parental, guardian, or familial legal rights and responsibilities to protect clients and make decisions on behalf of clients.

e. SUPPORT NETWORK INVOLVEMENT
Rehabilitation counselors recognize that support by others may be important to clients. Rehabilitation counselors consider enlisting the support, understanding, and involvement of others (e.g., religious/spiritual/community leaders, family members, friends, and guardians) as resources, when appropriate, with consent from clients.

A.4. Avoiding Harm and Avoiding Value Imposition

a. AVOIDING HARM
Rehabilitation counselors act to avoid harming clients, trainees, supervisees, and research participants and to minimize or to remedy unavoidable or unanticipated harm.

b. PERSONAL VALUES
Rehabilitation counselors are aware of their values, attitudes, beliefs, and behaviors and avoid imposing values that are inconsistent with rehabilitation counseling goals.

A.5. Roles and Relationships With Clients

a. PROHIBITION OF SEXUAL OR ROMANTIC RELATIONSHIPS WITH CURRENT CLIENTS
Sexual or romantic rehabilitation counselor–client interactions or relationships with current clients, their romantic partners, or their immediate family members are prohibited.

b. SEXUAL OR ROMANTIC RELATIONSHIPS WITH FORMER CLIENTS
Sexual or romantic rehabilitation counselor–client interactions or relationships with former clients, their romantic partners, or their immediate family members are prohibited for a period of five years following the last professional contact. Even after five years, rehabilitation counselors give careful consideration to the potential for sexual or romantic relationships to cause harm to former clients. In cases of potential exploitation and/or harm, rehabilitation counselors avoid entering such interactions or relationships.

c. PROHIBITION OF SEXUAL OR ROMANTIC RELATIONSHIPS WITH CERTAIN FORMER CLIENTS
If clients have a history of physical, emotional, or sexual abuse or if clients have ever been diagnosed with any form of psychosis or personality disorder, marked cognitive impairment, or if clients are likely to remain in need of therapy due to the intensity or chronicity of a problem, rehabilitation counselors do not engage in sexual activities or sexual contact with former clients, regardless of the length of time elapsed since termination of the client relationship.

d. NONPROFESSIONAL INTERACTIONS OR RELATIONSHIPS OTHER THAN SEXUAL OR ROMANTIC INTERACTIONS OR RELATIONSHIPS

Rehabilitation counselors avoid nonprofessional relationships with clients, former clients, their romantic partners, or their immediate family members, except when such interactions are potentially beneficial to clients or former clients. In cases where nonprofessional interactions may be potentially beneficial to clients or former clients, rehabilitation counselors must document in case records, prior to interactions (when feasible), the rationale for such interactions, the potential benefits, and anticipated consequences for the clients or former clients and other involved parties. Such interactions are initiated with appropriate consent from clients and are time-limited (e.g., extended free-standing friendships are prohibited) or context specific (e.g., constrained to an organizational or community setting). Where unintentional harm occurs to clients or former clients, or to other involved parties, due to nonprofessional interactions, rehabilitation counselors must show evidence of an attempt to remedy such harm. Examples of potentially beneficial interactions include, but are not limited to, attending a formal ceremony (e.g., a wedding/commitment ceremony or graduation); purchasing a service or product provided by clients or former clients (excepting unrestricted bartering); hospital visits to ill family members; or mutual membership in professional associations, organizations, or communities.

e. COUNSELING RELATIONSHIPS WITH FORMER ROMANTIC PARTNERS PROHIBITED

Rehabilitation counselors do not provide counseling services to individuals with whom they have had a prior sexual or romantic relationship.

f. ROLE CHANGES IN THE PROFESSIONAL RELATIONSHIP

When rehabilitation counselors change roles from the original or most recent contracted relationship, they obtain informed consent from clients or evaluees and explain the right to refuse services related to the change. Examples of role changes include: (1) changing from individual to group, relationship or family counseling, or vice versa; (2) changing from a forensic to a primary care role, or vice versa; (3) changing from a non-forensic evaluative role to a rehabilitation or therapeutic role, or vice versa; (4) changing from a rehabilitation counselor to a researcher role (e.g., enlisting clients as research participants), or vice versa; and, (5) changing from a rehabilitation counselor to a mediator role, or vice versa. The clients or evaluees must be fully informed of any anticipated consequences (e.g., financial, legal, personal, or therapeutic) due to a role change by the rehabilitation counselor.

g. RECEIVING GIFTS

Rehabilitation counselors understand the challenges of accepting gifts from clients and recognize that in some cultures, small gifts are a token of respect and gratitude. When determining whether to accept gifts from clients, rehabilitation counselors take into account the cultural or community practice, therapeutic relationship, the monetary value of gifts, the motivation of the client for giving gifts, and the motivation of the rehabilitation counselor for accepting or declining gifts.

A.6. Multiple Clients

When rehabilitation counselors agree to provide counseling services to two or more persons who have a relationship (e.g., husband/wife; parent/child), rehabilitation counselors clarify at the outset which person is, or which persons are, to be served and the nature of the relationship rehabilitation counselors have with each involved person. If it becomes apparent that rehabilitation counselors may be called upon to perform potentially conflicting roles, rehabilitation counselors clarify, adjust, or withdraw from roles appropriately.

A.7. Group Work

a. SCREENING
Rehabilitation counselors screen prospective group counseling/therapy participants. To the extent possible, rehabilitation counselors select members whose needs and goals are compatible with goals of the group, who do not impede the group process, and whose well-being is not jeopardized by the group experience.

b. PROTECTING CLIENTS
In a group setting, rehabilitation counselors take reasonable precautions to protect clients from harm or trauma.

A.8. Termination and Referral

a. ABANDONMENT PROHIBITED
Rehabilitation counselors do not abandon or neglect clients in counseling. Rehabilitation counselors assist in making appropriate arrangements for the continuation of services when necessary (e.g., during interruptions such as vacations, illness, and following termination).

b. INITIAL DETERMINATION OF INABILITY TO ASSIST CLIENTS
If rehabilitation counselors determine they are unable to be of professional assistance to clients, rehabilitation counselors avoid entering such counseling relationships.

c. APPROPRIATE TERMINATION AND REFERRAL
Rehabilitation counselors terminate counseling relationships when it becomes reasonably apparent that clients no longer need assistance, are not likely to benefit, or are being harmed by continued counseling. Rehabilitation counselors may terminate counseling when in jeopardy of harm by clients or other persons with whom clients have a relationship, or when clients do not pay agreed-upon fees. Rehabilitation counselors provide pre-termination counseling and recommend other clinically and culturally appropriate service sources when necessary.

d. APPROPRIATE TRANSFER OF SERVICES
When rehabilitation counselors transfer or refer clients to other practitioners, they ensure that appropriate counseling and administrative processes are completed in a timely manner and that open communication is maintained with both clients and

practitioners. Rehabilitation counselors prepare and disseminate, to identified colleagues or records custodian, a plan for the transfer of clients and files in the case of their incapacitation, death, or termination of practice.

A.9. End-of-Life Care for Terminally Ill Clients

a. QUALITY OF CARE
Rehabilitation counselors take measures that enable clients to: (1) obtain high quality end-of-life care for their physical, emotional, social, and spiritual needs; (2) exercise the highest degree of self-determination possible; (3) be given every opportunity possible to engage in informed decision-making regarding their end-of-life care; and, (4) receive complete and adequate assessment regarding their ability to make competent, rational decisions on their own behalf from mental health professionals who are experienced in end-of-life care practice.

b. REHABILITATION COUNSELOR COMPETENCE, CHOICE, AND REFERRAL
Rehabilitation counselors may choose to work or not work with terminally ill clients who wish to explore their end-of-life options. Rehabilitation counselors provide appropriate referral information if they are not competent to address such concerns.

c. CONFIDENTIALITY
Rehabilitation counselors who provide services to terminally ill individuals who are considering hastening their own deaths have the option of breaking or not breaking confidentiality on this matter, depending on applicable laws and the specific circumstances of the situation and after seeking consultation or supervision from appropriate professional and legal parties.

Section B: Confidentiality, Privileged Communication, and Privacy

B.1. Respecting Client Rights

a. CULTURAL DIVERSITY CONSIDERATIONS
Rehabilitation counselors maintain beliefs, attitudes, knowledge, and skills regarding cultural meanings of confidentiality and privacy. Rehabilitation counselors hold ongoing discussions with clients as to how, when, and with whom information is to be shared.

b. RESPECT FOR PRIVACY
Rehabilitation counselors respect privacy rights of clients. Rehabilitation counselors solicit private information from clients only when it is beneficial to the counseling process.

c. RESPECT FOR CONFIDENTIALITY
Rehabilitation counselors do not share confidential information without consent from clients or without sound legal or ethical justification.

d. EXPLANATION OF LIMITATIONS
At initiation and throughout the counseling process, rehabilitation counselors inform clients of the limitations of confidentiality and seek to identify foreseeable situations in which confidentiality must be breached.

B.2. Exceptions

a. DANGER AND LEGAL REQUIREMENTS
The general requirement that rehabilitation counselors keep information confidential does not apply when disclosure is required to protect clients or identified others from serious and foreseeable harm, or when legal requirements demand that confidential information must be revealed. Rehabilitation counselors consult with other professionals when in doubt as to the validity of an exception.

b. CONTAGIOUS, LIFE-THREATENING DISEASES
When clients disclose that they have a disease commonly known to be both communicable and life-threatening, rehabilitation counselors may be justified in disclosing information to identifiable third parties, if they are known to be at demonstrable and high risk of contracting the disease. Prior to making a disclosure, rehabilitation counselors confirm that there is such a diagnosis and assess the intent of clients to inform the third parties about their disease or to engage in any behaviors that may be harmful to identifiable third parties.

c. COURT-ORDERED DISCLOSURE
When subpoenaed to release confidential or privileged information without permission from clients, rehabilitation counselors obtain written, informed consent from clients or take steps to prohibit the disclosure or have it limited as narrowly as possible due to potential harm to clients or the counseling relationship. Whenever reasonable, rehabilitation counselors obtain a court directive to clarify the nature and extent of the response to a subpoena.

d. MINIMAL DISCLOSURE
When circumstances require the disclosure of confidential information, only essential information is revealed.

B.3. Information Shared With Others

a. WORK ENVIRONMENT
Rehabilitation counselors make every effort to ensure that privacy and confidentiality of clients is maintained by employees, supervisees, students, clerical assistants, and volunteers.

b. PROFESSIONAL COLLABORATION
If rehabilitation of clients involves the sharing of their information among team members, clients are advised of this fact and are informed of the team's existence and composition. Rehabilitation counselors carefully consider implications for clients in extending confidential information if participating in their service teams.

c. CLIENTS SERVED BY OTHERS

When rehabilitation counselors learn that clients have an ongoing professional relationship with another rehabilitation counselor or treating professional, they request release from clients to inform the other professionals and strive to establish a positive and collaborative professional relationship. File review, second-opinion services, and other indirect services are not considered an ongoing professional relationship.

d. CLIENT ASSISTANTS

When clients are accompanied by an individual providing assistance to clients (e.g., interpreter, personal care assistant), rehabilitation counselors ensure that the assistant is apprised of the need to maintain and document confidentiality. At all times, clients retain the right to decide who can be present as client assistants.

e. CONFIDENTIAL SETTINGS

Rehabilitation counselors discuss confidential information only in offices or settings in which they can reasonably ensure the privacy of clients.

f. THIRD-PARTY PAYERS

Rehabilitation counselors disclose information to third-party payers only when clients have authorized such disclosure, unless otherwise required by law or statute.

g. DECEASED CLIENTS

Rehabilitation counselors protect the confidentiality of deceased clients, consistent with legal requirements and agency policies.

B.4. Groups and Families

a. GROUP WORK

In group work, rehabilitation counselors clearly explain the importance and parameters of confidentiality for the specific group being entered.

b. COUPLES AND FAMILY COUNSELING

In couples and family counseling, rehabilitation counselors clearly define who the clients are and discuss expectations and limitations of confidentiality. Rehabilitation counselors seek agreement and document in writing such agreement among all involved parties having capacity to give consent concerning each individual's right to confidentiality. Rehabilitation counselors clearly define whether they share or do not share information with family members that is privately, individually communicated to rehabilitation counselors.

B.5. Responsibility to Minors or Clients Lacking Capacity to Consent

a. RESPONSIBILITY TO CLIENTS

When counseling minor clients or adult clients who lack the capacity to give voluntary, informed consent, rehabilitation counselors protect the confidentiality of information received in the counseling relationship as specified by national or local laws, written policies, and applicable ethical standards.

b. RESPONSIBILITY TO PARENTS AND LEGAL GUARDIANS

Rehabilitation counselors inform parents and legal guardians about the role of rehabilitation counselors and the confidential nature of the counseling relationship. Rehabilitation counselors are sensitive to the cultural diversity of families and respect the inherent rights and responsibilities of parents/guardians over the welfare of their children/charges according to law. Rehabilitation counselors work to establish, as appropriate, collaborative relationships with parents/guardians to best serve clients.

c. RELEASE OF CONFIDENTIAL INFORMATION

When minor clients or adult clients lack the capacity to give voluntary consent to release confidential information, rehabilitation counselors seek permission from parents or legal guardians to disclose information. In such instances, rehabilitation counselors inform clients consistent with their level of understanding and take culturally appropriate measures to safeguard the confidentiality of clients.

B.6. Records

a. REQUIREMENT OF RECORDS

Rehabilitation counselors include sufficient and timely documentation in the records of their clients to facilitate the delivery and continuity of needed services. Rehabilitation counselors take reasonable steps to ensure that documentation in records accurately reflects progress and services provided to clients. If errors are made in records, rehabilitation counselors take steps to properly note the correction of such errors according to agency or institutional policies.

b. CONFIDENTIALITY OF RECORDS

Rehabilitation counselors ensure that records are kept in a secure location and that only authorized persons have access to records.

c. CLIENT ACCESS

Rehabilitation counselors recognize that counseling records are kept for the benefit of clients and therefore provide access to records and copies of records when requested by clients, unless prohibited by law. In instances where the records contain information that may be sensitive, confusing, or detrimental to clients, rehabilitation counselors have a responsibility to educate clients regarding such information. In situations involving multiple clients, access to records is limited to those parts of records that do not include confidential information related to other clients. When rehabilitation counselors are in possession of records from others sources, they refer clients back to the original source.

d. DISCLOSURE OR TRANSFER

Unless exceptions to confidentiality exist, rehabilitation counselors obtain written permission from clients to disclose or transfer records to legitimate third parties. Steps are taken to ensure that recipients of counseling records are sensitive to their confidential nature.

e. STORAGE AND DISPOSAL AFTER TERMINATION
Rehabilitation counselors store the records of their clients following termination of services to ensure reasonable future access, maintain records in accordance with national or local statutes governing records, and dispose of records and other sensitive materials in a manner that protects the confidentiality of clients.

f. REASONABLE PRECAUTIONS
Rehabilitation counselors take reasonable precautions to protect the confidentiality of clients in the event of disaster or termination of practice, incapacity, or death of the rehabilitation counselor.

B.7. Consultation

a. AGREEMENTS
When acting as consultants, rehabilitation counselors seek agreement among parties involved concerning each individual's right to confidentiality, the obligation of each individual to preserve confidential information, and the limits of confidentiality of information shared by others.

b. RESPECT FOR PRIVACY
Rehabilitation counselors discuss information obtained in consultation only with persons directly involved with the case. Written and oral reports presented by rehabilitation counselors contain only data germane to the purposes of the consultation, and every effort is made to protect the identity of clients and to avoid undue invasion of privacy.

c. DISCLOSURE OF CONFIDENTIAL INFORMATION
When consulting with colleagues, rehabilitation counselors do not disclose confidential information that reasonably could lead to the identification of clients or other persons or organizations with whom they have a confidential relationship unless they have obtained the prior consent of the persons or organizations or the disclosure cannot be avoided. They disclose information only to the extent necessary to achieve the purpose of the consultation.

Section C: Advocacy and Accessibility

C.1. Advocacy

a. ATTITUDINAL BARRIERS
In direct service with clients, rehabilitation counselors address attitudinal barriers, including stereotyping and discrimination, toward individuals with disabilities. They increase their own awareness and sensitivity to individuals with disabilities.

b. ADVOCACY
Rehabilitation counselors provide clients with appropriate information to facilitate their self-advocacy actions whenever possible. They work with clients to help them

understand their rights and responsibilities, speak for themselves, make decisions, and contribute to society. When appropriate and with the consent of clients, rehabilitation counselors act as advocates on behalf of clients at the local, regional, and/or national levels.

c. ADVOCACY IN OWN AGENCY AND WITH COOPERATING AGENCIES
Rehabilitation counselors remain aware of actions taken by their own and cooperating agencies on behalf of clients and act as advocates for clients who cannot advocate for themselves to ensure effective service delivery.

d. ADVOCACY AND CONFIDENTIALITY
Rehabilitation counselors obtain the consent of clients prior to engaging in advocacy efforts on behalf of specific, identifiable clients to improve the provision of services and to work toward removal of systemic barriers or obstacles that inhibit access, growth, and development of clients.

e. AREAS OF KNOWLEDGE AND COMPETENCY
Rehabilitation counselors are knowledgeable about local, regional, and national systems and laws, and how they affect access to employment, education, transportation, housing, financial benefits, and medical services for people with disabilities. They obtain sufficient training in these systems in order to advocate effectively for clients and/or to facilitate self-advocacy of clients in these areas.

f. KNOWLEDGE OF BENEFIT SYSTEMS
Rehabilitation counselors are aware that disability benefit systems directly affect the quality of life of clients. They provide accurate and timely information or appropriate resources and referrals for these benefits.

C.2. Accessibility

a. COUNSELING PRACTICE
Rehabilitation counselors facilitate the provision of necessary accommodations, including physically and programmatically accessible facilities and services to individuals with disabilities.

b. BARRIERS TO ACCESS
Rehabilitation counselors collaborate with clients and/or others to identify barriers based on the functional limitations of clients. They communicate information on barriers to public and private authorities to facilitate removal of barriers to access.

c. REFERRAL ACCESSIBILITY
Prior to referring clients to a program, facility, or employment setting, rehabilitation counselors assist clients in ensuring that these are appropriately accessible, and do not engage in discrimination based on age, color, race, national origin, culture, disability, ethnicity, gender, gender identity, religion/spirituality, sexual orientation, marital status/partnership, language preference, socioeconomic status, or any basis proscribed by law.

Section D: Professional Responsibility

D.1. Professional Competence

a. BOUNDARIES OF COMPETENCE
Rehabilitation counselors practice only within the boundaries of their competence, based on their education, training, supervised experience, professional credentials, and appropriate professional experience. Rehabilitation counselors demonstrate beliefs, attitudes, knowledge, and skills pertinent to working with diverse client populations. Rehabilitation counselors do not misrepresent their role or competence to clients.

b. NEW SPECIALTY AREAS OF PRACTICE
Rehabilitation counselors practice in specialty areas new to them only after having obtained appropriate education, training, and supervised experience. While developing skills in new specialty areas, rehabilitation counselors take steps to ensure the competence of their work and to protect clients from possible harm.

c. QUALIFIED FOR EMPLOYMENT
Rehabilitation counselors accept employment for positions for which they are qualified by education, training, supervised experience, professional credentials, and appropriate professional experience. Rehabilitation counselors hire individuals for rehabilitation counseling positions who are qualified and competent for those positions.

d. MONITOR EFFECTIVENESS
Rehabilitation counselors continually monitor their effectiveness as professionals and take steps to improve when necessary. Rehabilitation counselors take reasonable steps to seek peer supervision as needed to evaluate their efficacy as rehabilitation counselors.

e. CONTINUING EDUCATION
Rehabilitation counselors recognize the need for continuing education to acquire and maintain a reasonable level of awareness of current scientific and professional information in their fields of activity. They take steps to maintain competence in the skills they use, are open to new procedures, and keep current with the diverse populations and specific populations with whom they work.

D.2. Cultural Competence/Diversity

a. INTERVENTIONS
Rehabilitation counselors develop and adapt interventions and services to incorporate consideration of cultural perspective of clients and recognition of barriers external to clients that may interfere with achieving effective rehabilitation outcomes.

b. NONDISCRIMINATION
Rehabilitation counselors do not discriminate against clients, students, employees, supervisees, or research participants in a manner that has a negative effect on these persons.

D.3. Functional Competence

a. IMPAIRMENT
Rehabilitation counselors are alert to the signs of impairment from their own physical, mental, or emotional problems, and refrain from offering or providing professional services when such impairment is likely to harm clients or others. They seek assistance for problems that reach the level of professional impairment, and, if necessary, they limit, suspend, or terminate their professional responsibilities until such time it is determined that they may safely resume their work. Rehabilitation counselors assist colleagues or supervisors in recognizing their own professional impairment and provide consultation and assistance when warranted with colleagues or supervisors showing signs of impairment and intervene as appropriate to prevent harm to clients.

b. DISASTER PREPARATION AND RESPONSE
Rehabilitation counselors make reasonable efforts to plan for facilitating continued services for clients in the event that rehabilitation counseling services are interrupted by disaster, such as acts of violence, terrorism, or a natural disaster.

D.4. Professional Credentials

a. ACCURATE REPRESENTATION
Rehabilitation counselors claim or imply only professional qualifications actually completed and correct any known misrepresentations of their qualifications by others. Rehabilitation counselors truthfully represent the qualifications of their professional colleagues. Rehabilitation counselors clearly distinguish between accredited and non-accredited degrees, paid and volunteer work experience, and accurately describe their continuing education and specialized training.

b. CREDENTIALS
Rehabilitation counselors claim only licenses or certifications that are current and in good standing.

c. EDUCATIONAL DEGREES
Rehabilitation counselors clearly differentiate between earned and honorary degrees.

d. IMPLYING DOCTORAL-LEVEL COMPETENCE
Rehabilitation counselors refer to themselves as "doctor" in a counseling context only when their doctorate is in counseling or a closely related field from an accredited university.

D.5. Responsibility to the Public and Other Professionals

a. SEXUAL HARASSMENT
Rehabilitation counselors do not condone or participate in sexual harassment.

b. REPORTS TO THIRD PARTIES
Rehabilitation counselors are accurate, honest, and objective in reporting their professional activities and judgments to appropriate third parties, including courts, health insurance companies, those who are the recipients of evaluation reports, and others.

c. MEDIA PRESENTATIONS
When rehabilitation counselors provide advice or comment by means of public lectures, demonstrations, radio or television programs, prerecorded tapes, technology-based applications, printed articles, mailed materials, or other media, they take reasonable precautions to ensure that: (1) the statements are based on appropriate professional counseling literature and practice; (2) the statements are otherwise consistent with the Code; and, (3) the recipients of the information are not encouraged to infer that a professional rehabilitation counseling relationship has been established.

d. EXPLOITATION OF OTHERS
Rehabilitation counselors do not exploit others in their professional relationships to seek or receive unjustified personal gains, sexual favors, unfair advantages, or unearned goods or services.

e. CONFLICT OF INTEREST
Rehabilitation counselors recognize that their own personal values, moral beliefs, or personal and professional relationships may interfere with their ability to practice competently. Under such circumstances, rehabilitation counselors are obligated to decline participation or to limit their assistance in a manner consistent with professional obligations.

f. VERACITY
Rehabilitation counselors do not engage in any act or omission of a dishonest, deceitful, or fraudulent nature in the conduct of their professional activities.

g. DISPARAGING REMARKS
Rehabilitation counselors do not disparage individuals or groups of individuals.

h. PERSONAL PUBLIC STATEMENTS
When making personal statements in a public context, rehabilitation counselors clarify that they are speaking from their personal perspective and that they are not speaking on behalf of all rehabilitation counselors, the profession, or any professional organizations with which they may be affiliated.

D.6. Scientific Bases for Interventions

a. TECHNIQUES/PROCEDURES/MODALITIES
Rehabilitation counselors use techniques/procedures/modalities that are grounded in theory and/or have an empirical or scientific foundation. When using techniques/procedures/modalities that are not grounded in theory and/or do not have an empirical or scientific foundation, rehabilitation counselors define the techniques/procedures/modalities as unproven or developing. They explain the potential risks and ethical considerations of using such techniques/procedures/modalities and take steps to protect clients from possible harm.

b. CREDIBLE RESOURCES
Rehabilitation counselors ensure that the resources used or accessed in counseling are credible and valid (e.g., Internet link, books used in bibliotherapy).

Section E: Relationships with Other Professionals

E.1. Relationships with Colleagues, Employers, and Employees

a. CULTURAL COMPETENCY CONSIDERATIONS
Rehabilitation counselors maintain beliefs, attitudes, knowledge, and skills regarding their interactions with people across cultures. Rehabilitation counselors are respectful of approaches to counseling services that differ from their own and of traditions and practices of other professional groups with which they work.

b. QUESTIONABLE CONDITIONS
Rehabilitation counselors alert their employers to conditions or inappropriate policies or practices that may be potentially disruptive or damaging to the professional responsibilities of rehabilitation counselors or that may limit their effectiveness. In those instances where rehabilitation counselors are critical of policies, they attempt to affect changes in such policies or procedures through constructive action within the organization. Such action may include referral to appropriate certification, accreditation, or licensure organizations, or voluntary termination of employment.

c. EMPLOYER POLICIES
The acceptance of employment in an agency or institution implies that rehabilitation counselors are in agreement with its general policies and principles. Rehabilitation counselors strive to reach agreement with employers as to acceptable standards of conduct that allow for changes in employer policies conducive to the growth and development of clients.

d. PROTECTION FROM PUNITIVE ACTION
Rehabilitation counselors take care not to harass or dismiss employees who have acted in a responsible and ethical manner to expose inappropriate employer policies or practices.

e. PERSONNEL SELECTION AND ASSIGNMENT
Rehabilitation counselors select competent staff and assign responsibilities compatible with their skills and experiences.

f. DISCRIMINATION
Rehabilitation counselors, as either employers or employees, engage in fair practices with regard to hiring, promoting, and training.

E.2. Consultation

a. CONSULTATION AS AN OPTION
Rehabilitation counselors may choose to consult with professionally competent persons about their clients. In choosing consultants, rehabilitation counselors avoid placing consultants in a conflict of interest situation that precludes the consultant from being a proper party to the efforts of rehabilitation counselors to help clients. If rehabilitation counselors are engaged in a work setting that compromises this

consultation standard, they consult with other professionals whenever possible to consider justifiable alternatives.

b. CONSULTANT COMPETENCY
Rehabilitation counselors take reasonable steps to ensure that they have the appropriate resources and competencies when providing consultation services. Rehabilitation counselors provide appropriate referral resources when requested or needed.

c. INFORMED CONSENT IN CONSULTATION
When providing consultation, rehabilitation counselors have an obligation to review, in writing and verbally, the rights and responsibilities of both rehabilitation counselors and consultees. Rehabilitation counselors use clear and understandable language to inform all parties involved about the purpose of the services to be provided, relevant costs, potential risks and benefits, and the limits of confidentiality. Working in conjunction with the consultees, rehabilitation counselors attempt to develop a clear definition of the problem, goals for change, and predicted consequences of interventions that are culturally responsive and appropriate to the needs of consultees.

E.3. Agency and Team Relationships

a. CLIENTS AS TEAM MEMBER
Rehabilitation counselors ensure that clients and/or their legally recognized representatives are afforded the opportunity for full participation in decisions related to the services they receive. Only those with a need to know are allowed access to the information of clients, and only then upon a properly executed release of information request or upon receipt of a court order.

b. INTERDISCIPLINARY TEAMWORK
Rehabilitation counselors who are members of interdisciplinary teams delivering multifaceted services to clients must keep the focus on how to serve clients best. They participate in and contribute to decisions that affect the well-being of clients by drawing on the perspectives, values, and experiences of the counseling profession and those of colleagues from other disciplines.

c. COMMUNICATION
Rehabilitation counselors ensure that there is fair and mutual understanding of rehabilitation plans by all parties cooperating in the rehabilitation of clients.

d. ESTABLISHING PROFESSIONAL AND ETHICAL OBLIGATIONS
Rehabilitation counselors who are members of interdisciplinary teams clarify professional and ethical obligations of the team as a whole and of its individual members. Rehabilitation counselors implement team decisions in rehabilitation plans and procedures, even when not personally agreeing with such decisions, unless these decisions breach the Code. When team decisions raise ethical concerns, rehabilitation counselors first attempt to resolve the concerns within the team. If they cannot reach resolution among team members, rehabilitation counselors consider other approaches to address their concerns consistent with the well-being of clients.

e. REPORTS
Rehabilitation counselors secure from other specialists appropriate reports and evaluations when such reports are essential for rehabilitation planning and/or service delivery.

Section F: Forensic and Indirect Services

F.1. Client or Evaluee Rights

a. PRIMARY OBLIGATIONS
Rehabilitation counselors produce unbiased, objective opinions and findings that can be substantiated by information and methodologies appropriate to the evaluation, which may include examination of individuals, research, and/or review of records. Rehabilitation counselors form opinions based on their professional knowledge and expertise that can be supported by the data gathered in evaluations. Rehabilitation counselors define the limits of their opinions or testimony, especially when an examination of individuals has not been conducted. Rehabilitation counselors acting as expert witnesses generate written documentation, either in the form of case notes or a report, as to their involvement and/or conclusions.

b. INFORMED CONSENT
Individuals being evaluated are informed in writing that the relationship is for the purpose of an evaluation and that a report of findings may be produced. Written consent for evaluations are obtained from those being evaluated or the individuals' legal representatives/guardians unless: (1) there is a clinical or cultural reason that this is not possible; (2) a court or legal jurisdiction orders evaluations to be conducted without the written consent of individuals being evaluated; and/or (3) deceased evaluees are the subject of evaluations. If written consent is not obtained, rehabilitation counselors document verbal consent and the reasons why obtaining written consent was not possible. When minors or vulnerable adults are evaluated, informed consent is obtained from parents or guardians.

c. DUAL ROLES
Rehabilitation counselors do not evaluate current or former clients for forensic purposes except under the conditions noted in A.5.f. or government statute. Likewise, rehabilitation counselors do not provide direct services to evaluees whom they have previously provided forensic services in the past except under the conditions noted in A.5.f. or government statute. In a forensic setting, rehabilitation counselors who are engaged as expert witnesses have no clients. The persons who are the subject of objective and unbiased evaluations are considered to be evaluees.

d. INDIRECT SERVICE PROVISION
Rehabilitation counselors who are employed by third parties as case consultants or expert witnesses, and who engage in communication with clients or evaluees, fully disclose to individuals (and/or their designees) the role of the rehabilitation counselor and limits of the relationship. Communication includes all forms of written or oral

interactions. When there is no intent to provide rehabilitation counseling services directly to clients or evaluees and when there is no in-person meeting or other communication, disclosure by rehabilitation counselors is not required.

e. CONFIDENTIALITY
When rehabilitation counselors are required by law, employers' policies, or extraordinary circumstances to serve in more than one role in judicial or administrative proceedings, they clarify role expectations and the parameters of confidentiality with their colleagues and with evaluees.

F.2. Rehabilitation Counselor Forensic Competency and Conduct

a. OBJECTIVITY
Rehabilitation counselors are aware of the standards governing their roles in performing forensic activities. Rehabilitation counselors are aware of the occasionally competing demands placed upon them by these standards and the requirements of the legal system, and attempt to resolve these conflicts by making known their commitment to this Code and taking steps to resolve conflicts in a responsible manner.

b. QUALIFICATION TO PROVIDE EXPERT TESTIMONY
Rehabilitation counselors have an obligation to present to the court, regarding specific matters to which they testify, the boundaries of their competence, the factual bases (knowledge, skill, experience, training, and education) for their qualifications as an expert, and the relevance of those factual bases to their qualifications as an expert on the specific matters at issue.

c. AVOID POTENTIALLY HARMFUL RELATIONSHIPS
Rehabilitation counselors who provide forensic evaluations avoid potentially harmful professional or personal relationships with individuals being evaluated, family members, romantic partners, and close friends of individuals they are evaluating. There may be circumstances however where not entering into professional or personal relationships is potentially more detrimental than providing services. When such is the case, rehabilitation counselors perform and document a risk assessment via use of an ethical decision-making model in order to arrive at an informed decision.

d. CONFLICT OF INTEREST
Rehabilitation counselors recognize that their own personal values, moral beliefs, or personal and professional relationships with parties to a legal proceeding may interfere with their ability to practice competently. Under such circumstances, rehabilitation counselors are obligated to decline participation or to limit their assistance in a manner consistent with professional obligations.

e. VALIDITY OF RESOURCES CONSULTED
Rehabilitation counselors ensure that the resources used or accessed in supporting opinions are credible and valid.

f. FOUNDATION OF KNOWLEDGE

Because of their special status as persons qualified as experts to the court, rehabilitation counselors have an obligation to maintain current knowledge of scientific, professional, and legal developments within their area of claimed competence. They are obligated also to use that knowledge, consistent with accepted clinical and scientific standards, in selected data collection methods and procedures for evaluation, treatment, consultation, or scholarly/empirical investigations.

g. DUTY TO CONFIRM INFORMATION

Where circumstances reasonably permit, rehabilitation counselors seek to obtain independent and personal verification of data relied upon as part of their professional services to the court or to parties to the legal proceedings.

h. CRITIQUE OF OPPOSING WORK PRODUCT

When evaluating or commenting upon the professional work products or qualifications of other experts or parties to legal proceedings, rehabilitation counselors represent their professional disagreements with reference to a fair and accurate evaluation of the data, theories, standards, and opinions of other experts or parties.

F.3. Forensic Practices

a. CASE ACCEPTANCE AND INDEPENDENT OPINION

While all rehabilitation counselors have the discretionary right to accept retention in any case or proceed within their area(s) of expertise, they decline involvement in any case when asked to take or support predetermined positions, assume invalid representation of facts, alter their methodology or process without foundation or compelling reasons, or where there are ethical concerns about the nature of the requested assignments.

b. TERMINATION AND ASSIGNMENT TRANSFER

If necessary to withdraw from a case after having been retained, rehabilitation counselors make reasonable efforts to assist evaluees and/or referral sources in locating another rehabilitation counselor to take over the assignment.

F.4. Forensic Business Practices

a. PAYMENTS AND OUTCOME

Rehabilitation counselors do not enter into financial commitments that may compromise the quality of their services or otherwise raise questions as to their credibility. Rehabilitation counselors neither give nor receive commissions, rebates, contingency or referral fees, gifts, or any other form of remuneration when accepting cases or referring evaluees for professional services. While liens should be avoided, they are sometimes standard practice in particular trial settings. Payment is never contingent on outcome or awards.

b. FEE DISPUTES

Should fee disputes arise during the course of evaluating cases and prior to trial, rehabilitation counselors have the ability to discontinue their involvement in cases as long as no harm comes to evaluees.

Section G: Evaluation, Assessment, and Interpretation

G.1. Informed Consent

a. EXPLANATION TO CLIENTS

Prior to assessment, rehabilitation counselors explain the nature and purposes of assessment and the specific use of results by potential recipients. The explanation is given in the language and/or developmental level of clients (or other legally authorized persons on behalf of clients), unless an explicit exception has been agreed upon in advance. Rehabilitation counselors consider personal or cultural context of clients, the level of their understanding of the results, and the impact of the results on clients. Regardless of whether scoring and interpretation are completed by rehabilitation counselors, by assistants, or by computer or other outside services, rehabilitation counselors take reasonable steps to ensure that appropriate explanations are given to clients.

b. RECIPIENTS OF RESULTS

Rehabilitation counselors consider the welfare of clients, explicit understandings, and prior agreements in determining who receives the assessment results. Rehabilitation counselors include accurate and appropriate interpretations with any release of individual or group assessment results. Issues of cultural diversity, when present, are taken into consideration when providing interpretations and releasing information.

G.2. Release of Information to Competent Professionals

a. MISUSE OF RESULTS

Rehabilitation counselors do not misuse assessment results, including test results and interpretations, and take reasonable steps to prevent the misuse of such by others.

b. RELEASE OF DATA TO QUALIFIED PROFESSIONALS

Rehabilitation counselors release assessment data in which clients are identified only with the consent of clients or their legal representatives, or court order. Such data is released only to professionals recognized as qualified to interpret the data.

G.3. Proper Diagnosis of Mental Disorders

a. PROPER DIAGNOSIS

If within their professional and individual scope of practice, rehabilitation counselors take special care to provide proper diagnosis of mental disorders. Assessment techniques (including personal interviews) used to determine care of clients (e.g., focus of treatment, types of treatment, or recommended follow-up) are carefully selected and appropriately used.

b. CULTURAL SENSITIVITY
Rehabilitation counselors recognize that culture affects the manner in which the disorders of clients are defined. The socioeconomic and cultural experiences of clients are considered when diagnosing.

c. HISTORICAL AND SOCIAL PREJUDICES IN DIAGNOSIS AND THE DIAGNOSIS OF PATHOLOGY
Rehabilitation counselors recognize historical and social prejudices in the misdiagnosis and pathologizing of certain individuals and groups. Rehabilitation counselors may refrain from making and/or reporting a diagnosis if they believe it would cause harm to clients or others.

G.4. Competence to Use and Interpret Tests

a. LIMITS OF COMPETENCE
Rehabilitation counselors utilize only those testing and assessment services for which they have been trained and are competent. Rehabilitation counselors take reasonable measures to ensure the proper use of psychological and career assessment techniques by persons under their supervision. The requirement to develop this competency applies regardless of whether tests are administered through standard or technology-based methods.

b. APPROPRIATE USE
Rehabilitation counselors are responsible for the appropriate applications, scoring, interpretations, and use of assessment instruments relevant to the needs of clients, whether they score and interpret such assessments themselves or use technology or other services. Generally new instruments are used within one year of publication, unless rehabilitation counselors document a valid reason why the normative data from previous versions are more applicable to clients.

c. RECOMMENDATIONS BASED ON RESULTS
Rehabilitation counselors are responsible for recommendations involving individuals that are based on assessment results, and have a thorough understanding of educational, psychological, and career measurements, including validation criteria, assessment research, and guidelines for assessment development and use. In addition to test results, rehabilitation counselors consider other factors present in the client's situation (e.g., disability or cultural factors) before making any recommendations, when relevant.

d. ACCURATE INFORMATION
Rehabilitation counselors provide accurate information and avoid false claims or misconceptions when making statements about assessment instruments or techniques. Special efforts are made to avoid utilizing test results to make inappropriate diagnoses or inferences.

G.5. Test Selection

a. APPROPRIATENESS OF INSTRUMENTS
Rehabilitation counselors carefully consider the validity, reliability, psychometric limitations, and appropriateness of instruments when selecting tests for use in given situations or with particular clients.

b. REFERRAL INFORMATION
If clients are referred to a third party for assessment, rehabilitation counselors provide specific referral questions and sufficient objective data about clients to ensure that appropriate assessment instruments are utilized.

c. CULTURALLY DIVERSE POPULATIONS
Rehabilitation counselors are cautious when selecting assessments for use with individuals from culturally diverse populations to avoid the use of instruments that lack appropriate psychometric properties for those client populations.

G.6. Conditions of Test Administration

a. ADMINISTRATION CONDITIONS
Rehabilitation counselors administer assessments under the same conditions that were established in the standardized development of the instrument. When assessments are not administered under standard conditions, as may be necessary to accommodate clients with disabilities, or when unusual behavior or irregularities occur during the administration, those conditions are noted in interpretation, and the results may be designated as invalid or of questionable validity.

b. TECHNOLOGICAL ADMINISTRATION
When using technology or electronic methods to administer assessments, rehabilitation counselors ensure that the instruments are functioning properly and provide accurate results.

c. UNSUPERVISED TEST-TAKING
Rehabilitation counselors do not permit unsupervised or inadequately supervised use of tests or assessments unless the tests or assessments are designed, intended, and validated for self-administration and/or scoring.

G.7. Test Scoring and Interpretation

a. REPORTING RESERVATIONS
In reporting assessment results, rehabilitation counselors indicate any reservations that exist regarding validity or reliability because of the circumstances of the assessments or the inappropriateness of the norms for persons tested.

b. CULTURAL DIVERSITY ISSUES IN ASSESSMENT
Rehabilitation counselors use caution with assessment techniques that were normed on populations other than that of the client. Rehabilitation counselors recognize the effects of age, color, race, national origin, culture, disability, ethnicity, gender, gender

identity, religion/spirituality, sexual orientation, marital status/partnership, language preference, socioeconomic status, or any basis proscribed by law on test administrations and interpretations, and place test results in proper perspective with other relevant factors.

c. RESEARCH INSTRUMENTS
Rehabilitation counselors exercise caution when interpreting the results of research instruments not having sufficient technical data to support respondent results. The specific purposes for the use of such instruments are stated explicitly to examinees.

G.8. Assessment Considerations

a. ASSESSMENT SECURITY
Rehabilitation counselors maintain the integrity and security of tests and other assessment techniques consistent with legal and contractual obligations. Rehabilitation counselors do not appropriate, reproduce, or modify published assessments or parts thereof without acknowledgment and permission from the publisher.

b. OBSOLETE ASSESSMENT AND OUTDATED RESULTS
Rehabilitation counselors do not use data or results from assessments that are obsolete or outdated. Rehabilitation counselors make every effort to prevent the misuse of obsolete measures and assessment data by others.

c. ASSESSMENT CONSTRUCTION
Rehabilitation counselors use established scientific procedures, relevant standards, and current professional knowledge for assessment design in the development, publication, and utilization of educational and psychological assessment techniques.

Section H: Teaching, Supervision, and Training

H.1. Rehabilitation Counselor Supervision and Client Welfare

a. CLIENT WELFARE
Rehabilitation counselor supervisors meet regularly with supervisees to review case notes, samples of clinical work, or live observations in order to ensure the welfare of clients. Supervisees have a responsibility to understand and follow the Code.

b. REHABILITATION COUNSELOR CREDENTIALS
Rehabilitation counselor supervisors work to ensure that clients are aware of the qualifications of the supervisees who render services to clients.

c. INFORMED CONSENT AND CLIENT RIGHTS
Rehabilitation counselor supervisors make supervisees aware of the rights of clients including the protection of their privacy and confidentiality in the counseling relationship. Supervisees provide clients with professional disclosure information and inform them of how the supervision process influences the limits of confidentiality.

Supervisees make clients aware of who has access to records of the counseling relationship and how these records are used.

H.2. Rehabilitation Counselor Supervision Competence

a. SUPERVISOR PREPARATION
Rehabilitation counselors who offer supervision services regularly pursue continuing education activities, including both counseling and supervision topics and skills.

b. CULTURAL DIVERSITY IN REHABILITATION COUNSELOR SUPERVISION
Rehabilitation counselor supervisors are aware of and address the role of cultural diversity in the supervisory relationship.

H.3. Roles and Relationships with Supervisees or Trainees

a. RELATIONSHIP BOUNDARIES WITH SUPERVISEES OR TRAINEES
Rehabilitation counselor supervisors or educators clearly define and maintain ethical professional, personal, and social relationships with their supervisees or trainees. Rehabilitation counselor supervisors or educators avoid nonprofessional relationships with current supervisees or trainees. If rehabilitation counselor supervisors or educators must assume other professional roles (e.g., clinical and/or administrative supervisors, instructors) with supervisees or trainees, they work to minimize potential conflicts and explain to supervisees or trainees the expectations and responsibilities associated with each role.

They do not engage in any form of nonprofessional interactions that may compromise the supervisory relationship.

b. SEXUAL OR ROMANTIC RELATIONSHIPS
Rehabilitation counselors do not engage in sexual or romantic interactions or relationships with current supervisees or trainees.

c. EXPLOITATIVE RELATIONSHIPS
Rehabilitation counselors do not engage in exploitative relationships with individuals with whom they have supervisory, evaluative, or instructional control or authority.

d. SEXUAL HARASSMENT
Rehabilitation counselor supervisors or educators do not condone or subject supervisees or trainees to sexual harassment.

e. RELATIONSHIPS WITH FORMER SUPERVISEES OR TRAINEES
Rehabilitation counselor supervisors or educators are aware of the power differential in their relationships with supervisees or trainees. Rehabilitation counselor supervisors or educators foster open discussions with former supervisees or trainees when considering engaging in a social, sexual, or other intimate relationships. Rehabilitation counselor supervisors or educators discuss with the former supervisees or trainees how their former relationship may affect the change in relationship.

f. NONPROFESSIONAL RELATIONSHIPS

Rehabilitation counselor supervisors or educators avoid nonprofessional or ongoing professional relationships with supervisees or trainees in which there is a risk of potential harm to supervisees or trainees or that may compromise the training experience or grades assigned. In addition, rehabilitation counselor supervisors or educators do not accept any form of professional services, fees, commissions, reimbursement, or remuneration from a site for supervisee or trainee placements.

g. CLOSE RELATIVES AND FRIENDS

Rehabilitation counselor supervisors or educators avoid accepting close relatives, romantic partners, or friends as supervisees or trainees. When such circumstances can not be avoided, rehabilitation counselor supervisors or educators utilize a formal review mechanism.

h. POTENTIALLY BENEFICIAL RELATIONSHIPS

Rehabilitation counselor supervisors or educators are aware of the power differential in their relationships with supervisees or trainees. If they believe nonprofessional relationships with supervisees or trainees may be potentially beneficial to supervisees or trainees, they take precautions similar to those taken by rehabilitation counselors when working with clients. Examples of potentially beneficial interactions or relationships include attending a formal ceremony; hospital visits; providing support during a stressful event; or mutual membership in professional associations, organizations, or communities. Rehabilitation counselor supervisors or educators engage in open discussions with supervisees or trainees when they consider entering into relationships with them outside of their role as clinical and/or administrative supervisors. Before engaging in nonprofessional relationships, rehabilitation counselor supervisors or educators discuss the rationale for such interactions, potential benefits or drawbacks, and anticipated consequences with supervisees or trainees. Rehabilitation counselor supervisors or educators clarify the specific nature and limitations of the additional role(s) they have with supervisees or trainees. Nonprofessional relationships with supervisees or trainees are time-limited or context specific and initiated with their consent.

H.4. Rehabilitation Counselor Supervisor Responsibilities

a. DISCLOSURE AND INFORMED CONSENT FOR SUPERVISION

Rehabilitation counselor supervisors provide professional disclosure that, at a minimum, is consistent with the jurisdiction in which they practice. Rehabilitation counselor supervisors are responsible for incorporating into their supervision the principles of informed consent. Rehabilitation counselor supervisors inform supervisees of the policies and procedures to which they are to adhere and the mechanisms for due process appeal of individual supervisory actions.

b. EMERGENCIES AND ABSENCES

Rehabilitation counselor supervisors establish and communicate to supervisees the procedures for contacting them or, in their absence, alternative on-call supervisors to assist in handling crises.

c. STANDARDS FOR REHABILITATION COUNSELOR SUPERVISEES

Rehabilitation counselor supervisors make their supervisees aware of professional and ethical standards and legal responsibilities. Rehabilitation counselor supervisors of post-degree rehabilitation counselors encourage these rehabilitation counselors to adhere to professional standards of practice.

d. RESOLVING DIFFERENCES

When cultural, ethical, or professional issues are crucial to the viability of the supervisory relationship, both parties make efforts to resolve differences. When termination is warranted, rehabilitation counselor supervisors make appropriate referrals to possible alternative supervisors.

H.5. Rehabilitation Counselor Supervisor Evaluation, Remediation, and Endorsement

a. EVALUATION

Rehabilitation counselor supervisors or educators clearly state to supervisees or trainees, prior to and throughout the training program, the levels of competency expected, appraisal methods, and timing of evaluations for both didactic and clinical competencies. Rehabilitation counselor supervisors or educators document and provide supervisees or trainees ongoing performance appraisal and evaluation feedback.

b. LIMITATIONS

Throughout ongoing evaluation and appraisal, rehabilitation counselor supervisors or educators are aware of and address the inability of some supervisees or trainees to achieve, improve, or maintain counseling competencies. Rehabilitation counselor supervisors or educators: (1) assist supervisees or trainees in securing remedial assistance when needed; (2) seek professional consultation and document their decision to dismiss or refer supervisees or trainees for assistance; (3) ensure that supervisees or trainees have recourse in a timely manner to address decisions that require them to seek assistance or to dismiss them; and (4) provide supervisees or trainees with due process according to organizational policies and procedures.

c. COUNSELING FOR SUPERVISEES

Rehabilitation counselor supervisors or educators address interpersonal competencies of supervisees or trainees in terms of the impact of these issues on clients, supervisory relationships, and professional functioning. With the exception of brief interventions to address situational distress, or as part of educational activities, rehabilitation counselor supervisors or educators do not provide counseling services to supervisees or trainees. If supervisees or trainees request counseling or if counseling is required as part of a remediation process, rehabilitation counselor supervisors or educators provide them with referrals.

d. ENDORSEMENT

Rehabilitation counselor supervisors or educators endorse supervisees or trainees for certification, licensure, employment, or completion of academic or training programs based on satisfactory progress and observations while under supervision or training.

Regardless of qualifications, supervisors or educators do not endorse supervisees or trainees whom they believe to be impaired in any way that would interfere with the performance of the duties associated with the endorsement.

H.6. Responsibilities of Rehabilitation Counselor Educators

a. REHABILITATION COUNSELOR EDUCATORS
Rehabilitation counselor educators who are responsible for developing, implementing, and supervising educational programs are skilled as teachers and practitioners. They are knowledgeable regarding the ethical, legal, and regulatory aspects of the profession, are skilled in applying that knowledge, and make students aware of their responsibilities. Rehabilitation counselor educators conduct rehabilitation counselor education and training programs in an ethical manner and serve as role models for professional behavior.

b. INFUSING CULTURAL DIVERSITY
Rehabilitation counselor educators infuse material related to cultural diversity into all courses and workshops for the development of professional rehabilitation counselors.

c. INTEGRATION OF STUDY AND PRACTICE
Rehabilitation counselor educators establish education and training programs that integrate academic study and supervised practice.

d. TEACHING ETHICS
Rehabilitation counselor educators make students aware of their ethical responsibilities, standards of the profession, and the ethical responsibilities of students to the profession. Rehabilitation counselor educators infuse ethical considerations throughout the curriculum.

e. PEER RELATIONSHIPS
Rehabilitation counselor educators make every effort to ensure that the rights of peers are not compromised when students lead counseling groups or provide clinical supervision. Rehabilitation counselor educators take steps to ensure that students understand they have the same ethical obligations as rehabilitation counselor educators, trainers, and supervisors.

f. INNOVATIVE TECHNIQUES/PROCEDURES/MODALITIES
When rehabilitation counselor educators teach counseling techniques/procedures/ modalities that are innovative, without an empirical foundation or without a well-grounded theoretical foundation, they define the counseling techniques/procedures/ modalities as unproven or developing and explain to students the potential risks and ethical considerations of using such techniques/procedures/modalities.

g. FIELD PLACEMENTS
Rehabilitation counselor educators develop clear policies within their training programs regarding field placement and other clinical experiences. Rehabilitation counselor educators provide clearly stated roles and responsibilities for students, site supervisors, and program supervisors. They confirm that site supervisors are qualified

to provide supervision and inform site supervisors of their professional and ethical responsibilities in this role.

h. PROFESSIONAL DISCLOSURE
Before initiating counseling services, rehabilitation counselors-in-training disclose their status as students and explain how this status affects the limits of confidentiality. Rehabilitation counselor educators ensure that clients at field placement are aware of the services rendered and the qualifications of the students and supervisees rendering those services. Students obtain permission from clients before they use any information concerning the counseling relationship in the training process.

H.7. Student Welfare

a. ORIENTATION
Rehabilitation counselor educators recognize that orientation is a developmental process that continues throughout the educational and clinical training of students. Rehabilitation counselor educators have an ethical responsibility to provide enough information to prospective or current students about program expectations for them to make informed decisions about entering into and continuing in a program.

b. SELF-GROWTH EXPERIENCES
Rehabilitation counselor education programs delineate requirements for self-disclosure as part of self-growth experiences in their admission and program materials. Rehabilitation counselor educators use professional judgment when designing training experiences they conduct that require student self-growth or self-disclosure. Students are made aware of the ramifications their self-disclosure may have when rehabilitation counselors whose primary role as teachers, trainers, or supervisors require acting on ethical obligations to the profession. Evaluative components of experiential training experiences explicitly delineate predetermined academic standards that are separate and do not depend on the level of self-disclosure of students. As a condition to remain in the program, rehabilitation counselor educators may require that students seek professional help to address any personal concerns that may be affecting their competency.

H.8. Cultural Diversity Competence in Rehabilitation Counselor Education Programs and Training Programs

a. DIVERSITY
Rehabilitation counselor educators actively attempt to recruit and retain a diverse faculty and student body. Rehabilitation counselor educators demonstrate commitment to cultural diversity competence by recognizing and valuing diverse cultures and types of abilities faculty and students bring to the training experience. Rehabilitation counselor educators provide appropriate accommodations as required to enhance and support the well-being and performance of students.

b. CULTURAL DIVERSITY COMPETENCE
Rehabilitation counselor educators actively infuse cultural diversity competency into their training and supervision practices. They actively educate trainees to develop and

maintain beliefs, attitudes, knowledge, and skills necessary for competent practice with people across cultures.

Section I: Research and Publication

I.1. Research Responsibilities

a. USE OF HUMAN PARTICIPANTS
Rehabilitation counselors plan, design, conduct, and report research in a manner that reflects cultural sensitivity, is culturally appropriate, and is consistent with pertinent ethical principles, laws, host institutional regulations, and scientific standards governing research with human participants. They seek consultation when appropriate.

b. DEVIATION FROM STANDARD PRACTICES
Rehabilitation counselors seek consultation and observe stringent safeguards to protect the rights of research participants when a research problem suggests a deviation from standard acceptable practices.

c. PRECAUTIONS TO AVOID INJURY
Rehabilitation counselors who conduct research with human participants are responsible for the welfare of participants throughout the research process and take reasonable precautions to avoid causing injurious psychological, emotional, physical, or social effects to participants.

d. PRINCIPAL RESEARCHER RESPONSIBILITY
The ultimate responsibility for ethical research practice lies with principal researchers. All others involved in the research activities share ethical obligations and responsibilities for their own actions.

e. MINIMAL INTERFERENCE
Rehabilitation counselors take precautions to avoid causing disruption in the lives of research participants that may result from their involvement in research.

I.2. Informed Consent and Disclosure

a. INFORMED CONSENT IN RESEARCH
Individuals have the right to consent to become research participants. In seeking consent, rehabilitation counselors use language that: (1) accurately explains the purpose and procedures to be followed; (2) identifies any procedures that are experimental or relatively untried; (3) describes any attendant discomforts and risks; (4) describes any benefits or changes in individuals or organizations that might be reasonably expected; (5) discloses appropriate alternative procedures that would be advantageous for participants; (6) offers to answer any inquiries concerning the procedures; (7) describes any limitations on confidentiality; describes formats and potential target audiences for the dissemination of research findings; and instructs participants that they are free to withdraw their consent and to discontinue participation in the project at any time without penalty.

b. DECEPTION

Rehabilitation counselors do not conduct research involving deception unless alternative procedures are not feasible. If such deception has the potential to cause physical or emotional harm to research participants, the research is not conducted, regardless of prospective value. When the methodological requirements of a study necessitate concealment or deception, the investigator explains the reasons for this action as soon as possible during the debriefing.

c. VOLUNTARY PARTICIPATION

Participation in research is typically voluntary and without any penalty for refusal to participate. Involuntary participation is appropriate only when it can be demonstrated that participation has no harmful effects on participants and is essential to the research.

d. CONFIDENTIALITY OF INFORMATION

Information obtained about participants during the course of research is confidential. When the possibility exists that others may obtain access to such information, ethical research practice requires that the possibility, together with the plans for protecting confidentiality, be explained to participants as part of the procedures for obtaining informed consent.

e. INDIVIDUALS NOT CAPABLE OF GIVING INFORMED CONSENT

When individuals are not capable of giving informed consent, rehabilitation counselors provide an appropriate explanation to and obtain agreement for participation and appropriate consent from a legally authorized person.

f. COMMITMENTS TO PARTICIPANTS

Rehabilitation counselors take reasonable measures to honor all commitments to research participants.

g. EXPLANATIONS AFTER DATA COLLECTION

After data is collected, rehabilitation counselors provide participants with full clarification of the nature of the study to remove any misconceptions participants might have regarding the research. Where scientific or human values justify delaying or withholding information, rehabilitation counselors take reasonable measures to avoid causing harm.

h. AGREEMENT OF CONTRIBUTORS

Rehabilitation counselors who conduct joint research establish agreements in advance regarding allocation of tasks, publication credit, and types of acknowledgment received, and incur an obligation to cooperate as agreed.

i. INFORMING SPONSORS

Rehabilitation counselors inform sponsors, institutions, and publication channels regarding research procedures and outcomes. Rehabilitation counselors ensure that appropriate bodies and authorities are given pertinent information and acknowledgment.

I.3. Reporting Results

a. ACCURATE RESULTS
Rehabilitation counselors plan, conduct, and report research accurately. They provide thorough discussions of the limitations of their data and alternative hypotheses. Rehabilitation counselors do not engage in misleading or fraudulent research, distort data, misrepresent data, or deliberately bias their results. They explicitly mention all variables and conditions known to the investigator(s) that may have affected the outcome of studies or interpretations of data. They describe the extent to which results are applicable for diverse populations.

b. OBLIGATION TO REPORT UNFAVORABLE RESULTS
Rehabilitation counselors report the results of any research of professional value. Results that reflect unfavorably on institutions, programs, services, prevailing opinions, or vested interests are not withheld.

c. IDENTITY OF PARTICIPANTS
Rehabilitation counselors who supply data, aid in the research of another person, report research results, or make original data available, take due care to disguise the identity of respective participants in the absence of specific authorization from the participants to do otherwise. In situations where participants self-identify their involvement in research studies, researchers take active steps to ensure that data is adapted/changed to protect the identities and welfare of all parties and that discussion of results does not cause harm to participants.

d. REPORTING ERRORS
If rehabilitation counselors discover significant errors in their published research, they take reasonable steps to correct such errors in a correction erratum or through other appropriate publication means.

e. REPLICATION STUDIES
Rehabilitation counselors are obligated to make available sufficient original research data to qualified professionals who may wish to replicate the study.

I.4. Publications and Presentations

a. RECOGNIZING CONTRIBUTIONS
When conducting and reporting research, rehabilitation counselors are familiar with and give recognition to previous work on the topic, observe copyright laws, and give full credit to those to whom credit is due.

b. CONTRIBUTORS
Rehabilitation counselors give credit through joint authorship, acknowledgment, footnote statements, or other appropriate means to those who have contributed significantly to research or concept development in accordance with such contributions. Principal contributors are listed first and minor technical or professional contributions are acknowledged in notes or introductory statements.

c. STUDENT RESEARCH

For articles that are substantially based on students' course papers, projects, dissertations or theses of students, and for which students have been the primary contributors, they are listed as principal authors.

d. DUPLICATE SUBMISSION

Rehabilitation counselors submit manuscripts for consideration to only one journal at a time. Manuscripts that are published in whole or in substantial part in another journal or published work are not submitted for publication without acknowledgment and permission from the previous publication.

e. PROFESSIONAL REVIEW

Rehabilitation counselors who review material submitted for publication, research, or other scholarly purposes respect the confidentiality and proprietary rights of those who submitted it. Rehabilitation counselors use care to make publication decisions based on valid and defensible standards. Rehabilitation counselors review article submissions in a timely manner and based on their scope and competency in research methodologies. Rehabilitation counselors who serve as reviewers at the request of editors or publishers make every effort to review only materials that are within their scope of competency and use care to avoid personal biases.

f. PLAGIARISM

Rehabilitation counselors do not plagiarize, that is, they do not present another person's work as their own work.

g. REVIEW/REPUBLICATION OF DATA OR IDEAS

Rehabilitation counselors fully acknowledge and make editorial reviewers aware of prior publication of ideas or data where such ideas or data are submitted for review or publication.

h. NONPROFESSIONAL RELATIONSHIPS

Rehabilitation counselors avoid nonprofessional relationships with research participants when research involves intensive or extensive interaction. When a nonprofessional interaction between researchers and research participants may be potentially beneficial, researchers must document, prior to the interaction (when feasible), the rationale for such interactions, the potential benefits, and anticipated consequences for research participants. Such interactions are initiated with appropriate consent of research participants. Where unintentional harm occurs to research participants due to nonprofessional interactions, researchers must show evidence of an attempt to remedy such harm.

i. SEXUAL OR ROMANTIC RELATIONSHIPS WITH RESEARCH PARTICIPANTS

Rehabilitation counselors do not engage in sexual or romantic rehabilitation counselor–research participant interactions or initiate relationships with current research participants.

j. SEXUAL HARASSMENT AND RESEARCH PARTICIPANTS

Rehabilitation counselors do not condone or subject research participants to sexual harassment.

I.5. Confidentiality

a. INSTITUTIONAL APPROVAL
When institutional review board approval is required, rehabilitation counselors provide accurate information about their research proposals and obtain approval prior to conducting their research. They conduct research in accordance with the approved research protocol.

b. ADHERENCE TO GUIDELINES
Rehabilitation counselors are responsible for understanding and adhering to national, local, agency, or institutional policies or applicable guidelines regarding confidentiality in their research practices.

c. CONFIDENTIALITY OF INFORMATION OBTAINED IN RESEARCH
Violations of participants' privacy and confidentiality are risks of participation in research involving human participants. Investigators maintain all research records in a secure manner. They explain to participants the risks of violations of privacy and confidentiality and disclose to participants any limits of confidentiality that reasonably can be expected.

d. DISCLOSURE OF RESEARCH INFORMATION
Rehabilitation counselors do not disclose confidential information that reasonably could lead to the identification of research participants unless they have obtained the prior consent of participants. Use of data derived from counseling relationships for purposes of training, research, or publication are confined to content that are disguised to ensure the anonymity of the individuals involved.

e. AGREEMENT FOR IDENTIFICATION
Rehabilitation counselors identify clients, students, or research participants in a presentation or publication only when it has been reviewed by those clients, students, or research participants and they have agreed to its presentation or publication.

Section J: Technology and Distance Counseling

J.1. Behavior and Identification

a. APPLICATION AND COMPETENCE
Rehabilitation counselors are held to the same level of expected behavior and competence as defined by the Code regardless of the technology used (e.g., cellular phones, email, facsimile, video, audio, audio-visual) or its application (e.g., assessment, research, data storage).

b. PROBLEMATIC USE OF THE INTERNET
Rehabilitation counselors are aware of behavioral differences with the use of the Internet, and/or methods of electronic communication, and how these may impact the counseling process.

c. POTENTIAL MISUNDERSTANDINGS
Rehabilitation counselors educate clients on how to prevent and address potential misunderstandings arising from the lack of visual cues and voice intonations when communicating electronically.

J.2. Accessibility

a. DETERMINING CLIENT CAPABILITIES
When providing technology-assisted services, rehabilitation counselors determine that clients are functionally and linguistically capable of using the application and that the technology is appropriate for the needs of clients. Rehabilitation counselors verify that clients understand the purpose and operation of technology applications and follow-up with clients to correct possible misconceptions, discover appropriate use, and assess subsequent steps.

b. ACCESSING TECHNOLOGY
Based on functional, linguistic, or cultural needs of clients, rehabilitation counselors guide clients in obtaining reasonable access to pertinent applications when providing technology-assisted services.

J.3. Confidentiality, Informed Consent, and Security

a. CONFIDENTIALITY AND INFORMED CONSENT
Rehabilitation counselors ensure that clients are provided sufficient information to adequately address and explain the limits of: (1) technology used in the counseling process in general; (2) ensuring and maintaining complete confidentiality of client information transmitted through electronic means; (3) a colleague, supervisor, and an employee, such as an Information Technology (IT) administrator or paraprofessional staff, who might have authorized or unauthorized access to electronic transmissions; (4) an authorized or unauthorized user including a family member and fellow employee who has access to any technology the client may use in the counseling process; (5) pertinent legal rights and limitations governing the practice of a profession over jurisdictional boundaries; (6) record maintenance and retention policies; (7) technology failure, unavailability, or crisis contact procedures; and, (8) protecting client information during the counseling process and at the termination of services.

b. TRANSMITTING CONFIDENTIAL INFORMATION
Rehabilitation counselors take precautions to ensure the confidentiality of information transmitted through the use of computers, email, facsimile machines, telephones, voicemail, answering machines, and other technology.

c. SECURITY
Rehabilitation counselors: (1) use encrypted and/or password-protected Internet sites and/or email communications to help ensure confidentiality when possible and take other reasonable precautions to ensure the confidentiality of information transmitted through the use of computers, email, facsimiles, telephones, voicemail, answering machines, or other technology; (2) notify clients of the inability to use encryption or

password protection, the hazards of not using these security measures; and, (3) limit transmissions to general communications that are not specific to clients, and/or use non-descript identifiers.

d. IMPOSTERS
In situations where it is difficult to verify the identity of rehabilitation counselors, clients, their guardians, and/or team members, rehabilitation counselors: (1) address imposter concerns, such as using code words, numbers, graphics, or other non-descript identifiers; and (2) establish methods for verifying identities.

J.4. Technology-Assisted Assessment

Rehabilitation counselors using technology-assisted test interpretations abide by the ethical standards for the use of such assessments regardless of administration, scoring, interpretation, or reporting method and ensure that persons under their supervision are aware of these standards.

J.5. Consultation Groups

When participating in electronic professional consultation or consultation groups (e.g., social networks, listservs, blogs, online courses, supervision, interdisciplinary teams), rehabilitation counselors: (1) establish and/or adhere to the group's norms promoting behavior that is consistent with ethical standards, and (2) limit disclosure of confidential information.

J.6. Records, Data Storage, and Disposal

a. RECORDS MANAGEMENT
Rehabilitation counselors are aware that electronic messages are considered to be part of the records of clients. Since electronic records are preserved, rehabilitation counselors inform clients of the retention method and period, of who has access to the records, and how the records are destroyed.

b. PERMISSION TO RECORD
Rehabilitation counselors obtain permission from clients prior to recording sessions through electronic or other means.

c. PERMISSION TO OBSERVE
Rehabilitation counselors obtain permission from clients prior to observing counseling sessions, reviewing session transcripts, and/or listening to or viewing recordings of sessions with supervisors, faculty, peers, or others within the training environment.

J.7. Legal

a. ETHICAL/LEGAL REVIEW
Rehabilitation counselors review pertinent legal and ethical codes for possible violations emanating from the practice of distance counseling and/or supervision.

b. LAWS AND STATUTES
Rehabilitation counselors ensure that the use of technology does not violate the laws of any local, regional, national, or international entity, observe all relevant statutes, and seek business, legal, and technical assistance when using technology in such a manner.

J.8. Advertising

a. ONLINE PRESENCE
Rehabilitation counselors maintaining sites on the Internet do so based on the advertising, accessibility, and cultural provisions of the Code. The Internet site is regularly maintained and includes avenues for communication with rehabilitation counselors.

b. VERACITY OF ELECTRONIC INFORMATION
Rehabilitation counselors assist clients in determining the validity and reliability of information found on the Internet and/or other technology applications.

J.9. Research and Publication

a. INFORMED CONSENT
Rehabilitation counselors are aware of the limits of technology-based research with regards to privacy, confidentiality, participant identities, venues used, accuracy, and/ or dissemination. They inform participants of those limitations whenever possible, and make provisions to safeguard the collection, dissemination, and storage of data collected.

b. INTELLECTUAL PROPERTY
When rehabilitation counselors possess intellectual property of people or entities (e.g., audio, visual, or written historical or electronic media), they take reasonable precautions to protect the technological dissemination of that information through disclosure, informed consent, password protection, encryption, copyright, or other security/intellectual property protection means.

J.10. Rehabilitation Counselor Unavailability

a. TECHNOLOGICAL FAILURE
Rehabilitation counselors explain to clients the possibility of technology failure and provide an alternative means of communication.

b. UNAVAILABILITY
Rehabilitation counselors provide clients with instructions for contacting them when they are unavailable through technological means.

c. CRISIS CONTACT
Rehabilitation counselors provide referral information for at least one agency or rehabilitation counselor-on-call for purposes of crisis intervention for clients within their geographical region.

J.11. Distance Counseling Credential Disclosure

Rehabilitation counselors practicing through Internet sites provide information to clients regarding applicable certification boards and/or licensure bodies to facilitate client rights and protection and to address ethical concerns.

J.12. Distance Counseling Relationships

a. BENEFITS AND LIMITATIONS

Rehabilitation counselors inform clients of the benefits and limitations of using technology applications in the counseling process and in business procedures. Such technologies include, but are not limited to, computer hardware and/or software, telephones, the Internet and other audio and/or video communication, assessment, research, or data storage devices or media.

b. INAPPROPRIATE APPLICATIONS

When technology-assisted distance counseling services are deemed inappropriate by rehabilitation counselors or clients, rehabilitation counselors pursue services face-to-face or by other means.

c. BOUNDARIES

Rehabilitation counselors discuss and establish boundaries with clients, family members, service providers, and/or team members regarding the appropriate use and/or application of technology and the limits of its use within the counseling relationship.

J.13. Distance Counseling Security and Business Practices

a. SELF-DESCRIPTION

Rehabilitation counselors practicing through Internet sites provide information about themselves (e.g., ethnicity, gender) as would be available if the counseling were to take place face-to-face.

b. INTERNET SITES

Rehabilitation counselors practicing through Internet sites: (1) obtain the written consent of legal guardians or other authorized legal representatives prior to rendering services in the event clients are minor children, adults who are legally incompetent, or adults incapable of giving informed consent; and (2) strive to provide translation and interpretation capabilities for clients who have a different primary language while also addressing the imperfect nature of such translations or interpretations.

c. BUSINESS PRACTICES

As part of the process of establishing informed consent, rehabilitation counselors: (1) discuss time zone differences, local customs, and cultural or language differences that might impact service delivery; and (2) educate clients when technology-assisted distance counseling services are not covered by insurance.

J.14. Distance Group Counseling

When participating in distance group counseling, rehabilitation counselors: (1) establish and/or adhere to the group's norms promoting behavior that is consistent with ethical standards; and (2) limit disclosure of confidential information.

J.15. Teaching, Supervision, and Training at a Distance

Rehabilitation counselors, educators, supervisors, or trainers working with trainees or supervisees at a distance, disclose to trainees or supervisees the limits of technology in conducting distance teaching, supervision, and training.

Section K: Business Practices

K.1. Advertising and Soliciting Clients

a. ACCURATE ADVERTISING
When advertising or otherwise representing their services to the public, rehabilitation counselors identify their credentials in an accurate manner that is not false, misleading, deceptive, or fraudulent.

b. TESTIMONIALS
Rehabilitation counselors who use testimonials do not solicit them from current clients or former clients or any other persons who may be vulnerable to undue influence.

c. STATEMENTS BY OTHERS
Rehabilitation counselors make reasonable efforts to ensure that statements made by others about them or the profession are accurate.

d. RECRUITING THROUGH EMPLOYMENT
Rehabilitation counselors do not use their places of employment or institutional affiliations to recruit or gain clients, supervisees, or consultees for their private practice.

e. PRODUCTS AND TRAINING ADVERTISEMENTS
Rehabilitation counselors who develop products related to their profession or conduct workshops or training events ensure that the advertisements concerning these products or events are accurate and disclose adequate information for clients to make informed choices.

f. PROMOTING TO THOSE SERVED
Rehabilitation counselors do not use counseling, teaching, training, or supervisory relationships to promote their products or training events in a manner that is deceptive or would exert undue influence on individuals who may be vulnerable. Rehabilitation counselor educators may adopt textbooks they have authored for appropriate instructional purposes.

K.2. Client Records

a. APPROPRIATE DOCUMENTATION
Rehabilitation counselors establish and maintain documentation consistent with agency policy that accurately, sufficiently, and in a timely manner reflects the services provided and that identifies who provided the services. If case notes need to be altered, it is done in a manner that preserves the original notes and is accompanied by the date of change, information that identifies who made the change, and the rationale for the change.

b. PRIVACY
Documentation generated by rehabilitation counselors protects the privacy of clients to the extent that it is possible and includes only relevant or appropriate counseling information.

c. RECORDS MAINTENANCE
Rehabilitation counselors maintain records necessary for rendering professional services to clients and as required by applicable laws, regulations, or agency/institution procedures. Subsequent to file closure, records are maintained for the number of years consistent with jurisdictional requirements or for longer periods during which maintenance of such records is necessary or helpful to provide reasonably anticipated future services to clients. After that time, records are destroyed in a manner assuring preservation of confidentiality.

K.3. Fees, Bartering, and Billing

a. ESTABLISHING FEES
In establishing fees for professional counseling services, rehabilitation counselors consider the financial status and locality of clients. In the event that the established fee structure is inappropriate for clients, rehabilitation counselors assist clients in attempting to find comparable services of acceptable cost.

b. ADVANCE UNDERSTANDING OF FEES
Prior to entering the counseling relationship, rehabilitation counselors clearly explain to clients all financial arrangements related to professional services. If rehabilitation counselors intend to use collection agencies or take legal measures to collect fees from clients who do not pay for services as agreed upon, they first inform clients of intended actions and offer clients the opportunity to make payment.

c. REFERRAL FEES
Rehabilitation counselors do not give or receive commissions, rebates, or any other form of remuneration when referring clients for professional services.

d. WITHHOLDING RECORDS FOR NONPAYMENT
Rehabilitation counselors may not withhold records under their control that are requested and needed for the emergency treatment of clients solely because payment has not been received.

e. BARTERING DISCOURAGED

Rehabilitation counselors ordinarily refrain from accepting goods or services from clients in return for rehabilitation counseling services because such arrangements create inherent potential for conflicts, exploitation, and distortion of the professional relationship. Rehabilitation counselors participate in bartering only if the relationship is not exploitative or harmful to clients, if clients request it, if a clear written contract is established, and if such arrangements are an accepted practice in the community or culture of clients.

f. BILLING RECORDS

Rehabilitation counselors establish and maintain billing records that are confidential and accurately reflect the services provided, the time engaged in the activity, and that clearly identify who provided the services.

K.4. Termination

Rehabilitation counselors in fee-for-service relationships may terminate services with clients due to nonpayment of fees under the following conditions: (1) clients were informed of payment responsibilities and the effects of nonpayment or the termination of payment by third parties; and (2) clients do not pose an imminent danger to self or others. As appropriate, rehabilitation counselors refer clients to other qualified professionals to address issues unresolved at the time of termination.

Section L: Resolving Ethical Issues

L.1. Knowledge of CRCC Standards

Rehabilitation counselors are responsible for reading, understanding, and following the Code, and seeking clarification of any standard that is not understood. Lack of knowledge or misunderstanding of an ethical responsibility is not a defense against a charge of unethical conduct.

L.2. Application of Standards

a. DECISION-MAKING MODELS AND SKILLS

Rehabilitation counselors must be prepared to recognize underlying ethical principles and conflicts among competing interests, as well as to apply appropriate decision-making models and skills to resolve dilemmas and act ethically.

b. ADDRESSING UNETHICAL BEHAVIOR

Rehabilitation counselors expect colleagues to adhere to the Code. When rehabilitation counselors possess knowledge that raises doubt as to whether another rehabilitation counselor is acting in an ethical manner, they take appropriate action.

c. CONFLICTS BETWEEN ETHICS AND LAWS

Rehabilitation counselors obey the laws and statutes of the legal jurisdiction in which they practice unless there is a conflict with the Code. If ethical responsibilities conflict with laws, regulations, or other governing legal authorities, rehabilitation counselors make known their commitment to the Code and take steps to resolve conflicts. If conflicts cannot be resolved by such means, rehabilitation counselors may adhere to the requirements of law, regulations, or other governing legal authorities.

d. KNOWLEDGE OF RELATED CODES OF ETHICS

Rehabilitation counselors understand applicable ethics codes from other professional organizations or from certification and licensure bodies of which they are members. Rehabilitation counselors are aware that the Code forms the basis for CRCC disciplinary actions, and understand that if there is a discrepancy between codes they are held to the CRCC standards.

e. CONSULTATION

When uncertain as to whether particular situations or courses of action may be in violation of the Code, rehabilitation counselors consult with other professionals who are knowledgeable about ethics, with supervisors, colleagues, and/or with appropriate authorities, such as CRCC, licensure boards, or legal counsel.

f. ORGANIZATION CONFLICTS

If the demands of organizations with which rehabilitation counselors are affiliated pose a conflict with the Code, rehabilitation counselors specify the nature of such conflicts and express to their supervisors or other responsible officials their commitment to the Code. When possible, rehabilitation counselors work toward change within organizations to allow full adherence to the Code. In doing so, they address any confidentiality issues.

L.3. Suspected Violations

a. INFORMAL RESOLUTION

When rehabilitation counselors have reason to believe that another rehabilitation counselor is violating or has violated an ethical standard, they attempt first to resolve the issue informally with the other rehabilitation counselor if feasible, provided such action does not violate confidentiality rights that may be involved.

b. REPORTING ETHICAL VIOLATIONS

When an informal resolution is not appropriate or feasible, or if an apparent violation has substantially harmed or is likely to substantially harm persons or organizations and is not appropriate for informal resolution or is not resolved properly, rehabilitation counselors take further action appropriate to the situation. Such action might include referral to local or national committees on professional ethics, voluntary national certification bodies, licensure boards, or to the appropriate institutional authorities. This standard does not apply when an intervention would violate confidentiality rights (e.g., when clients refuse to allow information or statements to be shared) or when rehabilitation counselors have been retained to review the work of another rehabilitation counselor whose professional conduct is in question by a regulatory agency.

c. UNWARRANTED COMPLAINTS

Rehabilitation counselors do not initiate, participate in, or encourage the filing of ethics complaints that are made with reckless disregard or willful ignorance of facts that would disprove the allegation, or are intended to harm rehabilitation counselors rather than to protect clients or the public.

L.4. Cooperation with Ethics Committees

Rehabilitation counselors assist in the process of enforcing the Code. Rehabilitation counselors cooperate with requests, proceedings, and requirements of the CRCC Ethics Committee or ethics committees of other duly constituted associations or boards having jurisdiction over those charged with a violation. Rehabilitation counselors are familiar with the Guidelines and Procedures for Processing Complaints and use it as a reference for assisting in the enforcement of the Code.

L.5. Unfair Discrimination Against Complainants and Respondents

Rehabilitation counselors do not deny individuals services, employment, advancement, admission to academic or other programs, tenure, or promotions based solely upon their having made or their being the subject of an ethics complaint. This does not preclude taking action based upon the outcome of such proceedings when rehabilitation counselors are found to be in violation of ethical standards.

NOTE: Rehabilitation counselors who violate the Code are subject to disciplinary action. Since the use of the Certified Rehabilitation Counselor (CRC®) and Canadian Certified Rehabilitation Counselor (CCRC®) designations are a privilege granted by the Commission on Rehabilitation Counselor Certification (CRCC®), CRCC reserves unto itself the power to suspend or to revoke the privilege or to approve other penalties for a violation. Disciplinary penalties are imposed as warranted by the severity of the offense and its attendant circumstances. All disciplinary actions are undertaken in accordance with published procedures and penalties designed to assure the proper enforcement of the Code within the framework of due process and equal protection under the law.

Glossary of Terms

ADVOCACY – promoting the well-being of individuals and groups and the rehabilitation counseling profession within systems and organizations. Advocacy seeks fair treatment and full physical and programmatic access for clients, and the removal of any barriers or obstacles that inhibit access, growth, and development.

ASSENT – agreement with a proposed course of action in relation to counseling services or plans when a person is otherwise not capable or competent to give formal or legal consent (e.g., informed consent).

AUTONOMY – the right of clients to be self-governing within their social and cultural framework. The right of clients to make decisions on their own behalf.

BENEFICENCE – to do good to others; to promote the well-being of clients.

CLIENTS – individuals with, or directly affected by, a disability, functional limitation(s), or medical condition and who receive services from rehabilitation counselors. At times, rehabilitation counseling services may be provided to individuals other than those with a disability.

CONFIDENTIALITY – a promise or contract to respect the privacy of clients by not disclosing anything revealed to rehabilitation counselors except under agreed-upon conditions.

CONFLICT OF INTEREST – a situation in which financial or other personal considerations have the potential to compromise or bias professional judgment and objectivity.

CONSULTATION – when one professional seeks the advice of another professional. It is a process in which consultants assist consultees to resolve a specific issue.

CONTINGENCY FEE – any fee for services provided where the fee is payable only if there is a favorable result (defined as part of the fee contract).

COURT ORDER – a directive from a tribunal or court directing certain actions or conduct which rehabilitation counselors are legally required to follow.

CULTURAL COMPETENCE – encompasses beliefs, attitudes, knowledge, and skills that result in an ability to understand, communicate with, and effectively interact with people across cultures.

CULTURALLY DIVERSE – age, color, race, national origin, culture, disability, ethnicity, gender, gender identity, religion/spirituality, sexual orientation, marital status/partnership, language preference, socioeconomic status, or any basis proscribed by law.

DISPARAGING REMARKS – public statements that degrade, belittle, minimize, defame, demean, humiliate, or scorn individuals or groups of individuals. These differ from critiques, which are intended to provide comparisons of thoughts, ideas, methods, work products, or conclusions. If statements criticize the individual as a person, their character or intellect, or are based on incorrect information or fictional claims, these are considered disparaging remarks.

DISTANCE COUNSELING OR EDUCATION – any rehabilitation counseling or education that occurs through electronic auditory and/or electronic visual means.

EVALUEES – in a forensic setting, the people who are the subject of the objective and unbiased evaluations.

EXPLOIT – to take advantage of a power differential in a relationship.

FIDELITY – to be faithful; to keep promises and honor the trust placed in rehabilitation counselors.

FORENSIC – to provide expertise involving the application of professional knowledge and the use of scientific, technical, or other specialized knowledge for the resolution of legal or administrative issues, proceedings, or decisions.

FUNCTIONAL – relating to cognitive, sensory, environmental, intellectual, mental, behavioral, emotional, and/or physical capabilities.

IMMEDIATE FAMILY MEMBERS – a child, spouse, parent, grandparent, or sibling. Immediate family members are also defined in a manner that is sensitive to cultural differences.

INFORMED CONSENT – a process of communication between rehabilitation counselors and clients that results in the authorization or decision by clients based upon an appreciation and understanding of the facts and implications of an action.

JUSTICE – to be fair in the treatment of all clients; to provide appropriate services to all.

NONMALEFICENCE – to do no harm to others.

PRIVACY – the right of clients to keep the counseling relationship to oneself (e.g., as a secret). Privacy is more inclusive than confidentiality, which addresses communications in the counseling context.

PRIVILEGED COMMUNICATION – established by statute and protects clients from having confidential communications with rehabilitation counselors disclosed in legal proceedings without their permission.

PROFESSIONAL DISCLOSURE – the process of communicating pertinent information to clients in order for clients to engage in informed consent.

REGIONAL – state, provincial, or other intermediate level.

RETAINER – a contract between an agency or individual(s) and rehabilitation counselors when the agency/individual(s) pays to reserve the time of rehabilitation counselors.

SEXUAL HARASSMENT – sexual solicitation, physical advances, or verbal or nonverbal conduct that is sexual in nature, that occurs in connection with professional activities or roles, and (1) rehabilitation counselors know or are told the act is unwelcome, offensive, or creates a hostile workplace or learning environment; and (2) is sufficiently severe or intense to be perceived as harassment to a reasonable person in the context in which the behavior occurred. Sexual harassment may consist of a single intense or severe act considered harassment by a reasonable person, or multiple persistent or pervasive acts.

STUDENTS – persons actively enrolled in an academic program.

TEAMS – groups of individuals who participate in a structured or agreed-upon form of collaboration.

TRAINEES – rehabilitation counselors-in-training, students, or participants in in-service or continuing education.

VERACITY – to be honest; truthfulness.

Acknowledgements – CRCC recognizes the American Counseling Association and the International Association of Rehabilitation Professionals for permitting CRCC to adopt, in part, the ACA Code of Ethics and the IARP Code of Ethics, Standards of Practice and Competencies, respectively.

Association for Addiction Professionals (NAADAC)
Code of Ethics

Introduction to NAADAC Ethical Standards

Ethics are generally regarded as the standards that govern the conduct of a person. Smith and Hodges define ethics as a "human reflecting self-consciously on the act of being a moral being." This implies a process of self-reflection and awareness of how to behave as a moral being. Some definitions are dictated by law, individual belief systems, religion or a mixture of all three.

NAADAC recognizes that its members and certified counselors live and work in many diverse communities. NAADAC has established a set of ethical best-practices that apply to universal ethical deliberation. Further, NAADAC recognizes and encourages the notion that personal and professional ethics cannot be dealt with as separate domains. NAADAC members, addiction professionals and/or licensed/certified treatment providers (subsequently referred to as addiction professionals) recognize that the ability to do well is based on an underlying concern for the well-being of others. This concern emerges from recognition that we are all stakeholders in each other's lives—the well-being of each is intimately bound to the well-being of all; that when the happiness of some is purchased by the unhappiness of others, the stage is set for the misery of all. Addiction professionals must act in such a way that they would have no embarrassment if their behavior became a matter of public knowledge and would have no difficulty defending their actions before any competent authority.

The NAADAC Code of Ethics was written to govern the conduct of its members and it is the accepted standard of conduct for addiction professionals certified by the National Certification Commission. The code of ethics reflects ideals of NAADAC and its members. When an ethics complaint is filed with NAADAC, it is evaluated by consulting the NAADAC Code of Ethics. The NAADAC Code of Ethics is designed as a statement of the values of the profession and as a guide for making clinical decisions. This code is also utilized by state certification boards and educational institutions to evaluate the behavior of addiction professionals and to guide the certification process.

In addition to identifying specific ethical standards, White (1993) suggested consideration of the following when making ethical decisions:
1. Autonomy: To allow others the freedom to choose their own destiny
2. Obedience: The responsibility to observe and obey legal and ethical directives
3. Conscientious Refusal: The responsibility to refuse to carry out directives that are illegal and/or unethical
4. Beneficence: To help others
5. Gratitude: To pass along the good that we receive to others
6. Competence: To possess the necessary skills and knowledge to treat the clientele in a chosen discipline and to remain current with treatment modalities, theories and techniques

7. Justice: Fair and equal treatment, to treat others in a just manner
8. Stewardship: To use available resources in a judicious and conscientious manner, to give back
9. Honesty and Candor: Tell the truth in all dealing with clients, colleagues, business associates and the community
10. Fidelity: To be true to your word, keeping promises and commitments
11. Loyalty: The responsibility to not abandon those with whom you work
12. Diligence: To work hard in the chosen profession, to be mindful, careful and thorough in the services delivered
13. Discretion: Use of good judgment, honoring confidentiality and the privacy of others
14. Self-improvement: To work on professional and personal growth to be the best you can be
15. Non-malfeasance: Do no harm to the interests of the client
16. Restitution: When necessary, make amends to those who have been harmed or injured
17. Self-interest: To protect yourself and your personal interests

The Revised Code of Ethics is divided under major headings and standards. The sections utilized are:

I. The Counseling Relationship
II. Evaluation, Assessment and Interpretation of Client Data
III. Confidentiality/Privileged Communication and Privacy
IV. Professional Responsibility
V. Working in a Culturally Diverse World
VI. Workplace Standards
VII. Supervision and Consultation
VIII. Resolving Ethical Issues
IX. Communication and Published Works
X. Policy and Political Involvement

I. The Counseling Relationship

It is the responsibility of the addiction professional to safeguard the integrity of the counseling relationship and to ensure that the client is provided with services that are most beneficial. The client will be provided access to effective treatment and referral giving consideration to individual educational, legal and financial resources needs. Addiction professionals also recognize their responsibility to the larger society and any specific legal obligations that may, on limited occasions, supersede loyalty to clients. The addiction professional shall provide the client and/or guardian with accurate and complete information regarding the extent of the potential professional relationship. In all areas of function, the addiction professional is likely to encounter individuals who are vulnerable and exploitable. In such relationships he/she seeks to nurture and support the development of a relationship of equals rather than to take unfair advantage. In personal relationships, the addiction professional seeks to foster self-sufficiency and healthy self-esteem in others. In relationships with clients he/she provides only that level and length of care that is necessary and acceptable.

Standard 1: Client Welfare

The addiction professional understands that the ability to do good is based on an underlying concern for the well-being of others. The addiction professional will act for the good of others and exercise respect, sensitivity and insight. The addiction professional understands that the primary professional responsibility and loyalty is to the welfare of his or her clients, and will work for the client irrespective of who actually pays his/her fees.

1. The addiction professional understands and supports actions that will assist clients to a better quality of life, greater freedom and true independence.
2. The addiction professional will support clients in accomplishing what they can readily do for themselves. Likewise, the addiction professional will not insist on pursuing treatment goals without incorporating what the client perceives as good and necessary.
3. The addiction professional understands that suffering is unique to a specific individual and not of some generalized or abstract suffering, such as might be found in the understanding of the disorder. On that basis, the action taken to relieve suffering must be uniquely suited to the suffering individual and not simply some universal prescription.
4. Services will be provided without regard to the compensation provided by the client or by a third party and shall render equally appropriate services to individuals whether they are paying a reduced fee or a full fee or are waived from fees.

Standard 2: Client Self-Determination

The addiction professional understands and respects the fundamental human right of all individuals to self-determination and to make decisions that they consider in their own best interest. In that regard, the counselor will be open and clear about the nature, extent, probable effectiveness and cost of those services to allow each individual to make an informed decision about his or her care. The addiction professional works toward increased competence in all areas of professional functioning; recognizing that at the heart of all roles is an ethical commitment contributing greatly to the well-being and happiness of others. He/she is especially mindful of the need for faithful competence in those relationships that are termed fiduciary—relationships of special trust in which the clients generally do not have the resources to adequately judge competence.

1. The addiction professional will provide the client and/or guardian with accurate and complete information regarding the extent of the potential professional relationship, including the Code of Ethics and documentation regarding professional loyalties and responsibilities.
2. Addiction professionals will provide accurate information about the efficacy of treatment and referral options available to the client.
3. The addiction professional will terminate work with a client when services are no longer required or no longer serve the client's best interest.

4. The addiction professional will take reasonable steps to avoid abandoning clients who are in need of services. Referral will be made only after careful consideration of all factors to minimize adverse effects.
5. The addiction professional recognizes that there are clients with whom he/she cannot work effectively. In such cases, arrangements for consultation, co-therapy or referral are made.
6. The addiction professional may terminate services to a client for nonpayment if the financial contractual arrangements have been made clear to the client and if the client does not pose an imminent danger to self or others. The addiction professional will document discussion of the consequences of nonpayment with the client.
7. When an addiction professional must refuse to accept the client due to inability to pay for services, ethical standards support the addiction professional in attempting to identify other care options. Funding constraints might interfere with this standard.
8. The addiction professional will refer a client to an appropriate resource when the client's mental, spiritual, physical or chemical impairment status is beyond the scope of the addiction professional's expertise.
9. The addiction professional will foster self-sufficiency and healthy self-esteem in others. In relationships with clients, students, employees and supervisors, he/she strives to develop full creative potential and mature, independent functioning.
10. Informed Consent: The addiction professional understands the client's right to be informed about treatment. Informed consent information will be presented in clear and understandable language that informs the client or guardian of the purpose of the services, risks related to the services, limits of services due to requirements from a third party payer, relevant costs, reasonable alternatives and the client's right to refuse or withdraw consent within the time frames covered by the consent. When serving coerced clients, the addiction professional will provide information about the nature and extent of services, treatment options and the extent to which the client has the right to refuse services. When services are provided via technology such as computer, telephone or web-based counseling, clients are fully informed of the limitations and risks associated with these services. Client questions will be addressed within a reasonable time frame.
11. Clients will be provided with full disclosure including the guarantee of confidentiality if and when they are to receive services by a supervised person in training. The consent to treat will outline the boundaries of the client-supervisee relationship, the supervisee's training status and confidentiality issues. Clients will have the option of choosing not to engage in services provided by a trainee as determined by agency policies. Any disclosure forms will provide information about grievance procedures.

Standard 3: Dual Relationships

The addiction professional understands that the goal of treatment services is to nurture and support the development of a relationship of equals of individuals to ensure protection and fairness of all parties.

Addiction professionals will provide services to clients only in the context of a professional setting. In rural settings and in small communities, dual relationships are evaluated carefully and avoided as much as possible.

1. Because a relationship begins with a power differential, the addiction professional will not exploit relationships with current or former clients, current or former supervisees or colleagues for personal gain, including social or business relationships.
2. The addiction professional avoids situations that might appear to be or could be interpreted as a conflict of interest. Gifts from clients, other treatment organizations or the providers of materials or services used in the addiction professional's practice will not be accepted, except when refusal of such gift would cause irreparable harm to the client relationship. Gifts of value over $25 will not be accepted under any circumstances.
3. The addiction professional will not engage in professional relationships or commitments that conflict with family members, friends, close associates or others whose welfare might be jeopardized by such a dual relationship.
4. The addiction professional will not, under any circumstances, engage in sexual behavior with current or former clients.
5. The addiction professional will not accept as clients anyone with whom they have engaged in romantic or sexual relationships.
6. The addiction professional makes no request of clients that does not directly pertain to treatment (giving testimonials about the program or participating in interviews with reporters or students).
7. The addiction professional recognizes that there are situations in which dual relationships are difficult to avoid. Rural areas, small communities and other situations necessitate discussion of the counseling relationship and take steps to distinguish the counseling relationship from other interactions.
8. When the addiction professional works for an agency such as department of corrections, military, an HMO or as an employee of the client's employer, the obligations to external individuals and organizations are disclosed prior to delivering any services.
9. The addiction professional recognizes the challenges resulting from increased role of the criminal justice system in making referrals for addiction treatment. Consequently he/she strives to remove coercive elements of such referrals as quickly as possible to encourage engagement in the treatment and recovery process.
10. The addiction professional encourages self-sufficiency among clients in making daily choices related to the recovery process and self care.
11. The addiction professional shall avoid any action that might appear to impose on others' acceptance of their religious/spiritual, political or other personal beliefs while also encouraging and supporting participation in recovery support groups.

Standard 4: Group Standards

Much of the work conducted with substance use disorder clients is performed in group settings. Addiction professionals shall take steps to provide the required services while providing clients physical, emotional, spiritual and psychological health and safety.

1. Confidentiality standards are established for each counseling group by involving the addiction professional and the clients in setting confidentiality guidelines.
2. To the extent possible, addiction professionals will match clients to a group in which other clients have similar needs and goals.

Standard 5: Preventing Harm

The addiction professional understands that every decision and action has ethical implication leading either to benefit or harm, and will carefully consider whether decisions or actions have the potential to produce harm of a physical, psychological, financial, legal or spiritual nature before implementing them. The addiction professional recognizes that even in a life well lived, harm may be done to others by thoughtless words and actions, If he/she becomes aware that any word or action has done harm to anyone, he/she readily admits it and does what is possible to repair or ameliorate the harm except where doing so might cause greater harm.

1. The addiction professional counselor will refrain from using any methods that could be considered coercive such as threats, negative labeling and attempts to provoke shame or humiliation.
2. The addiction professional develops treatment plans as a negotiation with the client, soliciting the client's input about the identified issues/needs, the goals of treatment and the means of reaching treatment goals.
3. The addiction professional will make no requests of clients that are not necessary as part of the agreed treatment plan. At the beginning of each session, the client will be informed of the intent of the session. Collaborative effort between the client and the addiction professional will be maintained as much as possible.
4. The addiction professional will terminate the counseling or consulting relationship when it is reasonably clear that the client is not benefiting from the exchange.
5. The addiction professional understands the obligation to protect individuals, institutions and the profession from harm that might be done by others. Consequently there is awareness when the conduct of another individual is an actual or likely source of harm to clients, colleagues, institutions or the profession. The addiction professional will assume an ethical obligation to report such conduct to competent authorities.
6. The addiction professional defers to review by a human subjects committee (Institutional Review Board) to ensure that research protocol is free of coercion and that the informed consent process is followed. Confidentiality and deceptive practices are avoided except when such procedures are essential to the research protocol and are approved by the designated review board or committee.
7. When research is conducted, the addiction professional is careful to ensure that compensation to subjects is not as great or attractive as to distort the client's ability to make free decisions about participation.

II. Evaluation, Assessment and Interpretation of Client Data

The addiction professional uses assessment instruments as one component of the counseling/treatment process taking into account the client's personal and cultural background. The assessment process promotes the well-being of individual clients or groups. Addiction professionals base their recommendations/reports on approved evaluation instruments and procedures. The designated assessment instruments are ones for which reliability has been verified by research.

Standard 1: Scope of Competency

The addiction professional uses only those assessment instruments for which they have been adequately trained to administer and interpret.

Standard 2: Informed Consent

Addiction professionals obtain informed consent documentation prior to conducting the assessment except when such assessment is mandated by governmental or judicial entities and such mandate eliminates the requirement for informed consent. When the services of an interpreter are required, addiction professionals must obtain informed consent documents and verification of confidentiality from the interpreter and client.

Addiction professionals shall respect the client's right to know the results of assessments and the basis for conclusions and recommendations. Explanation of assessment results is provided to the client and/or guardian unless the reasons for the assessment preclude such disclosure or if it is deemed that such disclosure will cause harm to the client.

Standard 3: Screening

The formal process of identifying individuals with particular issues/needs or those who are at risk for developing problems in certain areas is conducted as a preliminary procedure to determine whether or not further assessment is warranted at that time.

Standard 4: Basis for Assessment

Assessment tools are utilized to gain needed insight in the formulation of the most appropriate treatment plan. Assessment instruments are utilized with the goal of gaining an understanding of the extent of a person's issues/needs and the extent of addictive behaviors.

Standard 5: Release of Assessment Results

Addiction professionals shall consider the examinee's welfare, explicit understanding of the assessment process and prior agreements in determining where and when to report assessment results. The information shared shall include accurate and appropriate interpretations when individual or group assessment results are reported to another entity.

Standard 6: Release of Data to Qualified Professionals

Information related to assessments is released to other professionals only with a signed release of information form or such a release from the client's legal representative. Such information is released only to persons recognized as qualified to interpret the data.

Standard 7: Diagnosis of Mental Health Disorders

Diagnosis of mental health disorders shall be performed only by an authorized mental health professional licensed or certified to conduct mental health assessments or by a licensed or certified addictions counselor who has completed graduate level specific education on diagnosis of mental health disorders.

Standard 8: Unsupervised Assessments

Unless the assessment instrument being used is designed, intended and validated for self-administration and/or scoring, Addiction professional administered tests will be chosen and scored following the recommended methodology.

Standard 9: Assessment Security

Addiction professionals maintain the integrity and security of tests and other assessment procedures consistent with legal and contractual obligations.

Standard 10: Outdated Assessment Results

Addiction professionals avoid reliance on outdated or obsolete assessment instruments. Professionals will seek out and engage in timely training and/or education on the administration, scoring and reporting of data obtained through assessment and testing procedures. Intake data and other documentation obtained from clients to be used in recommending treatment level and in treatment planning are reviewed and approved by an authorized mental health professional or a licensed or qualified addiction professional with specific education on assessment and testing.

Standard 11: Cultural Sensitivity Diagnosis

Addiction professionals recognize that cultural background and socioeconomic status impact the manner in which client issues/needs are defined. These factors are carefully considered when making a clinical diagnosis. Assessment procedures are chosen carefully to ensure appropriate assessment of specific client populations During assessment the addiction professional shall take appropriate steps to evaluate the assessment results while considering the culture and ethnicity of the persons being evaluated.

Standard 12: Social Prejudice

Addiction professionals recognize the presence of social prejudices in the diagnosis of substance use disorders and are aware of the long term impact of recording such diagnoses. Addiction professionals refrain from making and/or reporting a diagnosis if they think it would cause harm to the client or others.

III. Confidentiality/Privileged Communication and Privacy

Addiction professionals shall provide information to clients regarding confidentiality and any reasons for releasing information in adherence with confidentiality laws. When providing services to families, couples or groups, the limits and exceptions to confidentiality must be reviewed and a written document describing confidentiality must be provided to each person. Once private information is obtained by the addiction professional, standards of confidentiality apply. Confidential information is disclosed when appropriate with valid consent from a client or guardian. Every effort is made to protect the confidentiality of client information, except in very specific cases or situations.

1. The addiction professional will inform each client of the exceptions to confidentiality and only make a disclosure to prevent or minimize harm to another person or group, to prevent abuse of protected persons, when a legal court order is presented, for purpose of research, audit, internal agency communication or in a medical emergency. In each situation, only the information essential to satisfy the reason for the disclosure is provided.

2. The addiction professional will do everything possible to safeguard the privacy and confidentiality of client information, except where the client has given specific, written, informed and limited consent or when the client poses a risk of harm to themselves or others.

3. The addiction professional will inform the client of his/her confidentiality rights in writing as a part of informing the client of any areas likely to affect the client's confidentiality.

4. The addiction professional will explain the impact of electronic records and use of electronic devices to transmit confidential information via fax, email or other electronic means. When client information is transmitted electronically, the addiction professional will, as much as possible, utilize secure, dedicated telephone lines or encryption programs to ensure confidentiality.

5. Clients are to be notified when a disclosure is made, to whom the disclosure was made and for what purposes.

6. The addiction professional will inform the client and obtain the client's agreement in areas likely to affect the client's participation including the recording of an interview, the use of interview material for training purposes and/or observation of an interview by another person.

7. The addiction professional will inform the client(s) of the limits of confidentiality prior to recording an interview or prior to using information from a session for training purposes.

IV. Professional Responsibility

The addiction professional espouses objectivity and integrity and maintains the highest standards in the services provided. The addiction professional recognizes that effectiveness in his/her profession is based on the ability to be worthy of trust. The professional has taken time to reflect on the ethical implications of clinical decisions and behavior using competent authority as a guide. Further, the addiction professional recognizes that those who assume the role of assisting others to live a more responsible life take on the ethical responsibility of living a life that is more than ordinarily responsible. The addiction professional recognizes that even in a life well-lived, harm might be done to others by words and actions. When he/she becomes aware that any work or action has done harm, he/she admits the error and does what is possible to repair or ameliorate the harm except when to do so would cause greater harm. Professionals recognize the many ways in which they influence clients and others within the community and take this fact into consideration as they make decisions in their personal conduct.

Standard 1: Counselor Attributes

1. Addiction professionals will maintain respect for institutional policies and management functions of the agencies and institutions within which the services are being performed, but will take initiative toward improving such policies when it will better serve the interest of the client.

2. The addiction professional, as an educator, has a primary obligation to help others acquire knowledge and skills in treating the disease of substance use disorders.

3. The addiction professional, as an advocate for his or her clients, understands that he/she has an obligation to support legislation and public policy that recognizes treatment as the first intervention of choice for non-violent substance-related offenses.

4. The addiction professional practices honesty and congruency in all aspects of practice including accurate billing for services, accurate accounting of expenses, faithful and accurate reporting of interactions with clients and accurate reporting of professional activities.

5. The addiction professional recognizes that much of the property in the substance use disorder profession is intellectual in nature. In this regard, the addiction professional is careful to give appropriate credit for the ideas, concepts and publications of others when speaking or writing as a professional and as an individual.

6. The addiction professional is aware that conflicts can arise among the duties and rights that are applied to various relationships and commitments of his/her life. Priorities are set among those relationships and family, friends and associates are informed to the priorities established in order to balance these relationships and the duties flowing from them.

7. When work involves addressing the needs of potentially violent clients, the addiction professional will ensure that adequate safeguards are in place to protect clients and staff from harm.

8. Addiction professionals shall continually seek out new and effective approaches to enhance their professional abilities including continuing education research, and participation in activities with professionals in other disciplines. Addiction professionals have a commitment to lifelong learning and continued education and skills to better serve clients and the community.

9. The addiction professional respects the differing perspectives that might arise from professional training and experience other than his/her own. In this regard, common ground is sought rather than striving for ascendance of one opinion over another.

10. Addiction professionals, whether they profess to be in recovery or not, must be cognizant of ways in which their use of psychoactive chemicals in public or in private might adversely affect the opinion of the public at large, the recovery community, other members of the addiction professional community or, most particularly, vulnerable individuals seeking treatment for their own problematic use of psychoactive chemicals. Addiction professionals who profess to be in recovery will avoid impairment in their professional or personal lives due to

psychoactive chemicals. If impairment occurs, they are expected to immediately report their impairment, to take immediate action to discontinue professional practice and to take immediate steps to address their impairment through professional assistance. (See Standard 2, item 3 below).

Standard 2: Legal and Ethical Standards

Addiction professionals will uphold the legal and ethical standards of the profession by being fully cognizant of all federal laws and laws that govern practice of substance use disorder counseling in their respective state. Furthermore, addiction professionals will strive to uphold not just the letter of the law and the Code, but will espouse aspirational ethical standards such as autonomy, beneficence, non-malfeasance, justice, fidelity and veracity.

1. Addiction professionals will honestly represent their professional qualifications, affiliations, credentials and experience.
2. Any services provided shall be identified and described accurately with no unsubstantiated claims for the efficacy of the services. Substance use disorders are to be described in terms of information that has been verified by scientific inquiry.
3. The addiction professional strives for a better understanding of substance use disorders and refuses to accept supposition and prejudice as if it were the truth.
4. The impact of impairment on professional performance is recognized; addiction professionals will seek appropriate treatment for him/herself or for a colleague. Addiction professionals support the work of peer assistance programs to assist in the recovery of colleagues or themselves.
5. The addiction professional will ensure that products or services associated with or provided by the member by means of teaching, demonstration, publications or other types of media meet the ethical standards of this code.
6. The addiction professional who is in recovery will maintain a support system outside the work setting to enhance his/her own well-being and personal growth as well as promoting continued work in the professional setting.
7. The addiction professional will maintain appropriate property, life and malpractice insurance policies that serve to protect personal and agency assets.

Standard 3: Records and Data

The addiction professional maintains records of professional services rendered, research conducted, interactions with other individuals, agencies, legal and medical entities regarding professional responsibilities to clients and to the profession as a whole.

1. The addiction professional creates, maintains, disseminates, stores, retains and disposes of records related to research, practice, payment for services, payment of debts and other work in accordance with legal standards and in a manner that permits/satisfies the ethics standards established. Documents will include data relating to the date, time and place of client contact, the services provided, referrals made, disclosures of confidential information, consultation regarding the client, notation of supervision meetings and the outcome of every service provided.
2. Client records are maintained and disposed of in accordance with law and in a manner that meets the current ethical standards.

3. Records of client interactions including group and individual counseling services are maintained in a document separate from documents recording financial transactions such as client payments, third party payments and gifts or donations.
4. Records shall be kept in a locked file cabinet or room that is not easily accessed by professionals other than those performing essential services in the care of clients or the operation of agency.
5. Electronic records shall be maintained in a manner that assures consistent service and confidentiality to clients.
6. Steps shall be taken to ensure confidentiality of all electronic data and transmission of data to other entities.
7. Notes kept by the addiction professional that assist the professional in making appropriate decisions regarding client care but are not relevant to client services shall be maintained in separate, locked locations.

Standard 4: Interprofessional Relationships

The addiction professional shall treat colleagues with respect, courtesy, fairness and good faith and shall afford the same to other professionals.
1. Addiction professionals shall refrain from offering professional services to a client in counseling with another professional except with the knowledge of the other professional or after the termination of the client's relationship with the other professional.
2. The addiction professional shall cooperate with duly constituted professional ethics committees and promptly supply necessary information unless constrained by the demands of confidentiality.
3. The addiction professional shall not in any way exploit relationships with supervisees, employees, students, research participants or volunteers.

V. Working in a Culturally Diverse World

Addiction professionals, understand the significance of the role that ethnicity and culture plays in an individual's perceptions and how he or she lives in the world. Addiction professionals shall remain aware that many individuals have disabilities which may or may not be obvious. Some disabilities are invisible and unless described might not appear to inhibit expected social, work and health care interactions. Included in the invisible disabled category are those persons who are hearing impaired, have a learning disability, have a history of brain or physical injuries and those affected by chronic illness. Persons having such limitations might be younger than age.

Part of the intake and assessment must then include a question about any additional factor that must be considered when working with the client.
1. Addiction professionals do not discriminate either in their professional or personal lives against other persons with respect to race, ethnicity, national origin, color, gender, sexual orientation, veteran status, gender identity or expression, age, marital status, political beliefs, religion, immigration status and mental or physical challenges.

2. Accommodations are made as needed for clients who are physically, mentally, educationally challenged or are experiencing emotional difficulties or speak a different language than the clinician.

VI. Workplace Standards

The addiction professional recognizes that the profession is founded on national standards of competency which promote the best interests of society, the client, the individual addiction professional and the profession as a whole. The addiction professional recognizes the need for ongoing education as a component of professional competency and development.

1. The addiction professional recognizes boundaries and limitations of their own competencies and does not offer services or use techniques outside of their own professional competencies.
2. Addiction professionals recognize the impact of impairment on professional performance and shall be willing to seek appropriate treatment for oneself or for a colleague.

Working Environment

Addiction professionals work to maintain a working/therapeutic environment in which clients, colleagues and employees can be safe. The working environment should be kept in good condition through maintenance, meeting sanitation needs and addressing structural defects.

1. The addiction professional seeks appropriate supervision/consultation to ensure conformance with workplace standards.
2. The clerical staff members of the treatment agency hired and supervised by addiction professionals are competent, educated in confidentiality standards and respectful of clients seeking services.
3. Private work areas that ensure confidentiality will be maintained.

VII. Supervision and Consultation

Addiction professionals who supervise others accept the obligation to facilitate further professional development of these individuals by providing accurate and current information, timely evaluations and constructive consultation. Counseling supervisors are aware of the power differential in their relationships with supervisees and take precautions to maintain ethical standards. In relationships with students, employees and supervisees he/she strives to develop full creative potential and mature independent functioning.

1. Addiction professionals must take steps to ensure appropriate resources are available when providing consultation to others. Consulting counselors use clear and understandable language to inform all parties involved of the purpose and expectations related to consultation.
2. Addiction professionals who provide supervision to employees, trainees and other counselors must have completed education and training specific to clinical and/or administrative supervision. The addiction professional who supervises counselors

in training shall ensure that counselors in training adhere to policies regarding client care.

3. Addiction professionals serving as supervisors shall clearly define and maintain ethical professional, personal and social relationships with those they supervise. If other professional roles must be assumed, standards must be established to minimize potential conflicts.
4. Sexual, romantic or personal relationships with current supervisees are prohibited.
5. Supervision of relatives, romantic partners or friends is prohibited.
6. Supervision meetings are conducted at specific regular intervals and documentation of each meeting is maintained.
7. Supervisors are responsible for incorporating the principles of informed consent into the supervision relationship.
8. Addiction professionals who serve as supervisors shall establish and communicate to supervisees the procedures for contacting them, or in their absence alternative on-call supervisors.
9. Supervising addiction professionals will assist those they supervise in identifying counter-transference and transference issues. When the supervisee is in need of counseling to address issues related to professional work or personal challenges, appropriate referrals shall be provided.

VIII. Resolving Ethical Issues

The addiction professional shall behave in accordance with legal, ethical and moral standards for his or her work. To this end, professionals will attempt to resolve ethical dilemmas with direct and open communication among all parties involved and seek supervision and/or consultation as appropriate.

1. When ethical responsibilities conflict with law, regulations or other governing legal authority, addiction professionals should take steps to resolve the issue through consultation and supervision.
2. When addiction professionals have knowledge that another counselor might be acting in an unethical manner, they are obligated to take appropriate action based, as appropriate, on the standards of this code of ethics, their state ethics committee and the National Certification Commission.
3. When an ethical dilemma involving a person not following the ethical standards cannot be resolved informally, the matter shall be referred to the state ethics committee and the National Certification Commission.
4. Addiction professionals will cooperate with investigations, proceedings and requirements of ethics committees.

IX. Communication and Published Works

The addiction professional who submits for publication or prepares handouts for clients, students or for general distribution shall be aware of and adhere to copyright laws.

1. The addiction professional honestly respects the limits of present knowledge in public statements related to alcohol and drug abuse. Statements of fact will be

based on what has been empirically validated as fact. Other opinions, speculations and conjectures related to the addictive process shall be represented as less than scientifically validated.

2. The addiction professional recognizes contributions of other persons to their written documents.
3. When a document is based on cooperative work, all contributors are recognized in documents or during a presentation.
4. The addiction professional who reviews material submitted for publication, research or other scholarly purposes must respect the confidentiality and proprietary rights of the authors.

X. Policy and Political Involvement

Standard 1: Societal Obligations

The addiction professional is strongly encouraged to the best of his/her ability, actively engage the legislative processes, educational institutions and the general public to change public policy and legislation to make possible opportunities and choice of service for all human beings of any ethnic or social background whose lives are impaired by alcoholism and drug abuse.

1. The addiction professional understands that laws and regulations exist for the good ordering of society and for the restraint of harm and evil and will follow them, while reserving the right to commit civil disobedience.
2. The one exception to this principle is a law or regulation that is clearly unjust, where compliance leads to greater harm than breaking a law.
3. The addiction professional understands that the determination that a law or regulation is unjust is not a matter of preference or opinion but a matter of rational investigation, deliberation and dispute, and will willingly accept that there may be a penalty for justified civil disobedience.

Standard 2: Public Participation

The addiction professional is strongly encouraged to actively participate in community activities designed to shape policies and institutions that impact on substance use disorders. Addiction professionals will provide appropriate professional services in public emergencies to the greatest extent possible.

Standard 3: Social and Political Action

The addiction professional is strongly encouraged to understand that personal and professional commitments and relationships create a network of rights and corresponding duties and will work to safeguard the natural and consensual rights of each individual within their community. The addiction professional, understands that social and political actions and opinions are an individual's right and will not work to impose their social or political views on individuals with whom they have a professional relationship.

This resource was designed to provide an ethics code and ethical standards that will be used by counseling professionals. These principles of ethical conduct outline the importance of having ethical standards and the importance of adhering to those standards. These principles can help professionals face ethical dilemmas in their practice and explore ways to avoid them.

Please use this resource and share it with your colleagues. For more information contact naad ac@naadac.org or 800.548.0497.
Revised March 28, 2011.
Page updated June 27, 2013.

CODE OF ETHICS
Canadian Counselling and Psychotherapy Association / L'Association Canadienne de Counseling et de Psychothérapie January 2007

Contents

Preamble

This Code of Ethics expresses the ethical principles and values of the Canadian Counselling and Psychotherapy Association and serves as a guide to the professional conduct of all its members. It also informs the public which they serve of the standards of ethical conduct for which members are to be responsible and accountable. The Code reflects such values as integrity, competence, responsibility and an understanding of and respect for the cultural diversity of society. It is part of a social contract, based on attitudes of mutual respect and trust by which society supports the autonomy of the profession in return for the commitment of its members to act ethically in the provision of professional services.

Members of CCPA have a responsibility to ensure that they are familiar with this Code of Ethics, to understand its application to their professional conduct, and to strive to adhere to its principles and values. Counsellors should also be familiar with the CCPA Standards of Practice for Counsellors, as well as with other sources of information which will assist them in making informed professional decisions. These include the laws, regulations, and policies which are professionally relevant to their working environment.

Members are accountable to both the public and their peers and are therefore subject to the complaints and disciplinary procedures of the Canadian Counselling and Psychotherapy Association. Violations of this Code, however, do not automatically imply legal liability. Such a determination can only be made by legal and judicial proceedings. This peer review process is intended to enable the Association to advise and to discipline its members in response to substantiated complaints originating either with peers or the public.

Although a Code of Ethics is essential to the maintenance of ethical integrity and accountability, it cannot be a substitute for the active process of ethical decision-making. Members increasingly confront challenging ethical demands and dilemmas in a complex and dynamic society to which a simple and direct application of this code may not be possible. Also, reasonable differences of opinion can and do exist among members with respect to how ethical principles and values should be rank-ordered when they are in conflict. Therefore, members must develop the ability and the courage to exercise a high level of ethical judgment. For these reasons, the Code includes a section on ethical decision-making.

This Code is not a static document but will need revisions over time because of the continuing development of ethical knowledge and the emergence of consensus on challenging ethical issues. Therefore, members and others, including members of the public, are invited to submit comments and suggestions at any time to CCPA.

Ethical Principles

The expectations for ethical conduct as expressed in this Code are based on the following fundamental principles:

a) Beneficence	-being proactive in promoting the client's best interests
b) Fidelity	-honouring commitments to clients and maintaining integrity in counselling relationship
c) Nonmaleficence	-not wilfully harming clients and refraining from actions that risk harm
d) Autonomy	-respecting the rights of clients to self-determination
e) Justice	-respecting the dignity and just treatment of all persons
f) Societal Interest	-respecting the need to be responsible to society

The CCPA Process of Ethical Decision-Making

This brief overview of approaches to the process of ethical decision-making is provided so that counsellors will have some direction when making ethical decisions and resolving ethical dilemmas.

1. Principle-Based Ethical Decision-Making

Step One — What are the key ethical issues in this situation?

Step Two — What ethical articles from the CCPA Code of Ethics are relevant to this situation?

Step Three — Which of the six ethical principles are of major importance in this situation? (This step also involves securing additional information, consulting with knowledgeable colleagues or the CCPA Ethics Committee, and examining the probable outcomes of various courses of action.)

Step Four — How can the relevant ethical articles be applied in this circumstance and any conflict between principles be resolved and what are the potential risks and benefits of this application and resolution?

Step Five — What do my feelings and intuitions tell me to do in this situation? (Counsellors may consider "**2. Virtue-Based Ethical Decision-Making**" at this point).

Step Six — What plan of action will be most helpful in this situation?

2. Virtue-Based Ethical Decision-Making

The virtue ethics approach is based on the belief that counsellors are motivated to be virtuous and caring because they believe it is the right thing to do. Virtue ethics focus on the counsellor as an ethical agent with the capacity to make complex ethical decisions. Although there is no step-by-step methodology for virtue ethics, the following questions may help the counsellor in the process of virtue-based ethical decision-making:
1. What emotions and intuition am I aware of as I consider this ethical dilemma and what are they telling me to do?
2. How can my values best show caring for the client in this situation?
3. How will my decision affect other relevant individuals in this ethical dilemma?
4. What decision would I feel best about publicizing?
5. What decision would best define who I am as a person?

3. Quick Check
1. **Publicity** — Would I want this ethical decision announced on the front page of a major newspaper?
2. **Universality** — Would I make the same decision for everyone? If every counsellor made this decision, would it be a good thing?
3. **Justice** — Is everyone being treated fairly by my decision?

For a more comprehensive treatment of Ethical Decision-Making, members are directed to the CCPA publication, *Counselling Ethics: Issues and Cases*, available from the CCPA National Office.

A. Professional Responsibility

A1. General Responsibility

Counsellors maintain high standards of professional competence and ethical behaviour, and recognize the need for continuing education and personal care in order to meet this responsibility. (See also **C1, F1**)

A2. Respect for Rights

Counsellors participate in only those practices which are respectful of the legal, civic, and moral rights of others, and act to safeguard the dignity and rights of their clients, students, and research participants.

A3. Boundaries of Competence

Counsellors limit their counselling services and practices to those which are within their professional competence by virtue of their education and professional experience, and consistent with any requirements for provincial and national credentials. They refer to other professionals, when the counselling needs of clients exceed their level of competence. (See also **F2**)

A4. Supervision and Consultation

Counsellors take reasonable steps to obtain supervision and/or consultation with respect to their counselling practices and, particularly, with respect to doubts or uncertainties which may arise during their professional work. (See also **B10, C4, C7**)

A5. Representation of Professional Qualifications

Counsellors claim or imply only those professional qualifications which they possess, and are responsible for correcting any known misrepresentation of their qualifications by others.

A6. Responsibility to Counsellors and Other Professionals

Counsellors understand that ethical behaviour among themselves and with other professionals is expected at all times.

A7. Unethical Behaviour by Other Counsellors

Counsellors have an obligation when they have serious doubts as to the ethical behaviour of another counsellor, to seek an informal resolution with the counsellor, when feasible and appropriate. When an informal resolution is not appropriate or feasible, or is unsuccessful, counsellors report their concerns to the CCPA Ethics Committee.

A8. Responsibility to Clients

When counsellors have reasonable grounds to believe that a client has an ethical complaint about the conduct of a CCPA member, counsellors inform the client of the CCPA Procedures for Processing Complaints of Ethical Violations and how to access these procedures.

A9. Sexual Harassment

Counsellors do not condone or engage in sexual harassment, which is defined as deliberate or repeated verbal or written comments, gestures, or physical contacts of a sexual nature.

A10. Sensitivity to Diversity

Counsellors strive to understand and respect the diversity of their clients, including differences related to age, ethnicity, culture, gender, disability, religion, sexual orientation and socio-economic status. (See also **B9, D10**)

A11. Extension of Ethical Responsibilities

Counselling services and products provided by counsellors through classroom instruction, public lectures, demonstrations, publications, radio and television programs, computer technology and other media must meet the appropriate ethical standards consistent with this Code of Ethics.

B. Counselling Relationships

B1. Primary Responsibility

Counsellors have a primary responsibility to respect the integrity and promote the welfare of their clients. They work collaboratively with clients to devise integrated, individualized counselling plans that offer reasonable promise of success and are consistent with the abilities and circumstances of clients.

B2. Confidentiality

Counselling relationships and information resulting therefrom are kept confidential.

However, there are the following exceptions to confidentiality:

(i)   when disclosure is required to prevent clear and imminent danger to the client or others;

(ii) when legal requirements demand that confidential material be revealed;

(iii) when a child is in need of protection. (See also **B15, B17, E6, E7, F8**)

B3. Duty to Warn

When counsellors become aware of the intention or potential of clients to place others in clear or imminent danger, they use reasonable care to give threatened persons such warnings as are essential to avert foreseeable dangers.

B4. Client's Rights and Informed Consent

When counselling is initiated, and throughout the counselling process as necessary, counsellors inform clients of the purposes, goals, techniques, procedures, limitations, potential risks and benefits of services to be performed, and other such pertinent information. Counsellors make sure that clients understand the implications of diagnosis, fees and fee collection arrangements, record-keeping, and limits of confidentiality. Clients have the right to participate in the ongoing counselling plans, to refuse any recommended services, and to be advised of the consequences of such refusal. (See also **C5, E5**)

B5. Children and Persons with Diminished Capacity

Counsellors conduct the informed consent process with those legally appropriate to give consent when counselling, assessing, and having as research subjects children and/or persons with diminished capacity. These clients also give consent to such services or involvement commensurate with their capacity to do so. Counsellors understand that the parental or guardian right to consent on behalf of children diminishes commensurate with the child's growing capacity to provide informed consent.

B6. Maintenance of Records

Counsellors maintain records in sufficient detail to track the sequence and nature of professional services rendered and consistent with any legal, regulatory, agency, or institutional requirement. They secure the safety of such records and create, maintain, transfer, and dispose of them in a manner compliant with the requirements of confidentiality and the other articles of this Code of Ethics.

B7. Access to Records

Counsellors understand that clients have a right of access to their counselling records, and that disclosure to others of information from these records only occurs with the written consent of the client and/or when required by law.

B8. Dual Relationships

Counsellors make every effort to avoid dual relationships with clients that could impair professional judgment or increase the risk of harm to clients. Examples of dual relationships include, but are not limited to, familial, social, financial, business, or close personal relationships. When a dual relationship cannot be avoided, counsellors take appropriate professional precautions such as role clarification, informed consent, consultation, and documentation to ensure that judgment is not impaired and no exploitation occurs. (See also **B11, B12, B13, C5, C7, F10**)

B9. Respecting Diversity

Counsellors actively work to understand the diverse cultural background of the clients with whom they work, and do not condone or engage in discrimination based on age, colour, culture, ethnicity, disability, gender, religion, sexual orientation, marital, or socio-economic status. (See also **D10**)

B10. Consulting With Other Professionals

Counsellors may consult with other professionally competent persons about the client. However, if the identity of the client is to be revealed, it is done with the written consent of the client. Counsellors choose professional consultants in a manner which will avoid placing the consultant in a conflict of interest situation.

B11. Relationships with Former Clients

Counsellors remain accountable for any relationships established with former clients. Those relationships could include, but are not limited to those of a friendship, social, financial, and business nature. Counsellors exercise caution about entering any such relationships and take into account whether or not the issues and relational dynamics present during the counselling have been fully resolved and properly terminated. In any case, counsellors seek consultation on such decisions.

B12. Sexual Intimacies

Counsellors avoid any type of sexual intimacies with clients and they do not counsel persons with whom they have had a sexual relationship. Counsellors do not engage in sexual intimacies with former clients within a minimum of three years after terminating the counselling relationship. This prohibition is not limited to the three year period but extends indefinitely if the client is clearly vulnerable, by reason of emotional or cognitive disorder, to exploitative influence by the counsellor. Counsellors, in all such circumstances, clearly bear the burden to ensure that no such exploitative influence has occurred, and to seek consultative assistance.

B13. **Multiple Clients**

When counsellors agree to provide counselling to two or more persons who have a relationship (such as husband and wife, or parents and children), counsellors clarify at the outset which person or persons are clients and the nature of the relationship they will have with each person. If conflicting roles emerge for counsellors, they must clarify, adjust, or withdraw from roles appropriately.

B14. **Multiple Helpers**

If, after entering a counselling relationship, a counsellor discovers the client is already in a counselling relationship, the counsellor is responsible for discussing the issues related to continuing or terminating counselling with the client. It may be necessary, with client consent, to discuss these issues with the other helper.

B15. **Group Work**

Counsellors have the responsibility to screen prospective group members, especially when group goals focus on self-understanding and growth through self-disclosure. Counsellors inform clients of group member rights, issues of confidentiality, and group techniques typically used. They take reasonable precautions to protect group members from physical and/or psychological harm resulting from interaction within the group, both during and following the group experience.

B16. **Computer Use**

When computer applications are used as a component of counselling services, counsellors ensure that: (a) client and counsellor identities are verified; (b) the client is capable of using the computer application; (c) the computer application is appropriate to the needs of the client; (d) the client understands the purpose and operation of client-assisted and/or self-help computer applications; and (e) a follow-up of client use of a computer application is provided to assist subsequent needs. In all cases, computer applications do not diminish the counsellor's responsibility to act in accordance with the CCPA Code of Ethics, and in particular, to ensure adherence to the principles of confidentiality, informed consent, and safeguarding against harmful effects. (See also **D5**)

B17. **Delivery of Services by Telephone, Teleconferencing, and Internet**

Counsellors follow all additional ethical guidelines for services delivered by telephone, teleconferencing, and the Internet, including appropriate precautions regarding confidentiality, security, informed consent, records and counselling plans, as well as determining the right to provide such services in regulatory jurisdictions.

B18. **Referral**

When counsellors determine their inability to be of professional assistance to clients, they avoid initiating a counselling relationship, or immediately terminate it. In either event, members suggest appropriate alternatives, including making a referral to resources about which they are knowledgeable. Should clients decline the suggested referral, counsellors are not obligated to continue the relationship.

B19. Termination of Counselling

Counsellors terminate counselling relationships, with client agreement whenever possible, when it is reasonably clear that: the goals of counselling have
been met, the client is no longer benefitting from counselling, the client does
not pay fees charged, previously disclosed agency or institutional limits do not
allow for the provision of further counselling services, and the client or another
person with whom the client has a relationship threatens or otherwise endan-
gers the counsellor. However, counsellors make reasonable efforts to facilitate
the continued access to counselling services when services are interrupted by
these factors and by counsellor illness, client or counsellor relocation, client financial difficulties and so forth.

C. Consulting and Private Practice

C1. General Responsibility

Counsellors provide consultative services only in those areas in which they have
demonstrated competency by virtue of their education and experience.

C2. Undiminished Responsibility and Liability

Counsellors who work in private practice, whether incorporated or not, must
ensure that there is no diminishing of their individual professional responsibility to act in accordance with the CCPA Code of Ethics, or in their liability for
any failure to do so.

C3. Accurate Advertising

Counsellors, when advertising services as private practitioners, do so in a
manner that accurately and clearly informs the public of their services and
areas of expertise.

C4. Consultative Relationships

Counsellors ensure that consultation occurs within a voluntary relationship
between a counsellor and a help-seeking individual, group, or organization, and
that the goals are understood by all parties concerned.

C5. Informed Consent

Counsellors who provide services for the use of third parties, acknowledge and
clarify for the informed consent of clients, all obligations of such multiple relationships, including purpose(s), entitlement to information, and any restrictions on confidentiality. Third parties include: courts, public and private
institutions, funding agencies, employees, and so forth.

C6. Respect for Privacy

Counsellors limit any discussion of client information obtained from a consulting relationship to persons clearly involved with the case. Any written and oral
reports restrict data to the purposes of the consultation and, every effort is
made to protect client identity and to avoid undue invasion of privacy.

C7.   Conflict of Interest

Counsellors who engage in consultation avoid circumstances where the duality of relationships or the prior possession of information could lead to a conflict of interest.

C8.   Sponsorship and Recruitment

Counsellors present any of their organizational affiliations or membership in such a way as to avoid misunderstanding regarding sponsorship or certification. They also avoid the use of any institutional affiliation to recruit private practice clients.

D. Evaluation and Assessment

D1.   General Orientation

Counsellors adequately orient and inform clients so that evaluation and assessment results can be placed in proper perspective along with other relevant information.

D2.   Purposes and Results of Evaluation and Assessment

Counsellors take responsibility to inform clients about the purpose of any evaluation and assessment instruments and procedures and the meaning of evaluation and assessment results.

D3.   Evaluation and Assessment Competence

Counsellors recognize the limits of their competence and offer only those evaluation and assessment services for which they have appropriate preparation and which meet established professional standards.

D4.   Administrative and Supervisory Conditions

Counsellors ensure that evaluation and assessment instruments and procedures are administered and supervised under established conditions consistent with professional standards. They note any departures from standard conditions and any unusual behaviour or irregularities which may affect the interpretation of results.

D5.   Use of Technology

Counsellors recognize that their ethical responsibilities are not altered, or in any way diminished, by the use of technology for the administration of evaluation and assessment instruments. Counsellors retain their responsibility for the maintenance of the ethical principles of privacy, confidentiality, and responsibility for decisions regardless of the technology used.

D6.   Appropriateness of Evaluation and Assessment

Counsellors ensure that evaluation and assessment instruments and procedures are valid, reliable, and appropriate to both the client and the intended purposes.

D7.   Reporting Evaluation and Assessment Results

Counsellors ensure that when reporting evaluation and assessment results to clients and other individuals care is taken to provide, in an appropriate manner, accurate and sufficient information for an understanding of any conclusions and recommendations made, and to identify the basis for any reservations which might exist.

D8. Release of Evaluation and Assessment Data

Counsellors ensure that evaluation and assessment data are released appropriately and only to the client and persons qualified to interpret and use them properly.

D9. Integrity of Evaluation and Assessment Instruments and Procedures

Counsellors who use psychological tests and other assessment instruments, the value of which depends on their novelty to the client, ensure that they are limited to and safeguarded by those with the professional interest and competence to do so.

D10. Sensitivity to Diversity when Assessing and Evaluating

Counsellors proceed with caution when judging and interpreting the performance of minority group members and any other persons not represented in the group on which the evaluation and assessment instruments and procedures were standardized. They recognize and take into account the potential effects of age, ethnicity, disability, culture, gender, religion, sexual orientation and socio-economic status on both the administration of, and the interpretation of data from, such instruments and procedures.

D11. Security Maintenance

Counsellors ensure the integrity and security of evaluation and assessment instruments and procedures consistent with any legal and contractual obligations. They refrain from appropriating, reproducing, or modifying established evaluation and assessment instruments without the expressed permission and adequate recognition of the original author, publisher and copyright holder.

E. Research and Publications

E1. Researcher Responsibility

Counsellors plan, conduct, and report on research in a manner consistent with relevant ethical principles, professional standards of practice, federal and provincial laws, institutional regulations, cultural norms, and standards governing research with human subjects.

E2. Subject Welfare

Counsellors are responsible for protecting the welfare of their research subjects during research, and avoid causing injurious psychological, physical or social effects to persons who participate in their research activities.

E3. Principal Researcher Responsibility

Counsellors, when in the role of principal researcher are responsible for ensuring that appropriate ethical research practices are followed and, with respect to research involving human subjects, for obtaining an independent and appropriate ethical review before proceeding with the research. Research associates involved in the research activities share ethical obligations and full responsibility for their own actions.

E4. Voluntary Participation

Counsellors ensure that participation in research is voluntary. However, involuntary participation may be appropriate when it can be shown that participation will have no harmful effects on subjects, is essential to the research, and meets ethical review requirements.

E5. Informed Consent of Research Subjects

Counsellors inform all research subjects of the purpose(s) of their research. In addition, subjects are made aware of any experimental procedures, possible risks, disclosures and limitations on confidentiality. Subjects are also informed that they are free to ask questions and to discontinue at anytime.

E6. Research Confidentiality

Counsellors ensure that research information on subjects is confidential and the identity of participants is protected unless otherwise authorized by them, consistent with all informed consent procedures.

E7. Use of Confidential Information for Didactic or Other Purposes

Counsellors do not disclose in their writings, public presentation, or public media, any personally identifiable information obtained in confidence about clients, research participants, students, or organizational clients unless (1) there is legal authorization to do so, (2) reasonable steps are taken not to identify the person or organization, or (3) the person or organizational client has given informed written consent.

E8. Further Research

Counsellors have an obligation to collaborate with colleagues by making available original research data to qualified researchers who may wish to replicate or verify the research.

E9. Research Sponsors

Counsellors, when conducting research, obtain informed consent from sponsors and institutions and ensure that sponsors and institutions are given feedback information and proper acknowledgement.

E10. Review of Manuscripts

Counsellors who review material submitted for publication, research or other scholarly purposes respect the confidentiality and proprietary rights of those who submitted the research.

E11. Reporting Results

In reporting research results, counsellors mention any variables and conditions that might affect the outcome of the investigation or the interpretation of the results, and provide information sufficient for others who might wish to replicate the research.

E12. Research Contributions

Counsellors give due credit through joint authorship, acknowledgement, footnote statements, or other appropriate means to those who have contributed significantly to the research and/or publication, and to those who have done previous work on the topic. For an article that is based mainly on a student thesis or dissertation, the student is listed as principal author.

E13. Submission for Publication

Counsellors do not submit the same manuscript or one essentially similar in content for simultaneous publication consideration by two or more journals. In addition, manuscripts published in whole or in substantial part in another journal or published work should not be submitted for publication without acknowledgement and permission from the previous publication.

F. Counsellor Education, Training and Supervision

F1. General Responsibility

Counsellors who are responsible for counsellor education, training and supervision adhere to current CCPA guidelines and standards with respect to such activities and conduct themselves in a manner consistent with the CCPA Code of Ethics and Standards of Practice for Counsellors.

F2. Boundaries of Competence

Counsellors who conduct counsellor education, training and supervision have the necessary knowledge and skills to do so, and limit their involvement to such competencies.

F3. Ethical Orientation

Counsellors who are responsible for counsellor education, training and supervision have an obligation to make their students, trainees, and supervisees aware of the ethical responsibilities as expressed in the CCPA Code of Ethics and Standards of Practice for Counsellors.

F4. Clarification of Roles and Responsibilities

Counsellors who engage in counselling supervision of students or trainees take responsibility for clarifying their respective roles and obligations.

F5. Welfare of Clients

Counsellors who engage in counselling supervision of students or trainees take steps to ensure the welfare of clients during the supervised practice period, and intervene, when necessary, to ensure that this obligation is met.

F6. Program Orientation

Counsellors responsible for counsellor education programs and training activities take responsibility to orient prospective students and trainees to all core elements of such programs and activities, including to a clear policy with respect to all supervised practice components, both those simulated and real.

F7. Relational Boundaries

Counsellors who work as counsellor educators, trainers, and supervisors establish relationships with their students, trainees and supervisees such that appropriate relational boundaries are clarified and maintained, and dual relationships avoided.

F8.   Obligation to Inform

Counsellors who work as counsellor educators, trainers, and supervisors take steps to inform students, trainees, and supervisees, at the beginning of activities associated with these roles, of all reasonably foreseeable circumstances under which confidentiality may be breached during such activities.

F9.   Self-Development and Self-Awareness

Counsellors who work as counsellor educators, trainers and supervisors, encourage and facilitate the self-development and self-awareness of students, trainees and supervisees, so that they learn to integrate their professional practice and personal insight.

F10.   Dealing with Personal Issues

Counsellors responsible for counsellor education, training, and supervision recognize when such activities evoke significant personal issues for students, trainees, and supervisees and refer to other sources when necessary to avoid counselling those for whom they hold administrative or evaluative responsibility.

F11.   Self-Growth Activities

Counsellors who work as counsellor educators, trainers, and supervisors, ensure that any professional experiences which require self-disclosure and engagement in self-growth activities are managed in a manner consistent with the principles of informed consent, confidentiality, and safeguarding against any harmful effects.

The Code of Ethics (1999) was developed by a Canadian Counselling and Psychotherapy Association (CCPA)
Committee consisting of:
Glenn W. Sheppard, Co-Chair
William E. Schulz, Co-Chair
Sylvia-Anne McMahon

The revisions in this 2007 Code of Ethics were prepared by:
Glenn W. Sheppard and William E. Schulz

Approved by CCPA Board of Directors, January, 2007

Canadian Counselling and Psychotherapy Association
114-223 Colonnade Rd
Ottawa, Ontario, K2E 7K3
Fax: (613) 237-9786
Toll free: 1-877-765-5565
Web www.ccpa-accp.ca

American School Counselor Association (ASCA)
Ethical Standards for School Counselors

Preamble

The American School Counselor Association (ASCA) is a professional organization whose members are school counselors certified/licensed in school counseling with unique qualifications and skills to address all students' academic, personal/social and career development needs. Members are also school counseling program directors/supervisors and counselor educators. These ethical standards are the ethical responsibility of school counselors. School counseling program directors/supervisors should know them and provide support for practitioners to uphold them. School counselor educators should know them, teach them to their students and provide support for school counseling candidates to uphold them.

Professional school counselors are advocates, leaders, collaborators and consultants who create opportunities for equity in access and success in educational opportunities by connecting their programs to the mission of schools and subscribing to the following tenets of professional responsibility:

- Each person has the right to be respected, be treated with dignity and have access to a comprehensive school counseling program that advocates for and affirms all students from diverse populations including: ethnic/racial identity, age, economic status, abilities/disabilities, language, immigration status, sexual orientation, gender, gender identity/expression, family type, religious/spiritual identity and appearance.
- Each person has the right to receive the information and support needed to move toward self-direction and self-development and affirmation within one's group identities, with special care being given to students who have historically not received adequate educational services, e.g., students of color, students living at a low socio-economic status, students with disabilities and students from non-dominant language backgrounds.
- Each person has the right to understand the full magnitude and meaning of his/her educational choices and how those choices will affect future opportunities.
- Each person has the right to privacy and thereby the right to expect the school-counselor/student relationship to comply with all laws, policies and ethical standards pertaining to confidentiality in the school setting.
- Each person has the right to feel safe in school environments that school counselors help create, free from abuse, bullying, neglect, harassment or other forms of violence.

In this document, ASCA specifies the principles of ethical behavior necessary to maintain the high standards of integrity, leadership and professionalism among its members. The Ethical Standards for School Counselors were developed to clarify the nature of ethical responsibilities held in common by school counselors, supervisors/

directors of school counseling programs and school counselor educators. The purposes of this document are to:

- Serve as a guide for the ethical practices of all professional school counselors, supervisors/directors of school counseling programs and school counselor educators regardless of level, area, population served or membership in this professional association;
- Provide self-appraisal and peer evaluations regarding school counselors' responsibilities to students, parents/guardians, colleagues and professional associates, schools, communities and the counseling profession; and
- Inform all stakeholders, including students, parents and guardians, teachers, administrators, community members and courts of justice, of best ethical practices, values and expected behaviors of the school counseling professional.

A.1. Responsibilities to Students

Professional school counselors:

a. Have a primary obligation to the students, who are to be treated with dignity and respect as unique individuals.
b. Are concerned with the educational, academic, career, personal and social needs and encourage the maximum development of every student.
c. Respect students' values, beliefs and cultural background and do not impose the school counselor's personal values on students or their families.
d. Are knowledgeable of laws, regulations and policies relating to students and strive to protect and inform students regarding their rights.
e. Promote the welfare of individual students and collaborate with them to develop an action plan for success.
f. Consider the involvement of support networks valued by the individual students.
g. Understand that professional distance with students is appropriate, and any sexual or romantic relationship with students whether illegal in the state of practice is considered a grievous breach of ethics and is prohibited regardless of a student's age.
h. Consider the potential for harm before entering into a relationship with former students or one of their family members.

A.2. Confidentiality

Professional school counselors:

a. Inform individual students of the purposes, goals, techniques and rules of procedure under which they may receive counseling. Disclosure includes the limits of confidentiality in a developmentally appropriate manner. Informed consent requires competence on the part of students to understand the limits of confidentiality and therefore, can be difficult to obtain from students of a certain developmental level. Professionals are aware that even though every attempt is made to obtain informed consent it is not always possible and when needed will make counseling decisions on students' behalf.
b. Explain the limits of confidentiality in appropriate ways such as classroom guidance lessons, the student handbook, school counseling brochures, school Web site,

verbal notice or other methods of student, school and community communication in addition to oral notification to individual students.

c. Recognize the complicated nature of confidentiality in schools and consider each case in context. Keep information confidential unless legal requirements demand that confidential information be revealed or a breach is required to prevent serious and foreseeable harm to the student. Serious and foreseeable harm is different for each minor in schools and is defined by students' developmental and chronological age, the setting, parental rights and the nature of the harm. School counselors consult with appropriate professionals when in doubt as to the validity of an exception.

d. Recognize their primary obligation for confidentiality is to the students but balance that obligation with an understanding of parents'/guardians' legal and inherent rights to be the guiding voice in their children's lives, especially in value-laden issues. Understand the need to balance students' ethical rights to make choices, their capacity to give consent or assent and parental or familial legal rights and responsibilities to protect these students and make decisions on their behalf.

e. Promote the autonomy and independence of students to the extent possible and use the most appropriate and least intrusive method of breach. The developmental age and the circumstances requiring the breach are considered and as appropriate students are engaged in a discussion about the method and timing of the breach.

f. In absence of state legislation expressly forbidding disclosure, consider the ethical responsibility to provide information to an identified third party who, by his/her relationship with the student, is at a high risk of contracting a disease that is commonly known to be communicable and fatal. Disclosure requires satisfaction of all of the following conditions:

- Student identifies partner or the partner is highly identifiable
- School counselor recommends the student notify partner and refrain from further high-risk behavior
- Student refuses
- School counselor informs the student of the intent to notify the partner
- School counselor seeks legal consultation from the school district's legal representative in writing as to the legalities of informing the partner

g. Request of the court that disclosure not be required when the release of confidential information may potentially harm a student or the counseling relationship.

h. Protect the confidentiality of students' records and release personal data in accordance with prescribed federal and state laws and school policies including the laws within the Family Education Rights and Privacy Act (FERPA). Student information stored and transmitted electronically is treated with the same care as traditional student records. Recognize the vulnerability of confidentiality in electronic communications and only transmit sensitive information electronically in a way that is untraceable to students' identity. Critical information such as a student who has a history of suicidal ideation must be conveyed to the receiving school in a personal contact such as a phone call.

A.3. Academic, Career/College/Post-Secondary Access and Personal/Social Counseling Plans

Professional school counselors:

a. Provide students with a comprehensive school counseling program that parallels the ASCA National Model with emphasis on working jointly with all students to develop personal/social, academic and career goals.
b. Ensure equitable academic, career, post-secondary access and personal/social opportunities for all students through the use of data to help close achievement gaps and opportunity gaps.
c. Provide and advocate for individual students' career awareness, exploration and post-secondary plans supporting the students' right to choose from the wide array of options when they leave secondary education.

A.4. Dual Relationships

Professional school counselors:

a. Avoid dual relationships that might impair their objectivity and increase the risk of harm to students (*e.g.*, counseling one's family members or the children of close friends or associates). If a dual relationship is unavoidable, the school counselor is responsible for taking action to eliminate or reduce the potential for harm to the student through use of safeguards, which might include informed consent, consultation, supervision and documentation.
b. Maintain appropriate professional distance with students at all times.
c. Avoid dual relationships with students through communication mediums such as social networking sites.
d. Avoid dual relationships with school personnel that might infringe on the integrity of the school counselor/student relationship.

A.5. Appropriate Referrals

Professional school counselors:

a. Make referrals when necessary or appropriate to outside resources for student and/or family support. Appropriate referrals may necessitate informing both parents/guardians and students of applicable resources and making proper plans for transitions with minimal interruption of services. Students retain the right to discontinue the counseling relationship at any time.
b. Help educate about and prevent personal and social concerns for all students within the school counselor's scope of education and competence and make necessary referrals when the counseling needs are beyond the individual school counselor's education and training. Every attempt is made to find appropriate specialized resources for clinical therapeutic topics that are difficult or inappropriate to address in a school setting such as eating disorders, sexual trauma, chemical dependency and other addictions needing sustained clinical duration or assistance.
c. Request a release of information signed by the student and/or parents/guardians when attempting to develop a collaborative relationship with other service providers assigned to the student.
d. Develop a reasonable method of termination of counseling when it becomes apparent that counseling assistance is no longer needed or a referral is necessary to better meet the student's needs.

A.6. Group Work

Professional school counselors:

a. Screen prospective group members and maintain an awareness of participants' needs, appropriate fit and personal goals in relation to the group's intention and focus. The school counselor takes reasonable precautions to protect members from physical and psychological harm resulting from interaction within the group.

b. Recognize that best practice is to notify the parents/guardians of children participating in small groups.

c. Establish clear expectations in the group setting, and clearly state that confidentiality in group counseling cannot be guaranteed. Given the developmental and chronological ages of minors in schools, recognize the tenuous nature of confidentiality for minors renders some topics inappropriate for group work in a school setting.

d. Provide necessary follow up with group members, and document proceedings as appropriate.

e. Develop professional competencies, and maintain appropriate education, training and supervision in group facilitation and any topics specific to the group.

f. Facilitate group work that is brief and solution-focused, working with a variety of academic, career, college and personal/social issues.

A.7. Danger to Self or Others

Professional school counselors:

a. Inform parents/guardians and/or appropriate authorities when a student poses a danger to self or others. This is to be done after careful deliberation and consultation with other counseling professionals.

b. Report risk assessments to parents when they underscore the need to act on behalf of a child at risk; never negate a risk of harm as students sometimes deceive in order to avoid further scrutiny and/or parental notification.

c. Understand the legal and ethical liability for releasing a student who is in danger to self or others without proper and necessary support for that student.

A.8. Student Records

Professional school counselors:

a. Maintain and secure records necessary for rendering professional services to the student as required by laws, regulations, institutional procedures and confidentiality guidelines.

b. Keep sole-possession records or individual student case notes separate from students' educational records in keeping with state laws.

c. Recognize the limits of sole-possession records and understand these records are a memory aid for the creator and in absence of privileged communication may be subpoenaed and may become educational records when they are shared or are accessible to others in either verbal or written form or when they include information other than professional opinion or personal observations.

d. Establish a reasonable timeline for purging sole-possession records or case notes. Suggested guidelines include shredding sole possession records when the student transitions to the next level, transfers to another school or graduates. Apply careful discretion and deliberation before destroying sole-possession records that may be needed by a court of law such as notes on child abuse, suicide, sexual harassment or violence.

e. Understand and abide by the Family Education Rights and Privacy Act (FERPA, 1974), which safeguards student's records and allows parents to have a voice in what and how information is shared with others regarding their child's educational records.

A.9. Evaluation, Assessment and Interpretation

Professional school counselors:

a. Adhere to all professional standards regarding selecting, administering and interpreting assessment measures and only utilize assessment measures that are within the scope of practice for school counselors and for which they are trained and competent.

b. Consider confidentiality issues when utilizing evaluative or assessment instruments and electronically based programs.

c. Consider the developmental age, language skills and level of competence of the student taking the assessments before assessments are given.

d. Provide interpretation of the nature, purposes, results and potential impact of assessment/evaluation measures in language the students can understand.

e. Monitor the use of assessment results and interpretations, and take reasonable steps to prevent others from misusing the information.

f. Use caution when utilizing assessment techniques, making evaluations and interpreting the performance of populations not represented in the norm group on which an instrument is standardized.

g. Assess the effectiveness of their program in having an impact on students' academic, career and personal/social development through accountability measures especially examining efforts to close achievement, opportunity and attainment gaps.

A.10. Technology

Professional school counselors:

a. Promote the benefits of and clarify the limitations of various appropriate technological applications. Professional school counselors promote technological applications (1) that are appropriate for students' individual needs, (2) that students understand how to use and (3) for which follow-up counseling assistance is provided.

b. Advocate for equal access to technology for all students, especially those historically underserved.

c. Take appropriate and reasonable measures for maintaining confidentiality of student information and educational records stored or transmitted through the use of computers, facsimile machines, telephones, voicemail, answering machines and other electronic or computer technology.

d. Understand the intent of FERPA and its impact on sharing electronic student records.

e. Consider the extent to which cyberbullying is interfering with students' educational process and base guidance curriculum and intervention programming for this pervasive and potentially dangerous problem on research-based and best practices.

A.11. Student Peer Support Program

Professional school counselors:

a. Have unique responsibilities when working with peer-helper or student-assistance programs and safeguard the welfare of students participating in peer-to-peer programs under their direction.

b. Are ultimately responsible for appropriate training and supervision for students serving as peer-support individuals in their school counseling programs.

B. Responsibilities to Parents/Guardians

B.1. Parent Rights and Responsibilities

Professional school counselors:

a. Respect the rights and responsibilities of parents/guardians for their children and endeavor to establish, as appropriate, a collaborative relationship with parents/guardians to facilitate students' maximum development.

b. Adhere to laws, local guidelines and ethical standards of practice when assisting parents/guardians experiencing family difficulties interfering with the student's effectiveness and welfare.

c. Are sensitive to diversity among families and recognize that all parents/guardians, custodial and noncustodial, are vested with certain rights and responsibilities for their children's welfare by virtue of their role and according to law.

d. Inform parents of the nature of counseling services provided in the school setting.

e. Adhere to the FERPA act regarding disclosure of student information.

f. Work to establish, as appropriate, collaborative relationships with parents/guardians to best serve student.

B.2. Parents/Guardians and Confidentiality

Professional school counselors:

a. Inform parents/guardians of the school counselor's role to include the confidential nature of the counseling relationship between the counselor and student.

b. Recognize that working with minors in a school setting requires school counselors to collaborate with students' parents/guardians to the extent possible.

c. Respect the confidentiality of parents/guardians to the extent that is reasonable to protect the best interest of the student being counseled.

d. Provide parents/guardians with accurate, comprehensive and relevant information in an objective and caring manner, as is appropriate and consistent with ethical responsibilities to the student.

e. Make reasonable efforts to honor the wishes of parents/guardians concerning information regarding the student unless a court order expressly forbids the involvement of a parent(s). In cases of divorce or separation, school counselors exercise a good-faith effort to keep both parents informed, maintaining focus on the student and avoiding supporting one parent over another in divorce proceedings.

C. Responsibilities to Colleagues and Professional Associates

C.1. Professional Relationships

Professional school counselors, the school counseling program director/site supervisor and the school counselor educator:

a. Establish and maintain professional relationships with faculty, staff and administration to facilitate an optimum counseling program.
b. Treat colleagues with professional respect, courtesy and fairness.
c. Recognize that teachers, staff and administrators who are high-functioning in the personal and social development skills can be powerful allies in supporting student success. School counselors work to develop relationships with all faculty and staff in order to advantage students.
d. Are aware of and utilize related professionals, organizations and other resources to whom the student may be referred.

C.2. Sharing Information with Other Professionals

Professional school counselors:

a. Promote awareness and adherence to appropriate guidelines regarding confidentiality, the distinction between public and private information and staff consultation.
b. Provide professional personnel with accurate, objective, concise and meaningful data necessary to adequately evaluate, counsel and assist the student.
c. Secure parental consent and develop clear agreements with other mental health professionals when a student is receiving services from another counselor or other mental health professional in order to avoid confusion and conflict for the student and parents/guardians.
d. Understand about the "release of information" process and parental rights in sharing information and attempt to establish a cooperative and collaborative relationship with other professionals to benefit students.
e. Recognize the powerful role of ally that faculty and administration who function high in personal/social development skills can play in supporting students in stress, and carefully filter confidential information to give these allies what they "need to know" in order to advantage the student. Consultation with other members of the school counseling profession is helpful in determining need-to-know information. The primary focus and obligation is always on the student when it comes to sharing confidential information.
f. Keep appropriate records regarding individual students, and develop a plan for transferring those records to another professional school counselor should the need occur. This documentation transfer will protect the confidentiality and benefit the needs of the student for whom the records are written.

C.3. Collaborating and Educating Around the Role of the School Counselor

The school counselor, school counseling program supervisor/director and school counselor educator:

a. Share the role of the school counseling program in ensuring data-driven academic, career/college and personal/social success competencies for every student, resulting in specific outcomes/indicators with all stakeholders.

b. Broker services internal and external to the schools to help ensure every student receives the benefits of a school counseling program and specific academic, career/college and personal/social competencies.

D. Responsibilities to School, Communities and Families

D.1. Responsibilities to the School

Professional school counselors:

a. Support and protect students' best interest against any infringement of their educational program.

b. Inform appropriate officials, in accordance with school policy, of conditions that may be potentially disruptive or damaging to the school's mission, personnel and property while honoring the confidentiality between the student and the school counselor.

c. Are knowledgeable and supportive of their school's mission, and connect their program to the school's mission.

d. Delineate and promote the school counselor's role, and function as a student advocate in meeting the needs of those served. School counselors will notify appropriate officials of systemic conditions that may limit or curtail their effectiveness in providing programs and services.

e. Accept employment only for positions for which they are qualified by education, training, supervised experience, state and national professional credentials and appropriate professional experience.

f. Advocate that administrators hire only qualified, appropriately trained and competent individuals for professional school counseling positions.

g. Assist in developing: (1) curricular and environmental conditions appropriate for the school and community; (2) educational procedures and programs to meet students' developmental needs; (3) a systematic evaluation process for comprehensive, developmental, standards-based school counseling programs, services and personnel; and (4) a data-driven evaluation process guiding the comprehensive, developmental school counseling program and service delivery.

D.2. Responsibility to the Community

Professional school counselors:

a. Collaborate with community agencies, organizations and individuals in students' best interest and without regard to personal reward or remuneration.

b. Extend their influence and opportunity to deliver a comprehensive school counseling program to all students by collaborating with community resources for student success.

c. Promote equity for all students through community resources.
d. Are careful not to use their professional role as a school counselor to benefit any type of private therapeutic or consultative practice in which they might be involved outside of the school setting.

E. Responsibilities to Self

E.1. Professional Competence
Professional school counselors:
a. Function within the boundaries of individual professional competence and accept responsibility for the consequences of their actions.
b. Monitor emotional and physical health and practice wellness to ensure optimal effectiveness. Seek physical or mental health referrals when needed to ensure competence at all times.
c. Monitor personal responsibility and recognize the high standard of care a professional in this critical position of trust must maintain on and off the job and are cognizant of and refrain from activity that may lead to inadequate professional services or diminish their effectiveness with school community members Professional and personal growth are ongoing throughout the counselor's career.
d. Strive through personal initiative to stay abreast of current research and to maintain professional competence in advocacy, teaming and collaboration, culturally competent counseling and school counseling program coordination, knowledge and use of technology, leadership, and equity assessment using data.
e. Ensure a variety of regular opportunities for participating in and facilitating professional development for self and other educators and school counselors through continuing education opportunities annually including: attendance at professional school counseling conferences; reading *Professional School Counseling* journal articles; facilitating workshops for education staff on issues school counselors are uniquely positioned to provide.
f. Enhance personal self-awareness, professional effectiveness and ethical practice by regularly attending presentations on ethical decision-making. Effective school counselors will seek supervision when ethical or professional questions arise in their practice.
g. Maintain current membership in professional associations to ensure ethical and best practices.

E.2. Multicultural and Social Justice Advocacy and Leadership
Professional school counselors:
a. Monitor and expand personal multicultural and social justice advocacy awareness, knowledge and skills. School counselors strive for exemplary cultural competence by ensuring personal beliefs or values are not imposed on students or other stakeholders.
b. Develop competencies in how prejudice, power and various forms of oppression, such as ableism, ageism, classism, familyism, genderism, heterosexism,

immigrationism, linguicism, racism, religionism and sexism, affect self, students and all stakeholders.

c. Acquire educational, consultation and training experiences to improve awareness, knowledge, skills and effectiveness in working with diverse populations: ethnic/racial status, age, economic status, special needs, ESL or ELL, immigration status, sexual orientation, gender, gender identity/expression, family type, religious/spiritual identity and appearance.

d. Affirm the multiple cultural and linguistic identities of every student and all stakeholders. Advocate for equitable school and school counseling program policies and practices for every student and all stakeholders including use of translators and bilingual/multilingual school counseling program materials that represent all languages used by families in the school community, and advocate for appropriate accommodations and accessibility for students with disabilities.

e. Use inclusive and culturally responsible language in all forms of communication.

f. Provide regular workshops and written/digital information to families to increase understanding, collaborative two-way communication and a welcoming school climate between families and the school to promote increased student achievement.

g. Work as advocates and leaders in the school to create equity-based school counseling programs that help close any achievement, opportunity and attainment gaps that deny all students the chance to pursue their educational goals.

F. Responsibilities to the Profession

F.1. Professionalism

Professional school counselors:

a. Accept the policies and procedures for handling ethical violations as a result of maintaining membership in the American School Counselor Association.

b. Conduct themselves in such a manner as to advance individual ethical practice and the profession.

c. Conduct appropriate research, and report findings in a manner consistent with acceptable educational and psychological research practices. School counselors advocate for the protection of individual students' identities when using data for research or program planning.

d. Seek institutional and parent/guardian consent before administering any research, and maintain security of research records.

e. Adhere to ethical standards of the profession, other official policy statements, such as ASCA's position statements, role statement and the ASCA National Model and relevant statutes established by federal, state and local governments, and when these are in conflict work responsibly for change.

f. Clearly distinguish between statements and actions made as a private individual and those made as a representative of the school counseling profession.

g. Do not use their professional position to recruit or gain clients, consultees for their private practice or to seek and receive unjustified personal gains, unfair advantage, inappropriate relationships or unearned goods or services.

F.2. Contribution to the Profession

Professional school counselors:

a. Actively participate in professional associations and share results and best practices in assessing, implementing and annually evaluating the outcomes of data-driven school counseling programs with measurable academic, career/college and personal/social competencies for every student.

b. Provide support, consultation and mentoring to novice professionals.

c. Have a responsibility to read and abide by the ASCA Ethical Standards and adhere to the applicable laws and regulations.

F.3. Supervision of School Counselor Candidates Pursuing Practicum and Internship Experiences:

Professional school counselors:

a. Provide support for appropriate experiences in academic, career, college access and personal/social counseling for school counseling interns.

b. Ensure school counselor candidates have experience in developing, implementing and evaluating a data-driven school counseling program model, such as the ASCA National Model.

c. Ensure the school counseling practicum and internship have specific, measurable service delivery, foundation, management and accountability systems.

d. Ensure school counselor candidates maintain appropriate liability insurance for the duration of the school counseling practicum and internship experiences.

e. Ensure a site visit is completed by a school counselor education faculty member for each practicum or internship student, preferably when both the school counselor trainee and site supervisor are present.

F.4. Collaboration and Education about School Counselors and School Counseling Programs with other Professionals

School counselors and school counseling program directors/supervisors collaborate with special educators, school nurses, school social workers, school psychologists, college counselors/admissions officers, physical therapists, occupational therapists and speech pathologists to advocate for optimal services for students and all other stakeholders.

G. Maintenance of Standards

Professional school counselors are expected to maintain ethical behavior at all times.

G.1. When there exists serious doubt as to the ethical behavior of a colleague(s) the following procedure may serve as a guide:

1. The school counselor should consult confidentially with a professional colleague to discuss the nature of a complaint to see if the professional colleague views the situation as an ethical violation.

2. When feasible, the school counselor should directly approach the colleague whose behavior is in question to discuss the complaint and seek resolution.

3. The school counselor should keep documentation of all the steps taken.
4. If resolution is not forthcoming at the personal level, the school counselor shall utilize the channels established within the school, school district, the state school counseling association and ASCA's Ethics Committee.
5. If the matter still remains unresolved, referral for review and appropriate action should be made to the Ethics Committees in the following sequence:
   - State school counselor association
   - American School Counselor Association
6. The ASCA Ethics Committee is responsible for:
   - Educating and consulting with the membership regarding ethical standards.
   - Periodically reviewing and recommending changes in code.
   - Receiving and processing questions to clarify the application of such standards. Questions must be submitted in writing to the ASCA Ethics Committee chair.
   - Handling complaints of alleged violations of the ASCA Ethical Standards for School Counselors. At the national level, complaints should be submitted in writing to the ASCA Ethics Committee, c/o the Executive Director, American School Counselor Association, 1101 King St., Suite 625, Alexandria, VA 22314.

G.2. When school counselors are forced to work in situations or abide by policies that do not reflect the ethics of the profession, the school counselor works responsibly through the correct channels to try and remedy the condition.

G.3. When faced with any ethical dilemma school counselors, school counseling program directors/supervisors and school counselor educators use an ethical decision-making model such as Solutions to Ethical Problems in Schools (STEPS) (Stone, 2001):

1. *Define the problem emotionally and intellectually*
2. *Apply the ASCA Ethical Standards and the law*
3. *Consider the students' chronological and developmental levels*
4. *Consider the setting, parental rights and minors' rights*
5. *Apply the moral principles*
6. *Determine Your potential courses of action and their consequences*
7. *Evaluate the selected action*
8. *Consult*
9. *Implement the course of action*

(Adopted 1984; revised 1992, 1998, 2004 and 2010)

American Psychological Association
Ethical Principles of Psychologists and Code of Conduct

Adopted August 21, 2002
Effective June 1, 2003
With the 2010 Amendments
Adopted February 20, 2010
Effective June 1, 2010

Contents

2010 Amendments to the 2002 "Ethical Principles of Psychologists and Code of Conduct"

Introduction and Applicability

The American Psychological Association's (APA's) Ethical Principles of Psychologists and Code of Conduct (hereinafter referred to as the Ethics Code) consists of an Introduction, a Preamble, five General Principles (A–E), and specific Ethical Standards. The Introduction discusses the intent, organization, procedural considerations, and scope of application of the Ethics Code. The Preamble and General Principles are aspirational goals to guide psychologists toward the highest ideals of psychology. Although the Preamble and General Principles are not themselves enforceable rules, they should be considered by psychologists in arriving at an ethical course of action. The Ethical Standards set forth enforceable rules for conduct as psychologists. Most of the Ethical Standards are written broadly, in order to apply to psychologists in varied roles, although the application of an Ethical Standard may vary depending on the context. The Ethical Standards are not exhaustive. The fact that a given conduct is not specifically addressed by an Ethical Standard does not mean that it is necessarily either ethical or unethical.

This Ethics Code applies only to psychologists' activities that are part of their scientific, educational, or professional roles as psychologists. Areas covered include but are not limited to the clinical, counseling, and school practice of psychology; research; teaching; supervision of trainees; public service; policy development; social intervention; development of assessment instruments; conducting assessments; educational counseling; organizational consulting; forensic activities; program design and evaluation; and administration. This Ethics Code applies to these activities across a variety of contexts, such as in person, postal, telephone, Internet, and other electronic transmissions. These activities shall be distinguished from the purely private conduct of psychologists, which is not within the purview of the Ethics Code.

Membership in the APA commits members and student affiliates to comply with the standards of the APA Ethics Code and to the rules and procedures used to enforce them. Lack of awareness or misunderstanding of an Ethical Standard is not itself a defense to a charge of unethical conduct.

The procedures for filing, investigating, and resolving complaints of unethical conduct are described in the current Rules and Procedures of the APA Ethics Committee. APA may impose sanctions on its members for violations of the standards of the Ethics Code, including termination of APA membership, and may notify other bodies and individuals of its actions. Actions that violate the standards of the Ethics Code may also lead to the imposition of sanctions on psychologists or students whether or not they are APA members by bodies other than APA, including state psychological associations, other professional groups, psychology boards, other state or federal agencies, and payors for health services. In addition, APA may take action against a member after his or her conviction of a felony, expulsion or suspension from an affiliated state psychological association, or suspension or loss of licensure. When the sanction to be imposed by APA is less than expulsion, the 2001 Rules and Procedures do not guarantee an opportunity for an in-person hearing, but generally provide that complaints will be resolved only on the basis of a submitted record.

The Ethics Code is intended to provide guidance for psychologists and standards of professional conduct that can be applied by the APA and by other bodies that choose to adopt them. The Ethics Code is not intended to be a basis of civil liability. Whether a psychologist has violated the Ethics Code standards does not by itself determine whether the psychologist is legally liable in a court action, whether a contract is enforceable, or whether other legal consequences occur.

The modifiers used in some of the standards of this Ethics Code (e.g., *reasonably, appropriate, potentially*) are included in the standards when they would (1) allow professional judgment on the part of psychologists, (2) eliminate injustice or inequality that would occur without the modifier, (3) ensure applicability across the broad range of activities conducted by psychologists, or (4) guard against a set of rigid rules that might be quickly outdated. As used in this Ethics Code, the term *reasonable* means the prevailing professional judgment of psychologists engaged in similar activities in similar circumstances, given the knowledge the psychologist had or should have had at the time.

The American Psychological Association's Council of Representatives adopted this version of the APA Ethics Code during its meeting on August 21, 2002. The Code became effective on June 1, 2003. The Council of Representatives amended this version of the Ethics Code on February 20, 2010. The amendments became effective on June 1, 2010 (see p. 15 of this pamphlet). Inquiries concerning the substance or interpretation of the APA Ethics Code should be addressed to the Director, Office of Ethics, American Psychological Association, 750 First Street, NE, Washington, DC 20002-4242. The Ethics Code and information regarding the Code can be found on the APA website, http://www.apa.org/ethics. The standards in this Ethics Code will be used to adjudicate complaints brought concerning alleged conduct occurring on or after the effective date. Complaints will be adjudicated on the basis of the version of the Ethics Code that was in effect at the time the conduct occurred.

The APA has previously published its Ethics Code as follows:

American Psychological Association. (1953). *Ethical standards of psychologists.* Washington, DC: Author.
American Psychological Association. (1959). Ethical standards of psychologists. *American Psychologist, 14,* 279–282.
American Psychological Association. (1963). Ethical standards of psychologists. *American Psychologist, 18,* 56–60.
American Psychological Association. (1968). Ethical standards of psychologists. *American Psychologist, 23,* 357–361.
American Psychological Association. (1977, March). Ethical standards of psychologists. *APA Monitor,* 22–23.
American Psychological Association. (1979). *Ethical standards of psychologists.* Washington, DC: Author.
American Psychological Association. (1981). Ethical principles of psychologists. *American Psychologist, 36,* 633–638.

American Psychological Association. (1990). Ethical principles of psychologists (Amended June 2, 1989). *American Psychologist, 45,* 390–395.

American Psychological Association. (1992). Ethical principles of psychologists and code of conduct. *American Psychologist, 47,* 1597–1611.

American Psychological Association. (2002). Ethical principles of psychologists and code of conduct. *American Psychologist, 57,* 1060-1073.

Request copies of the APA's Ethical Principles of Psychologists and Code of Conduct from the APA Order Department, 750 First Street, NE, Washington, DC 20002-4242, or phone (202) 336-5510.

In the process of making decisions regarding their professional behavior, psychologists must consider this Ethics Code in addition to applicable laws and psychology board regulations. In applying the Ethics Code to their professional work, psychologists may consider other materials and guidelines that have been adopted or endorsed by scientific and professional psychological organizations and the dictates of their own conscience, as well as consult with others within the field. If this Ethics Code establishes a higher standard of conduct than is required by law, psychologists must meet the higher ethical standard. If psychologists' ethical responsibilities conflict with law, regulations, or other governing legal authority, psychologists make known their commitment to this Ethics Code and take steps to resolve the conflict in a responsible manner in keeping with basic principles of human rights.

Preamble

Psychologists are committed to increasing scientific and professional knowledge of behavior and people's understanding of themselves and others and to the use of such knowledge to improve the condition of individuals, organizations, and society. Psychologists respect and protect civil and human rights and the central importance of freedom of inquiry and expression in research, teaching, and publication. They strive to help the public in developing informed judgments and choices concerning human behavior. In doing so, they perform many roles, such as researcher, educator, diagnostician, therapist, supervisor, consultant, administrator, social interventionist, and expert witness. This Ethics Code provides a common set of principles and standards upon which psychologists build their professional and scientific work.

This Ethics Code is intended to provide specific standards to cover most situations encountered by psychologists. It has as its goals the welfare and protection of the individuals and groups with whom psychologists work and the education of members, students, and the public regarding ethical standards of the discipline.

The development of a dynamic set of ethical standards for psychologists' work-related conduct requires a personal commitment and lifelong effort to act ethically; to encourage ethical behavior by students, supervisees, employees, and colleagues; and to consult with others concerning ethical problems.

General Principles

This section consists of General Principles. General Principles, as opposed to Ethical Standards, are aspirational in nature. Their intent is to guide and inspire psychologists toward the very highest ethical ideals of the profession. General Principles, in contrast to Ethical Standards, do not represent obligations and should not form the basis for imposing sanctions. Relying upon General Principles for either of these reasons distorts both their meaning and purpose.

Principle A: Beneficence and Nonmaleficence

Psychologists strive to benefit those with whom they work and take care to do no harm. In their professional actions, psychologists seek to safeguard the welfare and rights of those with whom they interact professionally and other affected persons, and the welfare of animal subjects of research. When conflicts occur among psychologists' obligations or concerns, they attempt to resolve these conflicts in a responsible fashion that avoids or minimizes harm. Because psychologists' scientific and professional judgments and actions may affect the lives of others, they are alert to and guard against personal, financial, social, organizational, or political factors that might lead to misuse of their influence. Psychologists strive to be aware of the possible effect of their own physical and mental health on their ability to help those with whom they work.

Principle B: Fidelity and Responsibility

Psychologists establish relationships of trust with those with whom they work. They are aware of their professional and scientific responsibilities to society and to the specific communities in which they work. Psychologists uphold professional standards of conduct, clarify their professional roles and obligations, accept appropriate responsibility for their behavior, and seek to manage conflicts of interest that could lead to exploitation or harm. Psychologists consult with, refer to, or cooperate with other professionals and institutions to the extent needed to serve the best interests of those with whom they work. They are concerned about the ethical compliance of their colleagues' scientific and professional conduct. Psychologists strive to contribute a portion of their professional time for little or no compensation or personal advantage.

Principle C: Integrity

Psychologists seek to promote accuracy, honesty, and truthfulness in the science, teaching, and practice of psychology. In these activities psychologists do not steal, cheat, or engage in fraud, subterfuge, or intentional misrepresentation of fact. Psychologists strive to keep their promises and to avoid unwise or unclear commitments. In situations in which deception may be ethically justifiable to maximize benefits and minimize harm, psychologists have a serious obligation to consider the need for, the possible consequences of, and their responsibility to correct any resulting mistrust or other harmful effects that arise from the use of such techniques.

Principle D: Justice

Psychologists recognize that fairness and justice entitle all persons to access to and benefit from the contributions of psychology and to equal quality in the processes, procedures, and services being conducted by psychologists. Psychologists exercise reasonable judgment and take precautions to ensure that their potential biases, the boundaries of their competence, and the limitations of their expertise do not lead to or condone unjust practices.

Principle E: Respect for People's Rights and Dignity

Psychologists respect the dignity and worth of all people, and the rights of individuals to privacy, confidentiality, and self-determination. Psychologists are aware that special safeguards may be necessary to protect the rights and welfare of persons or communities whose vulnerabilities impair autonomous decision-making. Psychologists are aware of and respect cultural, individual, and role differences, including those based on age, gender, gender identity, race, ethnicity, culture, national origin, religion, sexual orientation, disability, language, and socioeconomic status, and consider these factors when working with members of such groups. Psychologists try to eliminate the effect on their work of biases based on those factors, and they do not knowingly participate in or condone activities of others based upon such prejudices.

Ethical Standards

1. Resolving Ethical Issues

1.1 Misuse of Psychologists' Work

If psychologists learn of misuse or misrepresentation of their work, they take reasonable steps to correct or minimize the misuse or misrepresentation.

1.2 Conflicts Between Ethics and Law, Regulations, or Other Governing Legal Authority

If psychologists' ethical responsibilities conflict with law, regulations, or other governing legal authority, psychologists clarify the nature of the conflict, make known their commitment to the Ethics Code, and take reasonable steps to resolve the conflict consistent with the General Principles and Ethical Standards of the Ethics Code. Under no circumstances may this standard be used to justify or defend violating human rights.

1.3 Conflicts Between Ethics and Organizational Demands

If the demands of an organization with which psychologists are affiliated or for whom they are working are in conflict with this Ethics Code, psychologists clarify the nature of the conflict, make known their commitment to the Ethics Code, and take reasonable steps to resolve the conflict consistent with the General Principles and Ethical Standards of the Ethics Code. Under no circumstances may this standard be used to justify or defend violating human rights.

1.4 Informal Resolution of Ethical Violations

When psychologists believe that there may have been an ethical violation by another psychologist, they attempt to resolve the issue by bringing it to the attention of that individual, if an informal resolution appears appropriate and the intervention does not violate any confidentiality rights that may be involved. (See also Standards 1.02, Conflicts Between Ethics and Law, Regulations, or Other Governing Legal Authority, and 1.03, Conflicts Between Ethics and Organizational Demands.)

1.5 Reporting Ethical Violations

If an apparent ethical violation has substantially harmed or is likely to substantially harm a person or organization and is not appropriate for informal resolution under Standard 1.04, Informal Resolution of Ethical Violations, or is not resolved properly in that fashion, psychologists take further action appropriate to the situation. Such action might include referral to state or national committees on professional ethics, to state licensing boards, or to the appropriate institutional authorities. This standard does not apply when an intervention would violate confidentiality rights or when psychologists have been retained to review the work of another psychologist whose professional conduct is in question. (See also Standard 1.02, Conflicts Between Ethics and Law, Regulations, or Other Governing Legal Authority.)

1.6 Cooperating With Ethics Committees

Psychologists cooperate in ethics investigations, proceedings, and resulting requirements of the APA or any affiliated state psychological association to which they belong. In doing so, they address any confidentiality issues. Failure to cooperate is itself an ethics violation. However, making a request for deferment of adjudication of an ethics complaint pending the outcome of litigation does not alone constitute non-cooperation.

1.7 Improper Complaints

Psychologists do not file or encourage the filing of ethics complaints that are made with reckless disregard for or willful ignorance of facts that would disprove the allegation.

1.8 Unfair Discrimination Against Complainants and Respondents

Psychologists do not deny persons employment, advancement, admissions to academic or other programs, tenure, or promotion, based solely upon their having made or their being the subject of an ethics complaint. This does not preclude taking action based upon the outcome of such proceedings or considering other appropriate information.

2. Competence

2.1 Boundaries of Competence

a. Psychologists provide services, teach, and conduct research with populations and in areas only within the boundaries of their competence, based on their education, training, supervised experience, consultation, study, or professional experience.

b. Where scientific or professional knowledge in the discipline of psychology establishes that an understanding of factors associated with age, gender, gender identity, race, ethnicity, culture, national origin, religion, sexual orientation, disability, language, or socioeconomic status is essential for effective implementation of their services or research, psychologists have or obtain the training, experience, consultation, or supervision necessary to ensure the competence of their services, or they make appropriate referrals, except as provided in Standard 2.02, Providing Services in Emergencies.

c. Psychologists planning to provide services, teach, or conduct research involving populations, areas, techniques, or technologies new to them undertake relevant education, training, supervised experience, consultation, or study.

d. When psychologists are asked to provide services to individuals for whom appropriate mental health services are not available and for which psychologists have not obtained the competence necessary, psychologists with closely related prior training or experience may provide such services in order to ensure that services are not denied if they make a reasonable effort to obtain the competence required by using relevant research, training, consultation, or study.

e. In those emerging areas in which generally recognized standards for preparatory training do not yet exist, psychologists nevertheless take reasonable steps to ensure the competence of their work and to protect clients/patients, students, supervisees, research participants, organizational clients, and others from harm.

f. When assuming forensic roles, psychologists are or become reasonably familiar with the judicial or administrative rules governing their roles.

2.2 Providing Services in Emergencies

In emergencies, when psychologists provide services to individuals for whom other mental health services are not available and for which psychologists have not obtained the necessary training, psychologists may provide such services in order to ensure that services are not denied. The services are discontinued as soon as the emergency has ended or appropriate services are available.

2.3 Maintaining Competence

Psychologists undertake ongoing efforts to develop and maintain their competence.

2.4 Bases for Scientific and Professional Judgments

Psychologists' work is based upon established scientific and professional knowledge of the discipline. (See also Standards 2.01e, Boundaries of Competence, and 10.01b, Informed Consent to Therapy.)

2.5 Delegation of Work to Others

Psychologists who delegate work to employees, supervisees, or research or teaching assistants or who use the services of others, such as interpreters, take reasonable steps to (1) avoid delegating such work to persons who have a multiple relationship with those being served that would likely lead to exploitation or loss of objectivity; (2) authorize only those responsibilities that such persons can be expected to perform competently on the basis of their education, training, or experience, either independently or with the level of supervision being provided; and (3) see that such persons perform these services competently. (See also Standards 2.02, Providing Services in Emergencies; 3.05, Multiple Relationships; 4.01, Maintaining Confidentiality; 9.01, Bases for Assessments; 9.02, Use of Assessments; 9.03, Informed Consent in Assessments; and 9.07, Assessment by Unqualified Persons.)

2.6 Personal Problems and Conflicts

(a) Psychologists refrain from initiating an activity when they know or should know that there is a substantial likelihood that their personal problems will prevent them from performing their work-related activities in a competent manner.

(b) When psychologists become aware of personal problems that may interfere with their performing work-related duties adequately, they take appropriate measures, such as obtaining professional consultation or assistance, and determine whether they should limit, suspend, or terminate their work-related duties. (See also Standard 10.10, Terminating Therapy.)

3. Human Relations

3.1 Unfair Discrimination

In their work-related activities, psychologists do not engage in unfair discrimination based on age, gender, gender identity, race, ethnicity, culture, national origin, religion, sexual orientation, disability, socioeconomic status, or any basis proscribed by law.

3.2 Sexual Harassment

Psychologists do not engage in sexual harassment. Sexual harassment is sexual solicitation, physical advances, or verbal or nonverbal conduct that is sexual in nature, that occurs in connection with the psychologist's activities or roles as a psychologist, and that either (1) is unwelcome, is offensive, or creates a hostile workplace or educational environment, and the psychologist knows or is told this or (2) is sufficiently severe or intense to be abusive to a reasonable person in the context. Sexual harassment can consist of a single intense or severe act or of multiple persistent or pervasive acts. (See also Standard 1.08, Unfair Discrimination Against Complainants and Respondents.)

3.3 Other Harassment

Psychologists do not knowingly engage in behavior that is harassing or demeaning to persons with whom they interact in their work based on factors such as those persons' age, gender, gender identity, race, ethnicity, culture, national origin, religion, sexual orientation, disability, language, or socioeconomic status.

3.4 Avoiding Harm

Psychologists take reasonable steps to avoid harming their clients/patients, students, supervisees, research participants, organizational clients, and others with whom they work, and to minimize harm where it is foreseeable and unavoidable.

3.5 Multiple Relationships

(a) A multiple relationship occurs when a psychologist is in a professional role with a person and (1) at the same time is in another role with the same person, (2) at the same time is in a relationship with a person closely associated with or related to the person with whom the psychologist has the professional relationship, or (3) promises to enter into another relationship in the future with the person or a person closely associated with or related to the person.

A psychologist refrains from entering into a multiple relationship if the multiple relationship could reasonably be expected to impair the psychologist's objectivity, competence, or effectiveness in performing his or her functions as a psychologist, or otherwise risks exploitation or harm to the person with whom the professional relationship exists.

Multiple relationships that would not reasonably be expected to cause impairment or risk exploitation or harm are not unethical.

(b) If a psychologist finds that, due to unforeseen factors, a potentially harmful multiple relationship has arisen, the psychologist takes reasonable steps to resolve it with due regard for the best interests of the affected person and maximal compliance with the Ethics Code.

(c) When psychologists are required by law, institutional policy, or extraordinary circumstances to serve in more than one role in judicial or administrative proceedings, at the outset they clarify role expectations and the extent of confidentiality and thereafter as changes occur. (See also Standards 3.04, Avoiding Harm, and 3.07, Third-Party Requests for Services.)

3.6 Conflict of Interest

Psychologists refrain from taking on a professional role when personal, scientific, professional, legal, financial, or other interests or relationships could reasonably be expected to (1) impair their objectivity, competence, or effectiveness in performing their functions as psychologists or (2) expose the person or organization with whom the professional relationship exists to harm or exploitation.

3.7 Third-Party Requests for Services

When psychologists agree to provide services to a person or entity at the request of a third party, psychologists attempt to clarify at the outset of the service the nature of the relationship with all individuals or organizations involved. This clarification includes the role of the psychologist (e.g., therapist, consultant, diagnostician, or expert witness), an identification of who is the client, the probable uses of the services provided or the information obtained, and the fact that there may be limits to confidentiality. (See also Standards 3.05, Multiple Relationships, and 4.02, Discussing the Limits of Confidentiality.)

3.8 Exploitative Relationships

Psychologists do not exploit persons over whom they have supervisory, evaluative, or other authority such as clients/patients, students, supervisees, research participants, and employees. (See also Standards 3.05, Multiple Relationships; 6.04, Fees and Financial Arrangements; 6.05, Barter With Clients/Patients; 7.07, Sexual Relationships With Students and Supervisees; 10.05, Sexual Intimacies With Current Therapy Clients/Patients; 10.06, Sexual Intimacies With Relatives or Significant Others of Current Therapy Clients/Patients; 10.07, Therapy With Former Sexual Partners; and 10.08, Sexual Intimacies With Former Therapy Clients/Patients.)

3.9 Cooperation With Other Professionals

When indicated and professionally appropriate, psychologists cooperate with other professionals in order to serve their clients/patients effectively and appropriately. (See also Standard 4.05, Disclosures.)

3.10 Informed Consent

(a) When psychologists conduct research or provide assessment, therapy, counseling, or consulting services in person or via electronic transmission or other forms of communication, they obtain the informed consent of the individual or individuals using language that is reasonably understandable to that person or persons except when conducting such activities without consent is mandated by law or governmental regulation or as otherwise provided in this Ethics Code. (See also Standards 8.02, Informed Consent to Research; 9.03, Informed Consent in Assessments; and 10.01, Informed Consent to Therapy.)

(b) For persons who are legally incapable of giving informed consent, psychologists nevertheless (1) provide an appropriate explanation, (2) seek the individual's assent, (3) consider such persons' preferences and best interests, and (4) obtain appropriate permission from a legally authorized person, if such substitute consent is permitted or required by law. When consent by a legally authorized person is not permitted or required by law, psychologists take reasonable steps to protect the individual's rights and welfare.

(c) When psychological services are court ordered or otherwise mandated, psychologists inform the individual of the nature of the anticipated services, including whether the services are court ordered or mandated and any limits of confidentiality, before proceeding.

(d) Psychologists appropriately document written or oral consent, permission, and assent. (See also Standards 8.02, Informed Consent to Research; 9.03, Informed Consent in Assessments; and 10.01, Informed Consent to Therapy.)

3.11 Psychological Services Delivered to or Through Organizations

(a) Psychologists delivering services to or through organizations provide information beforehand to clients and when appropriate those directly affected by the services about (1) the nature and objectives of the services, (2) the intended recipients, (3) which of the individuals are clients, (4) the relationship the psychologist will have with each person and the organization, (5) the probable uses of services provided and information obtained, (6) who will have access to the information, and (7) limits of confidentiality. As soon as feasible, they provide information about the results and conclusions of such services to appropriate persons.

(b) If psychologists will be precluded by law or by organizational roles from providing such information to particular individuals or groups, they so inform those individuals or groups at the outset of the service.

3.12 Interruption of Psychological Services

Unless otherwise covered by contract, psychologists make reasonable efforts to plan for facilitating services in the event that psychological services are interrupted by factors such as the psychologist's illness, death, unavailability, relocation, or retirement or by the client's/patient's relocation or financial limitations. (See also Standard 6.02c, Maintenance, Dissemination, and Disposal of Confidential Records of Professional and Scientific Work.)

4. Privacy and Confidentiality

4.1 Maintaining Confidentiality
Psychologists have a primary obligation and take reasonable precautions to protect confidential information obtained through or stored in any medium, recognizing that the extent and limits of confidentiality may be regulated by law or established by institutional rules or professional or scientific relationship. (See also Standard 2.05, Delegation of Work to Others.)

4.2 Discussing the Limits of Confidentiality
(a) Psychologists discuss with persons (including, to the extent feasible, persons who are legally incapable of giving informed consent and their legal representatives) and organizations with whom they establish a scientific or professional relationship (1) the relevant limits of confidentiality and (2) the foreseeable uses of the information generated through their psychological activities. (See also Standard 3.10, Informed Consent.)
(b) Unless it is not feasible or is contraindicated, the discussion of confidentiality occurs at the outset of the relationship and thereafter as new circumstances may warrant.
(c) Psychologists who offer services, products, or information via electronic transmission inform clients/patients of the risks to privacy and limits of confidentiality.

4.3 Recording
Before recording the voices or images of individuals to whom they provide services, psychologists obtain permission from all such persons or their legal representatives. (See also Standards 8.03, Informed Consent for Recording Voices and Images in Research; 8.05, Dispensing With Informed Consent for Research; and 8.07, Deception in Research.)

4.4 Minimizing Intrusions on Privacy
(a) Psychologists include in written and oral reports and consultations, only information germane to the purpose for which the communication is made.
(b) Psychologists discuss confidential information obtained in their work only for appropriate scientific or professional purposes and only with persons clearly concerned with such matters.

4.5 Disclosures
(a) Psychologists may disclose confidential information with the appropriate consent of the organizational client, the individual client/patient, or another legally authorized person on behalf of the client/patient unless prohibited by law.
(b) Psychologists disclose confidential information without the consent of the individual only as mandated by law, or where permitted by law for a valid purpose such as to (1) provide needed professional services; (2) obtain appropriate

professional consultations; (3) protect the client/patient, psychologist, or others from harm; or (4) obtain payment for services from a client/patient, in which instance disclosure is limited to the minimum that is necessary to achieve the purpose. (See also Standard 6.04e, Fees and Financial Arrangements.)

4.6 Consultations
When consulting with colleagues, (1) psychologists do not disclose confidential information that reasonably could lead to the identification of a client/patient, research participant, or other person or organization with whom they have a confidential relationship unless they have obtained the prior consent of the person or organization or the disclosure cannot be avoided, and (2) they disclose information only to the extent necessary to achieve the purposes of the consultation. (See also Standard 4.01, Maintaining Confidentiality.)

4.7 Use of Confidential Information for Didactic or Other Purposes
Psychologists do not disclose in their writings, lectures, or other public media, confidential, personally identifiable information concerning their clients/patients, students, research participants, organizational clients, or other recipients of their services that they obtained during the course of their work, unless (1) they take reasonable steps to disguise the person or organization, (2) the person or organization has consented in writing, or (3) there is legal authorization for doing so.

5. Advertising and Other Public Statements

5.1 Avoidance of False or Deceptive Statements
(a) Public statements include but are not limited to paid or unpaid advertising, product endorsements, grant applications, licensing applications, other credentialing applications, brochures, printed matter, directory listings, personal resumes or curricula vitae, or comments for use in media such as print or electronic transmission, statements in legal proceedings, lectures and public oral presentations, and published materials. Psychologists do not knowingly make public statements that are false, deceptive, or fraudulent concerning their research, practice, or other work activities or those of persons or organizations with which they are affiliated.
(b) Psychologists do not make false, deceptive, or fraudulent statements concerning (1) their training, experience, or competence; (2) their academic degrees; (3) their credentials; (4) their institutional or association affiliations; (5) their services; (6) the scientific or clinical basis for, or results or degree of success of, their services; (7) their fees; or (8) their publications or research findings.
(c) Psychologists claim degrees as credentials for their health services only if those degrees (1) were earned from a regionally accredited educational institution or (2) were the basis for psychology licensure by the state in which they practice.

5.2 Statements By Others
(a) Psychologists who engage others to create or place public statements that promote their professional practice, products, or activities retain professional responsibility for such statements.

(b) Psychologists do not compensate employees of press, radio, television, or other communication media in return for publicity in a news item. (See also Standard 1.01, Misuse of Psychologists' Work.)

(c) A paid advertisement relating to psychologists' activities must be identified or clearly recognizable as such.

5.3 Descriptions of Workshops and Non-Degree-Granting Educational Programs

To the degree to which they exercise control, psychologists responsible for announcements, catalogs, brochures, or advertisements describing workshops, seminars, or other non-degree-granting educational programs ensure that they accurately describe the audience for which the program is intended, the educational objectives, the presenters, and the fees involved.

5.4 Media Presentations

When psychologists provide public advice or comment via print, Internet, or other electronic transmission, they take precautions to ensure that statements (1) are based on their professional knowledge, training, or experience in accord with appropriate psychological literature and practice; (2) are otherwise consistent with this Ethics Code; and (3) do not indicate that a professional relationship has been established with the recipient. (See also Standard 2.04, Bases for Scientific and Professional Judgments.)

5.5 Testimonials

Psychologists do not solicit testimonials from current therapy clients/patients or other persons who because of their particular circumstances are vulnerable to undue influence.

5.6 In-Person Solicitation

Psychologists do not engage, directly or through agents, in uninvited in-person solicitation of business from actual or potential therapy clients/patients or other persons who because of their particular circumstances are vulnerable to undue influence. However, this prohibition does not preclude (1) attempting to implement appropriate collateral contacts for the purpose of benefiting an already engaged therapy client/patient or (2) providing disaster or community outreach services.

6. Record Keeping and Fees

6.1 Documentation of Professional and Scientific Work and Maintenance of Records

Psychologists create, and to the extent the records are under their control, maintain, disseminate, store, retain, and dispose of records and data relating to their professional and scientific work in order to (1) facilitate provision of services later by them or by other professionals, (2) allow for replication of research design and analyses, (3) meet institutional requirements, (4) ensure accuracy of billing and payments, and (5) ensure compliance with law. (See also Standard 4.01, Maintaining Confidentiality.)

6.2 Maintenance, Dissemination, and Disposal of Confidential Records of Professional and Scientific Work

(a) Psychologists maintain confidentiality in creating, storing, accessing, transferring, and disposing of records under their control, whether these are written, automated, or in any other medium. (See also Standards 4.01, Maintaining Confidentiality, and 6.01, Documentation of Professional and Scientific Work and Maintenance of Records.)

(b) If confidential information concerning recipients of psychological services is entered into databases or systems of records available to persons whose access has not been consented to by the recipient, psychologists use coding or other techniques to avoid the inclusion of personal identifiers.

(c) Psychologists make plans in advance to facilitate the appropriate transfer and to protect the confidentiality of records and data in the event of psychologists' withdrawal from positions or practice. (See also Standards 3.12, Interruption of Psychological Services, and 10.09, Interruption of Therapy.)

6.3 Withholding Records for Nonpayment

Psychologists may not withhold records under their control that are requested and needed for a client's/patient's emergency treatment solely because payment has not been received.

6.4 Fees and Financial Arrangements

(a) As early as is feasible in a professional or scientific relationship, psychologists and recipients of psychological services reach an agreement specifying compensation and billing arrangements.

(b) Psychologists' fee practices are consistent with law.

(c) Psychologists do not misrepresent their fees.

(d) If limitations to services can be anticipated because of limitations in financing, this is discussed with the recipient of services as early as is feasible. (See also Standards 10.09, Interruption of Therapy, and 10.10, Terminating Therapy.)

(e) If the recipient of services does not pay for services as agreed, and if psychologists intend to use collection agencies or legal measures to collect the fees, psychologists first in-form the person that such measures will be taken and provide that person an opportunity to make prompt payment. (See also Standards 4.05, Disclosures; 6.03, Withholding Records for Nonpayment; and 10.01, Informed Consent to Therapy.)

6.5 Barter With Clients/Patients

Barter is the acceptance of goods, services, or other nonmonetary remuneration from clients/patients in return for psychological services. Psychologists may barter only if (1) it is not clinically contraindicated, and (2) the resulting arrangement is not exploitative. (See also Standards 3.05, Multiple Relationships, and 6.04, Fees and Financial Arrangements.)

6.6 Accuracy in Reports to Payors and Funding Sources

In their reports to payors for services or sources of research funding, psychologists take reasonable steps to ensure the accurate reporting of the nature of the service provided or research conducted, the fees, charges, or payments, and where applicable, the identity of the provider, the findings, and the diagnosis. (See also Standards 4.01, Maintaining Confidentiality; 4.04, Minimizing Intrusions on Privacy; and 4.05, Disclosures.)

6.7 Referrals and Fees
When psychologists pay, receive payment from, or divide fees with another professional, other than in an employer–employee relationship, the payment to each is based on the services provided (clinical, consultative, administrative, or other) and is not based on the referral itself. (See also Standard 3.09, Cooperation With Other Professionals.)

7. Education and Training

7.1 Design of Education and Training Programs
Psychologists responsible for education and training programs take reasonable steps to ensure that the programs are designed to provide the appropriate knowledge and proper experiences, and to meet the requirements for licensure, certification, or other goals for which claims are made by the program. (See also Standard 5.03, Descriptions of Workshops and Non-Degree-Granting Educational Programs.)

7.2 Descriptions of Education and Training Programs
Psychologists responsible for education and training programs take reasonable steps to ensure that there is a current and accurate description of the program content (including participation in required course- or program-related counseling, psychotherapy, experiential groups, consulting projects, or community service), training goals and objectives, stipends and benefits, and requirements that must be met for satisfactory completion of the program. This information must be made readily available to all interested parties.

7.3 Accuracy in Teaching
(a) Psychologists take reasonable steps to ensure that course syllabi are accurate regarding the subject matter to be covered, bases for evaluating progress, and the nature of course experiences. This standard does not preclude an instructor from modifying course content or requirements when the instructor considers it pedagogically necessary or desirable, so long as students are made aware of these modifications in a manner that enables them to fulfill course requirements. (See also Standard 5.01, Avoidance of False or Deceptive Statements.)
(b) When engaged in teaching or training, psychologists present psychological information accurately. (See also Standard 2.03, Maintaining Competence.)

7.4 Student Disclosure of Personal Information
Psychologists do not require students or supervisees to disclose personal information in course- or program-related activities, either orally or in writing, regarding sexual history, history of abuse and neglect, psychological treatment, and relationships with parents, peers, and spouses or significant others except if (1) the program or training facility has clearly identified this requirement in its admissions and program materials

or (2) the information is necessary to evaluate or obtain assistance for students whose personal problems could reasonably be judged to be preventing them from performing their training- or professionally related activities in a competent manner or posing a threat to the students or others.

7.5 Mandatory Individual or Group Therapy

(a) When individual or group therapy is a program or course requirement, psychologists responsible for that program allow students in undergraduate and graduate programs the option of selecting such therapy from practitioners unaffiliated with the program. (See also Standard 7.02, Descriptions of Education and Training Programs.)
(b) Faculty who are or are likely to be responsible for evaluating students' academic performance do not themselves provide that therapy. (See also Standard 3.05, Multiple Relationships.)

7.6 Assessing Student and Supervisee Performance

(a) In academic and supervisory relationships, psychologists establish a timely and specific process for providing feedback to students and supervisees. Information regarding the process is provided to the student at the beginning of supervision.
(b) Psychologists evaluate students and supervisees on the basis of their actual performance on relevant and established program requirements.

7.7 Sexual Relationships With Students and Supervisees

Psychologists do not engage in sexual relationships with students or supervisees who are in their department, agency, or training center or over whom psychologists have or are likely to have evaluative authority. (See also Standard 3.05, Multiple Relationships.)

8. Research and Publication

8.1 Institutional Approval

When institutional approval is required, psychologists provide accurate information about their research proposals and obtain approval prior to conducting the research. They conduct the research in accordance with the approved research protocol.

8.2 Informed Consent to Research

(a) When obtaining informed consent as required in Standard 3.10, Informed Consent, psychologists inform participants about (1) the purpose of the research, expected duration, and procedures; (2) their right to decline to participate and to withdraw from the research once participation has begun; (3) the foreseeable consequences of declining or withdrawing; (4) reasonably foreseeable factors that may be expected to influence their willingness to participate such as potential risks, discomfort, or adverse effects; (5) any prospective research benefits; (6) limits of confidentiality; (7) incentives for participation; and (8) whom to contact for questions about the research and research participants' rights. They provide opportunity for the prospective participants to ask questions and receive answers. (See also Standards 8.03, Informed Consent for Recording Voices and Images in Research; 8.05, Dispensing With Informed Consent for Research; and 8.07, Deception in Research.)

(b) Psychologists conducting intervention research involving the use of experimental treatments clarify to participants at the outset of the research (1) the experimental nature of the treatment; (2) the services that will or will not be available to the control group(s) if appropriate; (3) the means by which assignment to treatment and control groups will be made; (4) available treatment alternatives if an individual does not wish to participate in the research or wishes to withdraw once a study has begun; and (5) compensation for or monetary costs of participating including, if appropriate, whether reimbursement from the participant or a third-party payor will be sought. (See also Standard 8.02a, Informed Consent to Research.)

8.3 Informed Consent for Recording Voices and Images in Research

Psychologists obtain informed consent from research participants prior to recording their voices or images for data collection unless (1) the research consists solely of naturalistic observations in public places, and it is not anticipated that the recording will be used in a manner that could cause personal identification or harm, or (2) the research design includes deception, and consent for the use of the recording is obtained during debriefing. (See also Standard 8.07, Deception in Research.)

8.4 Client/Patient, Student, and Subordinate Research Participants

(a) When psychologists conduct research with clients/patients, students, or subordinates as participants, psychologists take steps to protect the prospective participants from adverse consequences of declining or withdrawing from participation.
(b) When research participation is a course requirement or an opportunity for extra credit, the prospective participant is given the choice of equitable alternative activities.

8.5 Dispensing With Informed Consent for Research

Psychologists may dispense with informed consent only (1) where research would not reasonably be assumed to create distress or harm and involves (a) the study of normal educational practices, curricula, or classroom management methods conducted in educational settings; (b) only anonymous questionnaires, naturalistic observations, or archival research for which disclosure of responses would not place participants at risk of criminal or civil liability or damage their financial standing, employability, or reputation, and confidentiality is protected; or (c) the study of factors related to job or organization effectiveness conducted in organizational settings for which there is no risk to participants' employability, and confidentiality is protected or (2) where otherwise permitted by law or federal or institutional regulations.

8.6 Offering Inducements for Research Participation

(a) Psychologists make reasonable efforts to avoid offering excessive or inappropriate financial or other inducements for research participation when such inducements are likely to coerce participation.
(b) When offering professional services as an inducement for research participation, psychologists clarify the nature of the services, as well as the risks, obligations, and limitations. (See also Standard 6.05, Barter With Clients/Patients.)

8.7 Deception in Research

(a) Psychologists do not conduct a study involving deception unless they have determined that the use of deceptive techniques is justified by the study's significant prospective scientific, educational, or applied value and that effective nondeceptive alternative procedures are not feasible.

(b) Psychologists do not deceive prospective participants about research that is reasonably expected to cause physical pain or severe emotional distress.

(c) Psychologists explain any deception that is an integral feature of the design and conduct of an experiment to participants as early as is feasible, preferably at the conclusion of their participation, but no later than at the conclusion of the data collection, and permit participants to withdraw their data. (See also Standard 8.08, Debriefing.)

8.8 Debriefing

(a) Psychologists provide a prompt opportunity for participants to obtain appropriate information about the nature, results, and conclusions of the research, and they take reasonable steps to correct any misconceptions that participants may have of which the psychologists are aware.

(b) If scientific or humane values justify delaying or withholding this information, psychologists take reasonable measures to reduce the risk of harm.

(c) When psychologists become aware that research procedures have harmed a participant, they take reasonable steps to minimize the harm.

8.9 Humane Care and Use of Animals in Research

(a) Psychologists acquire, care for, use, and dispose of animals in compliance with current federal, state, and local laws and regulations, and with professional standards.

(b) Psychologists trained in research methods and experienced in the care of laboratory animals supervise all procedures involving animals and are responsible for ensuring appropriate consideration of their comfort, health, and humane treatment.

(c) Psychologists ensure that all individuals under their supervision who are using animals have received instruction in research methods and in the care, maintenance, and handling of the species being used, to the extent appropriate to their role. (See also Standard 2.05, Delegation of Work to Others.)

(d) Psychologists make reasonable efforts to minimize the discomfort, infection, illness, and pain of animal subjects.

(e) Psychologists use a procedure subjecting animals to pain, stress, or privation only when an alternative procedure is unavailable and the goal is justified by its prospective scientific, educational, or applied value.

(f) Psychologists perform surgical procedures under appropriate anesthesia and follow techniques to avoid infection and minimize pain during and after surgery.

(g) When it is appropriate that an animal's life be terminated, psychologists proceed rapidly, with an effort to minimize pain and in accordance with accepted procedures.

8.10 Reporting Research Results

(a) Psychologists do not fabricate data. (See also Standard 5.01a, Avoidance of False or Deceptive Statements.)

(b) If psychologists discover significant errors in their published data, they take reasonable steps to correct such errors in a correction, retraction, erratum, or other appropriate publication means.

8.11 Plagiarism

Psychologists do not present portions of another's work or data as their own, even if the other work or data source is cited occasionally.

8.12 Publication Credit

(a) Psychologists take responsibility and credit, including authorship credit, only for work they have actually performed or to which they have substantially contributed. (See also Standard 8.12b, Publication Credit.)

(b) Principal authorship and other publication credits accurately reflect the relative scientific or professional contributions of the individuals involved, regardless of their relative status. Mere possession of an institutional position, such as department chair, does not justify authorship credit. Minor contributions to the research or to the writing for publications are acknowledged appropriately, such as in footnotes or in an introductory statement.

(c) Except under exceptional circumstances, a student is listed as principal author on any multiple-authored article that is substantially based on the student's doctoral dissertation. Faculty advisors discuss publication credit with students as early as feasible and throughout the research and publication process as appropriate. (See also Standard 8.12b, Publication Credit.)

8.13 Duplicate Publication of Data

Psychologists do not publish, as original data, data that have been previously published. This does not preclude republishing data when they are accompanied by proper acknowledgment.

8.14 Sharing Research Data for Verification

(a) After research results are published, psychologists do not withhold the data on which their conclusions are based from other competent professionals who seek to verify the substantive claims through reanalysis and who intend to use such data only for that purpose, provided that the confidentiality of the participants can be protected and unless legal rights concerning proprietary data preclude their release. This does not preclude psychologists from requiring that such individuals or groups be responsible for costs associated with the provision of such information.

(b) Psychologists who request data from other psychologists to verify the substantive claims through reanalysis may use shared data only for the declared purpose. Requesting psychologists obtain prior written agreement for all other uses of the data.

8.15 Reviewers

Psychologists who review material submitted for presentation, publication, grant, or research proposal review respect the confidentiality of and the proprietary rights in such information of those who submitted it.

9. Assessment

9.1 Bases for Assessments

(a) Psychologists base the opinions contained in their recommendations, reports, and diagnostic or evaluative statements, including forensic testimony, on information and techniques sufficient to substantiate their findings. (See also Standard 2.04, Bases for Scientific and Professional Judgments.)

(b) Except as noted in 9.01c, psychologists provide opinions of the psychological characteristics of individuals only after they have conducted an examination of the individuals adequate to support their statements or conclusions. When, despite reasonable efforts, such an examination is not practical, psychologists document the efforts they made and the result of those efforts, clarify the probable impact of their limited information on the reliability and validity of their opinions, and appropriately limit the nature and extent of their conclusions or recommendations. (See also Standards 2.01, Boundaries of Competence, and 9.06, Interpreting Assessment Results.)

(c) When psychologists conduct a record review or provide consultation or supervision and an individual examination is not warranted or necessary for the opinion, psychologists explain this and the sources of information on which they based their conclusions and recommendations.

9.2 Use of Assessments

(a) Psychologists administer, adapt, score, interpret, or use assessment techniques, interviews, tests, or instruments in a manner and for purposes that are appropriate in light of the research on or evidence of the usefulness and proper application of the techniques.

(b) Psychologists use assessment instruments whose validity and reliability have been established for use with members of the population tested. When such validity or reliability has not been established, psychologists describe the strengths and limitations of test results and interpretation.

(c) Psychologists use assessment methods that are appropriate to an individual's language preference and competence, unless the use of an alternative language is relevant to the assessment issues.

9.3 Informed Consent in Assessments

(a) Psychologists obtain informed consent for assessments, evaluations, or diagnostic services, as described in Standard 3.10, Informed Consent, except when (1) testing is mandated by law or governmental regulations; (2) informed consent is implied because testing is conducted as a routine educational, institutional, or organizational activity (e.g., when participants voluntarily agree to assessment when applying for a job); or (3) one purpose of the testing is to evaluate decisional capacity. Informed consent includes an explanation of the nature and purpose of the assessment, fees, involvement of third parties, and limits of confidentiality and sufficient opportunity for the client/patient to ask questions and receive answers.

(b) Psychologists inform persons with questionable capacity to consent or for whom testing is mandated by law or governmental regulations about the nature and purpose of the proposed assessment services, using language that is reasonably understandable to the person being assessed.

(c) Psychologists using the services of an interpreter obtain informed consent from the client/patient to use that interpreter, ensure that confidentiality of test results and test security are maintained, and include in their recommendations, reports, and diagnostic or evaluative statements, including forensic testimony, discussion of any limitations on the data obtained. (See also Standards 2.05, Delegation of Work to Others; 4.01, Maintaining Confidentiality; 9.01, Bases for Assessments; 9.06, Interpreting Assessment Results; and 9.07, Assessment by Unqualified Persons.)

9.4 Release of Test Data

(a) The term *test data* refers to raw and scaled scores, client/patient responses to test questions or stimuli, and psychologists' notes and recordings concerning client/patient statements and behavior during an examination. Those portions of test materials that include client/patient responses are included in the definition of *test data*. Pursuant to a client/ patient release, psychologists provide test data to the client/ patient or other persons identified in the release. Psychologists may refrain from releasing test data to protect a client/ patient or others from substantial harm or misuse or misrepresentation of the data or the test, recognizing that in many instances release of confidential information under these circumstances is regulated by law. (See also Standard 9.11, Maintaining Test Security.)

(b) In the absence of a client/patient release, psychologists provide test data only as required by law or court order.

9.5 Test Construction

Psychologists who develop tests and other assessment techniques use appropriate psychometric procedures and current scientific or professional knowledge for test design, standardization, validation, reduction or elimination of bias, and recommendations for use.

9.6 Interpreting Assessment Results

When interpreting assessment results, including automated interpretations, psychologists take into account the purpose of the assessment as well as the various test factors, test-taking abilities, and other characteristics of the person being assessed, such as situational, personal, linguistic, and cultural differences, that might affect psychologists' judgments or reduce the accuracy of their interpretations. They indicate any significant limitations of their interpretations. (See also Standards 2.01b and c, Boundaries of Competence, and 3.01, Unfair Discrimination.)

9.7 Assessment by Unqualified Persons

Psychologists do not promote the use of psychological assessment techniques by unqualified persons, except when such use is conducted for training purposes with appropriate supervision. (See also Standard 2.05, Delegation of Work to Others.)

9.8 Obsolete Tests and Outdated Test Results

(a) Psychologists do not base their assessment or intervention decisions or recommendations on data or test results that are outdated for the current purpose.

(b) Psychologists do not base such decisions or recommendations on tests and measures that are obsolete and not useful for the current purpose.

9.9 Test Scoring and Interpretation Services

(a) Psychologists who offer assessment or scoring services to other professionals accurately describe the purpose, norms, validity, reliability, and applications of the procedures and any special qualifications applicable to their use.

(b) Psychologists select scoring and interpretation services (including automated services) on the basis of evidence of the validity of the program and procedures as well as on other appropriate considerations. (See also Standard 2.01b and c, Boundaries of Competence.)

(c) Psychologists retain responsibility for the appropriate application, interpretation, and use of assessment instruments, whether they score and interpret such tests themselves or use automated or other services.

9.10 Explaining Assessment Results

Regardless of whether the scoring and interpretation are done by psychologists, by employees or assistants, or by automated or other outside services, psychologists take reasonable steps to ensure that explanations of results are given to the individual or designated representative unless the nature of the relationship precludes provision of an explanation of results (such as in some organizational consulting, preemployment or security screenings, and forensic evaluations), and this fact has been clearly explained to the person being assessed in advance.

9.11 Maintaining Test Security

The term *test materials* refers to manuals, instruments, protocols, and test questions or stimuli and does not include *test data* as defined in Standard 9.04, Release of Test Data. Psychologists make reasonable efforts to maintain the integrity and security of test materials and other assessment techniques consistent with law and contractual obligations, and in a manner that permits adherence to this Ethics Code.

10. Therapy

10.1 Informed Consent to Therapy

(a) When obtaining informed consent to therapy as required in Standard 3.10, Informed Consent, psychologists inform clients/patients as early as is feasible in the therapeutic relationship about the nature and anticipated course of therapy, fees, involvement of third parties, and limits of confidentiality and provide sufficient opportunity for the client/patient to ask questions and receive answers. (See also Standards 4.02, Discussing the Limits of Confidentiality, and 6.04, Fees and Financial Arrangements.)

(b) When obtaining informed consent for treatment for which generally recognized techniques and procedures have not been established, psychologists inform their clients/patients of the developing nature of the treatment, the potential risks involved, alternative treatments that may be available, and the voluntary nature of their participation. (See also Standards 2.01e, Boundaries of Competence, and 3.10, Informed Consent.)

(c) When the therapist is a trainee and the legal responsibility for the treatment provided resides with the supervisor, the client/patient, as part of the informed consent procedure, is informed that the therapist is in training and is being supervised and is given the name of the supervisor.

10.2 Therapy Involving Couples or Families

(a) When psychologists agree to provide services to several persons who have a relationship (such as spouses, significant others, or parents and children), they take reasonable steps to clarify at the outset (1) which of the individuals are clients/patients and (2) the relationship the psychologist will have with each person. This clarification includes the psychologist's role and the probable uses of the services provided or the information obtained. (See also Standard 4.02, Discussing the Limits of Confidentiality.)

(b) If it becomes apparent that psychologists may be called on to perform potentially conflicting roles (such as family therapist and then witness for one party in divorce proceedings), psychologists take reasonable steps to clarify and modify, or withdraw from, roles appropriately. (See also Standard 3.05c, Multiple Relationships.)

10.3 Group Therapy

When psychologists provide services to several persons in a group setting, they describe at the outset the roles and responsibilities of all parties and the limits of confidentiality.

10.4 Providing Therapy to Those Served by Others

In deciding whether to offer or provide services to those already receiving mental health services elsewhere, psychologists carefully consider the treatment issues and the potential client's/patient's welfare. Psychologists discuss these issues with the client/patient or another legally authorized person on behalf of the client/patient in order to minimize the risk of confusion and conflict, consult with the other service providers when appropriate, and proceed with caution and sensitivity to the therapeutic issues.

10.5 Sexual Intimacies With Current Therapy Clients/Patients

Psychologists do not engage in sexual intimacies with current therapy clients/patients.

10.6 Sexual Intimacies With Relatives or Significant Others of Current Therapy Clients/Patients

Psychologists do not engage in sexual intimacies with individuals they know to be close relatives, guardians, or significant others of current clients/patients. Psychologists do not terminate therapy to circumvent this standard.

10.7 Therapy With Former Sexual Partners

Psychologists do not accept as therapy clients/patients persons with whom they have engaged in sexual intimacies.

10.8 Sexual Intimacies With Former Therapy Clients/Patients

(a) Psychologists do not engage in sexual intimacies with former clients/patients for at least two years after cessation or termination of therapy.

(b) Psychologists do not engage in sexual intimacies with former clients/patients even after a two-year interval except in the most unusual circumstances. Psychologists who engage in such activity after the two years following cessation or termination of therapy and of having no sexual contact with the former client/patient bear the burden of demonstrating that there has been no exploitation, in light of all relevant factors, including (1) the amount of time that has passed since therapy terminated; (2) the nature, duration, and intensity of the therapy; (3) the circumstances of termination; (4) the client's/patient's personal history; (5) the client's/patient's current mental status; (6) the likelihood of adverse impact on the client/patient; and (7) any statements or actions made by the therapist during the course of therapy suggesting or inviting the possibility of a posttermination sexual or romantic relationship with the client/patient. (See also Standard 3.05, Multiple Relationships.)

10.9 Interruption of Therapy

When entering into employment or contractual relationships, psychologists make reasonable efforts to provide for orderly and appropriate resolution of responsibility for client/patient care in the event that the employment or contractual relationship ends, with paramount consideration given to the welfare of the client/patient. (See also Standard 3.12, Interruption of Psychological Services.)

10.10 Terminating Therapy

(a) Psychologists terminate therapy when it becomes reasonably clear that the client/patient no longer needs the service, is not likely to benefit, or is being harmed by continued service.

(b) Psychologists may terminate therapy when threatened or otherwise endangered by the client/patient or another person with whom the client/patient has a relationship.

(c) Except where precluded by the actions of clients/ patients or third-party payors, prior to termination psychologists provide pretermination counseling and suggest alternative service providers as appropriate.

2010 Amendments to the 2002 "Ethical Principles of Psychologists and Code of Conduct"

The American Psychological Association's Council of Representatives adopted the following amendments to the 2002 "Ethical Principles of Psychologists and Code of Conduct" at its February 2010 meeting. Changes are indicated by underlining for additions and striking through for deletions. A history of amending the Ethics Code is provided in the "Report of the Ethics Committee, 2009" in the July-August 2010 issue of the *American Psychologist* (Vol. 65, No. 5).

Original Language With Changes Marked

1.1 Introduction and Applicability

If psychologists' ethical responsibilities conflict with law, regulations, or other governing legal authority, psychologists make known their commitment to this Ethics Code and take steps to resolve the conflict in a responsible manner. If the conflict is unresolvable via such means, psychologists may adhere to the requirements of the law, regulations, or other governing authority in keeping with basic principles of human rights.

1.2 Conflicts Between Ethics and Law, Regulations, or Other Governing Legal Authority

If psychologists' ethical responsibilities conflict with law, regulations, or other governing legal authority, psychologists clarify the nature of the conflict, make known their commitment to the Ethics Code, and take reasonable steps to resolve the conflict consistent with the General Principles <u>and Ethical Standards of the Ethics Code</u>. If the conflict is unresolvable via such means, psychologists may adhere to the requirements of the law, regulations, or other governing legal authority. Under no circumstances may this standard be used to justify or defend violating human rights.

1.3 Conflicts Between Ethics and Organizational Demands

If the demands of an organization with which psychologists are affiliated or for whom they are working <u>are in</u> conflict with this Ethics Code, psychologists clarify the nature of the conflict, make known their commitment to the Ethics Code, and ~~to the extent feasible, resolve the conflict in a way that permits adherence to the Ethics Code.~~ *take reasonable steps to resolve the conflict consistent with the General Principles and Ethical Standards of the Ethics Code. Under no circumstances may this standard be used to justify or defend violating human rights.*

American Psychiatric Association
The Principles of Medical Ethics With Annotations
Especially Applicable to Psychiatry 2013 Edition

In 1973, the American Psychiatric Association (APA) published the first edition of *The Principles of Medical Ethics with Annotations Especially Applicable to Psychiatry*. Subsequently, revisions were published as the APA Board of Trustees and the APA Assembly approved additional annotations. In July of 1980, the American Medical Association (AMA) approved a new version of the *Principles of Medical Ethics* (the first revision since 1957), and the APA Ethics Committee[1] incorporated many of its annotations into the new *Principles*, which resulted in the 1981 edition and subsequent revisions. This version includes changes to the *Principles* approved by the AMA in 2001.

Foreword

ALL PHYSICIANS should practice in accordance with the medical code of ethics set forth in the *Principles of Medical Ethics* of the American Medical Association. An up-to-date expression and elaboration of these statements is found in the Opinions and Reports of the Council on Ethical and Judicial Affairs of the American Medical Association.[2] Psychiatrists are strongly advised to be familiar with these documents.[3]

However, these general guidelines have sometimes been difficult to interpret for psychiatry, so further annotations to the basic principles are offered in this document. While psychiatrists have the same goals as all physicians, there are special ethical problems in psychiatric practice that differ in coloring and degree from ethical problems in other branches of medical practice, even though the basic principles are the same. The annotations are not designed as absolutes and will be revised from time to time so as to be applicable to current practices and problems.

Following are the AMA *Principles of Medical Ethics*, printed in their entirety, and then each principle printed separately along with an annotation especially applicable to psychiatry.

---

[1]The committee included Herbert Klemmer, M.D., Chairperson, Miltiades Zaphiropoulos, M.D., Ewald Busse, M.D., John R. Saunders, M.D., and Robert McDevitt, M.D. J. Brand Brickman, M.D., William P. Camp, M.D., and Robert A. Moore, M.D., served as consultants to the APA Ethics Committee.

[2]*Current Opinions with Annotations of the Council on Ethical and Judicial Affairs*, Chicago, American Medical Association, 2002–2003.

[3]Chapter 7, Section 1 of the Bylaws of the American Psychiatric Association (May 2003 edition) states, "All members of the Association shall be bound by the ethical code of the medical profession, specifically defined in the *Principles of Medical Ethics* of the American Medical Association and in the Association's *Principles of Medical Ethics With Annotations Especially Applicable to Psychiatry*." In interpreting the Bylaws, it is the opinion of the APA Board of Trustees that inactive status in no way removes a physician member from responsibility to abide by the *Principles of Medical Ethics*.

Preamble

The medical profession has long subscribed to a body of ethical statements developed primarily for the benefit of the patient. As a member of this profession, a physician must recognize responsibility to patients first and foremost, as well as to society, to other health professionals, and to self. The following *Principles* adopted by the American Medical Association are not laws, but standards of conduct which define the essentials of honorable behavior for the physician.

Section 1

A physician shall be dedicated to providing competent medical care, with compassion and respect for human dignity and rights.

Section 2

A physician shall uphold the standards of professionalism, be honest in all professional interactions, and strive to report physicians deficient in character or competence, or engaging in fraud or deception, to appropriate entities.

Section 3

A physician shall respect the law and also recognize a responsibility to seek changes in those requirements which are contrary to the best interests of the patient.

Section 4

A physician shall respect the rights of patients, colleagues, and other health professionals, and shall safeguard patient confidences and privacy within the constraints of the law.

Section 5

A physician shall continue to study, apply, and advance scientific knowledge, maintain a commitment to medical education, make relevant information available to patients, colleagues, and the public, obtain consultation, and use the talents of other health professionals when indicated.

Section 6

A physician shall, in the provision of appropriate patient care, except in emergencies, be free to choose whom to serve, with whom to associate, and the environment in which to provide medical care.

Section 7

A physician shall recognize a responsibility to participate in activities contributing to the improvement of the community and the betterment of public health.

Section 8

A physician shall, while caring for a patient, regard responsibility to the patient as paramount.

Section 9

A physician shall support access to medical care for all people.

Principles With Annotations

Following are each of the AMA *Principles of Medical Ethics* printed separately along with annotations especially applicable to psychiatry.

Preamble

The medical profession has long subscribed to a body of ethical statements developed primarily for the benefit of the patient. As a member of this profession, a physician must recognize responsibility to patients first and foremost, as well as to society, to other health professionals, and to self. The following Principles adopted by the American Medical Association are not laws, but standards of conduct which define the essentials of honorable behavior for the physician.[4]

Section 1

A physician shall be dedicated to providing competent medical care with compassion and respect for human dignity and rights.

1. A psychiatrist shall not gratify his or her own needs by exploiting the patient. The psychiatrist shall be ever vigilant about the impact that his or her conduct has upon the boundaries of the doctor–patient relationship, and thus upon the well-being of the patient. These requirements become particularly important because of the essentially private, highly personal, and sometimes intensely emotional nature of the relationship established with the psychiatrist.
2. A psychiatrist should not be a party to any type of policy that excludes, segregates, or demeans the dignity of any patient because of ethnic origin, race, sex, creed, age, socioeconomic status, or sexual orientation.
3. In accord with the requirements of law and accepted medical practice, it is ethical for a physician to submit his or her work to peer review and to the ultimate authority of the medical staff executive body and the hospital administration and its governing body. In case of dispute, the ethical psychiatrist has the following steps available:
   a. Seek appeal from the medical staff decision to a joint conference committee, including members of the medical staff executive committee and the executive committee of the governing board. At this appeal, the ethical psychiatrist could request that outside opinions be considered.
   b. Appeal to the governing body itself.

---

[4]Statements in italics are taken directly from the American Medical Association's *Principles of Medical Ethics*.

    c. Appeal to state agencies regulating licensure of hospitals if, in the particular state, they concern themselves with matters of professional competency and quality of care.

    d. Attempt to educate colleagues through development of research projects and data and presentations at professional meetings and in professional journals.

    e. Seek redress in local courts, perhaps through an enjoining injunction against the governing body.

    f. Public education as carried out by an ethical psychiatrist would not utilize appeals based solely upon emotion, but would be presented in a professional way and without any potential exploitation of patients through testimonials.

4. A psychiatrist should not be a participant in a legally authorized execution.

Section 2

A physician shall uphold the standards of professionalism, be honest in all professional interactions and strive to report physicians deficient in character or competence, or engaging in fraud or deception to appropriate entities.

1. The requirement that the physician conduct himself/herself with propriety in his or her profession and in all the actions of his or her life is especially important in the case of the psychiatrist because the patient tends to model his or her behavior after that of his or her psychiatrist by identification. Further, the necessary intensity of the treatment relationship may tend to activate sexual and other needs and fantasies on the part of both patient and psychiatrist, while weakening the objectivity necessary for control. Additionally, the inherent inequality in the doctor-patient relationship may lead to exploitation of the patient. Sexual activity with a current or former patient is unethical.

2. The psychiatrist should diligently guard against exploiting information furnished by the patient and should not use the unique position of power afforded him/her by the psychotherapeutic situation to influence the patient in any way not directly relevant to the treatment goals.

3. A psychiatrist who regularly practices outside his or her area of professional competence should be considered unethical. Determination of professional competence should be made by peer review boards or other appropriate bodies.

4. Special consideration should be given to those psychiatrists who, because of mental illness, jeopardize the welfare of their patients and their own reputations and practices. It is ethical, even encouraged, for another psychiatrist to intercede in such situations.

5. Psychiatric services, like all medical services, are dispensed in the context of a contractual arrangement between the patient and the physician. The provisions of the contractual arrangement, which are binding on the physician as well as on the patient, should be explicitly established.

6. It is ethical for the psychiatrist to make a charge for a missed appointment when this falls within the terms of the specific contractual agreement with the patient. Charging for a missed appointment or for one not canceled 24 hours in advance need not, in itself, be considered unethical if a patient is fully advised that the

physician will make such a charge. The practice, however, should be resorted to infrequently and always with the utmost consideration for the patient and his or her circumstances.

7. An arrangement in which a psychiatrist provides supervision or administration to other physicians or nonmedical persons for a percentage of their fees or gross income is not acceptable; this would constitute fee splitting. In a team of practitioners, or a multidisciplinary team, it is ethical for the psychiatrist to receive income for administration, research, education, or consultation. This should be based on a mutually agreed-upon and set fee or salary, open to renegotiation when a change in the time demand occurs. (See also Section 5, Annotations 2, 3, and 4.)

Section 3

A physician shall respect the law and also recognize a responsibility to seek changes in those requirements which are contrary to the best interests of the patient.

1. It would seem self-evident that a psychiatrist who is a law-breaker might be ethically unsuited to practice his or her profession. When such illegal activities bear directly upon his or her practice, this would obviously be the case. However, in other instances, illegal activities such as those concerning the right to protest social injustices might not bear on either the image of the psychiatrist or the ability of the specific psychiatrist to treat his or her patient ethically and well. While no committee or board could offer prior assurance that any illegal activity would not be considered unethical, it is conceivable that an individual could violate a law without being guilty of professionally unethical behavior. Physicians lose no right of citizenship on entry into the profession of medicine.

2. Where not specifically prohibited by local laws governing medical practice, the practice of acupuncture by a psychiatrist is not unethical per se. The psychiatrist should have professional competence in the use of acupuncture. Or, if he or she is supervising the use of acupuncture by nonmedical individuals, he or she should provide proper medical supervision. (See also Section 5, Annotations 3 and 4.)

Section 4

A physician shall respect the rights of patients, colleagues, and other health professionals, and shall safeguard patient confidences and privacy within the constraints of the law.

1. Psychiatric records, including even the identification of a person as a patient, must be protected with extreme care. Confidentiality is essential to psychiatric treatment. This is based in part on the special nature of psychiatric therapy as well as on the traditional ethical relationship between physician and patient. Growing concern regarding the civil rights of patients and the possible adverse effects of computerization, duplication equipment, and data banks makes the dissemination of confidential information an increasing hazard. Because of the sensitive and private nature of the information with which the psychiatrist deals, he or she must be circumspect in the information that he or she chooses to disclose to others about a patient. The welfare of the patient must be a continuing consideration.

132

2. A psychiatrist may release confidential information only with the authorization of the patient or under proper legal compulsion. The continuing duty of the psychiatrist to protect the patient includes fully apprising him/her of the connotations of waiving the privilege of privacy. This may become an issue when the patient is being investigated by a government agency, is applying for a position, or is involved in legal action. The same principles apply to the release of information concerning treatment to medical departments of government agencies, business organizations, labor unions, and insurance companies. Information gained in confidence about patients seen in student health services should not be released without the students' explicit permission.
3. Clinical and other materials used in teaching and writing must be adequately disguised in order to preserve the anonymity of the individuals involved.
4. The ethical responsibility of maintaining confidentiality holds equally for the consultations in which the patient may not have been present and in which the consultee was not a physician. In such instances, the physician consultant should alert the consultee to his or her duty of confidentiality.
5. Ethically, the psychiatrist may disclose only that information which is relevant to a given situation. He or she should avoid offering speculation as fact. Sensitive information such as an individual's sexual orientation or fantasy material is usually unnecessary.
6. Psychiatrists are often asked to examine individuals for security purposes, to determine suitability for various jobs, and to determine legal competence. The psychiatrist must fully describe the nature and purpose and lack of confidentiality of the examination to the examinee at the beginning of the examination.
7. Careful judgment must be exercised by the psychiatrist in order to include, when appropriate, the parents or guardian in the treatment of a minor. At the same time, the psychiatrist must assure the minor proper confidentiality.
8. When, in the clinical judgment of the treating psychiatrist, the risk of danger is deemed to be significant, the psychiatrist may reveal confidential information disclosed by the patient."
9. When the psychiatrist is ordered by the court to reveal the confidences entrusted to him/her by patients, he or she may comply or he/ she may ethically hold the right to dissent within the framework of the law. When the psychiatrist is in doubt, the right of the patient to confidentiality and, by extension, to unimpaired treatment should be given priority. The psychiatrist should reserve the right to raise the question of adequate need for disclosure. In the event that the necessity for legal disclosure is demonstrated by the court, the psychiatrist may request the right to disclosure of only that information which is relevant to the legal question at hand.
10. With regard for the person's dignity and privacy and with truly informed consent, it is ethical to present a patient to a scientific gathering if the confidentiality of the presentation is understood and accepted by the audience.
11. It is ethical to present a patient or former patient to a public gathering or to the news media only if the patient is fully informed of enduring loss of confidentiality, is competent, and consents in writing without coercion.

12. When involved in funded research, the ethical psychiatrist will advise human subjects of the funding source, retain his or her freedom to reveal data and results, and follow all appropriate and current guidelines relative to human subject protection.
13. Ethical considerations in medical practice preclude the psychiatric evaluation of any person charged with criminal acts prior to access to, or availability of, legal counsel. The only exception is the rendering of care to the person for the sole purpose of medical treatment.
14. Sexual involvement between a faculty member or supervisor and a trainee or student, in those situations in which an abuse of power can occur, often takes advantage of inequalities in the working relationship and may be unethical because:
    a. Any treatment of a patient being supervised may be deleteriously affected.
    b. It may damage the trust relationship between teacher and student.
    c. Teachers are important professional role models for their trainees and affect their trainees' future professional behavior.

Section 5

A physician shall continue to study, apply, and advance scientific knowledge, maintain a commitment to medical education, make relevant information available to patients, colleagues, and the public, obtain consultation, and use the talents of other health professionals when indicated.

1. Psychiatrists are responsible for their own continuing education and should be mindful of the fact that theirs must be a lifetime of learning.
2. In the practice of his or her specialty, the psychiatrist consults, associates, collaborates, or integrates his or her work with that of many professionals, including psychologists, psychometricians, social workers, alcoholism counselors, marriage counselors, public health nurses, and the like. Furthermore, the nature of modern psychiatric practice extends his or her contacts to such people as teachers, juvenile and adult probation officers, attorneys, welfare workers, agency volunteers, and neighborhood aides. In referring patients for treatment, counseling, or rehabilitation to any of these practitioners, the psychiatrist should ensure that the allied professional or paraprofessional with whom he or she is dealing is a recognized member of his or her own discipline and is competent to carry out the therapeutic task required. The psychiatrist should have the same attitude toward members of the medical profession to whom he or she refers patients. Whenever he or she has reason to doubt the training, skill, or ethical qualifications of the allied professional, the psychiatrist should not refer cases to him/her.
3. When the psychiatrist assumes a collaborative or supervisory role with another mental health worker, he or she must expend sufficient time to assure that proper care is given. It is contrary to the interests of the patient and to patient care if the psychiatrist allows himself/herself to be used as a figurehead.
4. In relationships between psychiatrists and practicing licensed psychologists, the physician should not delegate to the psychologist or, in fact, to any nonmedical person any matter requiring the exercise of professional medical judgment.

5. The psychiatrist should agree to the request of a patient for consultation or to such a request from the family of an incompetent or minor patient. The psychiatrist may suggest possible consultants, but the patient or family should be given free choice of the consultant. If the psychiatrist disapproves of the professional qualifications of the consultant or if there is a difference of opinion that the primary therapist cannot resolve, he or she may, after suitable notice, withdraw from the case. If this disagreement occurs within an institution or agency framework, the differences should be resolved by the mediation or arbitration of higher professional authority within the institution or agency.

Section 6

A physician shall, in the provision of appropriate patient care, except in emergencies, be free to choose whom to serve, with whom to associate, and the environment in which to provide medical care.

1. Physicians generally agree that the doctor-patient relationship is such a vital factor in effective treatment of the patient that preservation of optimal conditions for development of a sound working relationship between a doctor and his or her patient should take precedence over all other considerations. Professional courtesy may lead to poor psychiatric care for physicians and their families because of embarrassment over the lack of a complete give-and-take contract.
2. An ethical psychiatrist may refuse to provide psychiatric treatment to a person who, in the psychiatrist's opinion, cannot be diagnosed as having a mental illness amenable to psychiatric treatment.

Section 7

A physician shall recognize a responsibility to participate in activities contributing to the improvement of the community and the betterment of public health.

1. Psychiatrists should foster the cooperation of those legitimately concerned with the medical, psychological, social, and legal aspects of mental health and illness. Psychiatrists are encouraged to serve society by advising and consulting with the executive, legislative, and judiciary branches of the government. A psychiatrist should clarify whether he/ she speaks as an individual or as a representative of an organization. Furthermore, psychiatrists should avoid cloaking their public statements with the authority of the profession (e.g., "Psychiatrists know that").
2. Psychiatrists may interpret and share with the public their expertise in the various psychosocial issues that may affect mental health and illness. Psychiatrists should always be mindful of their separate roles as dedicated citizens and as experts in psychological medicine.
3. On occasion psychiatrists are asked for an opinion about an individual who is in the light of public attention or who has disclosed information about himself/herself through public media. In such circumstances, a psychiatrist may share with the public his or her expertise about psychiatric issues in general. However, it is unethical for a psychiatrist to offer a professional opinion unless he or she has conducted an examination and has been granted proper authorization for such a statement.

4. The psychiatrist may permit his or her certification to be used for the involuntary treatment of any person only following his or her personal examination of that person. To do so, he or she must find that the person, because of mental illness, cannot form a judgment as to what is in his/ her own best interests and that, without such treatment, substantial impairment is likely to occur to the person or others.
5. Psychiatrists shall not participate in torture.

Section 8

A physician shall, while caring for a patient, regard responsibility to the patient as paramount.
1. Psychiatrists' relationships with companies, organizations, the community, or larger society can affect their interactions with patients.
2. When the psychiatrist's outside relationships conflict with the clinical needs of the patient, the psychiatrist must always consider the impact of such relationships and strive to resolve conflicts in a manner that the psychiatrist believes is likely to be beneficial to the patient.
3. When significant relationships exist that may conflict with patients' clinical needs, it is especially important to inform the patient or decision maker about these relationships and potential conflicts with clinical needs.
4. In informing a patient of treatment options, the psychiatrist should assist the patient in identifying relevant options that promote an informed treatment decision, including those that are not available from the psychiatrist or from the organization with which the psychiatrist is affiliated.

Section 9

A physician shall support access to medical care for all people.

Procedures for Handling Complaints of Unethical Conduct

Introduction

The medical profession has long subscribed to a body of ethical statements developed primarily for the benefit of the patient. As a member of this profession, a physician must recognize responsibility not only to patients but also to society, the profession, other health professionals, and to self. The *Principles of Medical Ethics with Annotations Especially Applicable to Psychiatry* (hereafter referred to as the "*Principles*"), adopted from the American Medical Association, are not laws but standards of conduct that define the essentials of honorable behavior for the physician.

Complaints charging members of the American Psychiatric Association (APA) with unethical behavior or practices shall be investigated and resolved in accordance with procedures approved by the APA Assembly and the APA Board of Trustees. These procedures are congruent with the minimum requirements under the Health Care Quality Improvement Act. A District Branch (DB) of the APA may adopt additional requirements to comply with any additional or more stringent requirements of state law. A District Branch should notify the APA if additional requirements are adopted.

Ethics cases are confidential. The allegations, the names of the parties and other information are made available only to persons directly participating in the proceedings. Information regarding an ethics case is made public in limited circumstance as set forth in these procedures and only after a final determination has been reached when required by law or necessary to protect the public.

Part I: Initial Procedures

A. The Complaint
1. An ethics complaint can be filed by a patient or guardian, a family member of a patient, an APA member or other individual with personal knowledge of the alleged unethical conduct.
2. The individual submitting the complaint is the "Complainant" and the APA member charged with ethics violations is the "Accused Member."
3. Complaints charging an APA member with unethical behavior shall be:
   a. In writing;
   b. Signed by the Complainant and
   c. Addressed to the DB of the Accused Member. If addressed to the APA, the complaint shall be referred by the APA to the Accused Member's DB.

B. Proceeding on Extrinsic Evidence:
1. A complaint may be based on extrinsic evidence, including any documents attached to the complaint.
2. A DB may initiate an ethical proceeding without a Complaint based upon extrinsic evidence which it receives or otherwise becomes aware that a member has potentially acted unethically in violation of the *Principles*. In such proceeding, there is no Complainant.
3. Extrinsic evidence includes formal judicial or administrative reports, sworn deposition or trial testimony, medical or hospital records, and similar reliable documents.

C. Review for Jurisdiction
1. Once a complaint is received, the DB shall review the complaint to determine if the DB has jurisdiction over the matter. This review shall take place before the Accused Member is notified that a complaint was filed.
2. This review will consider:
   a. Is the Accused Member a member of the APA and the DB? Only complaints against APA members can be investigated. If the Accused Member is not a member, the DB shall notify the Complainant that it cannot pursue the complaint because the Accused Member is not a member of the APA and no further action can be taken.
   b. Is the Accused Member a member of the DB? If not, the complaint shall be forwarded to the APA Office of Ethics.

    c. Does the complaint allege unethical conduct that took place over ten (10) years ago? A complaint alleging unethical conduct must be received within ten (10) years of the alleged conduct. In the case of a minor patient, the ten (10) year limit will not begin until the patient reaches the age of 18. If the alleged conduct took place outside of the ten year limit, the DB shall notify the Complainant in writing that no further action can be taken.

3. If the complaint meets these jurisdictional standards, the DB shall evaluate the complaint as set forth in Part II below to determine whether it alleges conduct that violates the *Principles*.
4. The DB's determination that a complaint does not meet these jurisdictional standards is final and there is no review by the Chair of the APA Ethics Committee.

D. Notice

Any "Notice" required in these procedures should be sent by a delivery system that requires a verifying of receipt, such as certified or overnight mail.

Part II: Review of Allegations

The DB Ethics Committee (DBEC) shall review the complaint to determine whether it alleges a recognized ethics violation of the *Principles*.

A. Preliminary Determinations
1. The DBEC shall determine whether the complaint alleges on its face an ethics violation(s) as set forth in the *Principles*.
2. This is not a determination on the merits of the complaint. Rather, it is a determination of whether a recognized ethics violation is alleged assuming the facts in the complaint are true. This review is limited to reviewing the allegations in the complaint and a determination of whether those allegations assert a recognized ethics violation as set forth in the *Principles*.
3. If the complaint alleges conduct that does not violate the *Principles*, the DBEC shall notify the Complainant in writing (with a copy to the APA Ethics Office) that no further action will be taken and also inform the Complainant that he/she may request within 30 days a review of this decision by the Chair of the APA Ethics Committee as set forth in Part II.C.1.
4. Before initiating this below Review phase, a signed Confidentiality Agreement shall be obtained from the Complainant (including any attorney representing the Complainant) by which the Complainant agrees that all information and documents concerning the ethical procedures and all communications from the APA and DB, including their ethics committees and Hearing Panels, are confidential and shall be used solely in connection with the ethical proceedings and not for other purposes or legal proceedings.

B. Review of Allegations
1. This phase is the period during which the DBEC begins to look at the merits of the case. The purpose of this process is to assess all information provided by the Complainant and then evaluate whether there is a basis for the allegation of

unethical conduct. The DBEC can choose whether or not to contact and advise the Accused Member of the ethics complaint during this stage.

2. The DB ethics chair shall appoint a member(s) to review the allegations in the complaint. The individual(s) shall submit a written or oral report to the DBEC.

3. To help ensure fairness, it is desirable that the DBEC arrange for those who do the review and those who serve on the hearing panel to be separate teams. Sometimes what surfaces during this review is not always relevant to or admissible at the hearing, and thus this separation of functions minimizes the chances that the hearing panel will have been influenced by an earlier phase of the case.

4. The review is accomplished by reviewing the allegations and any related materials provided to them by the Complainant. During the review phase, the reviewer(s) may seek additional information from the Complainant. The additional information can be obtained by written request, phone conference or in person interview.

5. During this Review of Allegations phase, the DBEC may, but is not required to, notify the Accused Member of the complaint and invite additional information from him or her. The additional information can be obtained by written request, phone conference or in person interview.

6. If the DBEC finds the complaint does state a potential ethics violation, it shall notify the Accused Member and invite additional information from him or her before proceeding with a formal investigation of the member pursuant to Part III.

7. If the DBEC finds the complaint does not state a potential ethics violation under the ethical standards established by the *Principles* and thus there is no basis to proceed, it shall notify the Complainant in writing of the conclusion. This Notice shall also inform the Complainant that he/she has 30 days to request a review of this decision by the Chair of the APA Ethics Committee as set forth in Part II.C.1.

8. If the DBEC determines there is a basis to proceed, it must notify the APA Secretary as well as the Complainant and the Accused Member and proceed to the exchange of information phase.

9. DBECs should postpone adjudication of ethics complaints until all other pending actions such as civil, criminal or licensing board proceedings have been resolved.

C. Review by the Chair of the APA Ethics Committee

1. If the DBEC determines the complaint does not allege an ethics violation of the *Principles*, the Complainant may request a review of a DB's decision by the Chair of the APA Ethics Committee. The request for a review must be sent to the DB and the Chair of the APA Ethics Committee within 30 days of the date of the Notice by the DB not to proceed.

2. If the Chair of the APA Ethics Committee determines that the complaint identifies a potential violation, he/she will request that the DB proceed with processing the complaint, and will provide the DB with a written explanation for this decision.

3. If the Chair of the APA Ethics Committee determines that the complaint does not warrant further action, then he/she will notify the Complainant and DB of this decision and that the case is closed.

Part III: Exchange of Information

A. Notice to Accused Member
   1. If the DBEC decides to proceed, the DBEC must notify the Accused Member of the ethics complaint and that the DBEC will proceed to determine whether the Accused Member violated the *Principles*. The Notice should include:
      a. A copy of the complaint;
      b. All documents that were attached to the complaint or obtained during the initial review phase; and
      c. Copies of the Principles and Procedures for Handling Complaints of Unethical Conduct;
      d. The ethical principle(s) the Accused Member is accused of violating.
   2. The DBEC should also notify the Accused Member of his or her due process rights.
      These include the right:
      a. To request a hearing;
      b. To be represented by an attorney or other person of the Accused Member's choice (hereafter referred to as "Counsel");
      c. To have a record made of the proceedings (but not the Ethics Committee's subsequent deliberations, which will not have been preserved), copies of which may be obtained by the Accused Member upon payment of any reasonable charges;
      d. To call, examine, and cross-examine witnesses;
      e. To present evidence determined to be relevant by the hearing panel, regardless of its admissibility in a court of law;
      f. To submit a written statement or make an oral statement at the close of the hearing;
      g. To receive a written decision; and
      h. To appeal any adverse decision to the APA Ethics Committee.
   3. When applicable, the DBEC shall obtain and provide the Accused Member with valid written authorization(s) from the patient(s) involved to provide relevant medical records and other information about the patient, and, if applicable, psychotherapy notes.

B. Accused Member's Response
   1. The Accused Member shall provide a written response to the complaint, including copies of all documents and a list of all witnesses he or she intends to present at the hearing. The Accused Member is not limited at the hearing to the evidence and witnesses identified in his or her response.
   2. The DBEC may also consider additional information prior to any scheduled hearing. On the basis of information in the Accused Member's response, or other information that surfaces during the Exchange of Information phase but prior to the hearing, the DBEC may decide to dismiss the case. A decision by the DBEC to dismiss in this phase requires review by the APA Ethics Committee as set forth in Part VI.

140

3. The name of any member who resigns from the APA after an ethics complaint against him/her is received and before it is resolved shall be reported in *Psychiatric News* and in the district branch newsletter or other usual means of communication with its membership.

C. Appointment of Hearing Panel

The DBEC shall appoint a panel of no less than three members to hear the complaint. All members should be ethics committee members when possible, and at least one must be. One member of the panel shall be selected to chair the Hearing Panel (Hearing Panel Chair) and shall be a voting member of the panel. The Accused Member may request those with whom he/she has a conflict of interest be excused, and reasonable requests should be honored.

D. Notice of Hearing

1. No less than 30 days before the scheduled hearing, the DBEC shall provide a Notice to the Complainant and the Accused Member. The Notice should supply the following information:
   a. The place, date and time of the hearing;
   b. The names of the Hearing Panel Chair and the other panel members who will hear the case; and
   c. A list of witnesses expected to testify.

2. Any reasonable requests by the parties for alternative hearing dates should be honored.

E. Education Option

1. At any time before a final determination of whether the Accused Member violated the ethical standards established by the *Principles*, and with the agreement of the Accused Member, the complaint may be resolved in accordance with the Educational Option rather than determine whether the Accused Member violated the *Principles*. In deciding whether to use this approach, the DBEC shall consider such factors as the nature and seriousness of the alleged misconduct and any prior findings or allegations of unethical conduct.

2. If the DBEC decides to attempt to resolve the complaint by using the Educational Option as described in paragraph 1 above, it shall proceed only after:
   a. Accused Member has been informed (1) that he/she is entitled to proceed under enforcement procedures, and (2) that the DBEC reserves the right to proceed on the complaint to determine whether the Accused Member violated the *Principles* if, in its sole discretion, it determines that the Accused Member has not satisfactorily cooperated.
   b. Accused Member agrees to proceed under the Educational Option;
   c. There are appropriate education opportunities available and the DBEC has the resources to monitor compliance;
   d. The Accused Member will have the opportunity to respond to the suggestion to use the Education Option. The DBEC shall determine the procedures to be used to obtain the responses, including written submissions and/or meeting with the parties separately or together. However, in determining the procedure it will use, the DBEC shall seek to provide a format that will

facilitate the Accused Member's understanding of the ethical issues raised by the complaint, including the reasons for or sources of the Complainant's concern, and to permit the DB to assess the Accused Member's understanding of these matters.

3. The DBEC shall identify a specific educational program including courses, reading and/or consultation for the Accused Member to complete within a specified period and shall notify the Accused Member and the APA Ethics Committee of the required program. The DBEC will monitor the Accused Member's compliance with any such educational requirements. The Accused Member's failure to complete the specified educational program may result in the proceedings being reopened to determine whether the Accused Member violated the *Principles*. It is preferable, but not required, that the subsequent proceeding be conducted by DBEC members other than those who participated in the process previously.

4. The DBEC shall retain records of complaints considered pursuant to this Part and of any education thereafter required of an Accused Member. The DB may consider such information in connection with a decision as to how to handle any later complaints involving the Accused Member.

5. Once the DBEC decides to resolve the complaint by using the Educational Option, it shall notify both the Complainant and Accused Member.

6. Upon completion of an Education Option requirements, the proceeding shall be terminated.

Part IV: The Hearing

A. Basic Requirements

1. While the spirit of this process is a collegial one based on mutual respect among professional colleagues—and not a court of law—procedural safeguards are an integral aspect in order to preserve the rights of the Accused Member and provide fairness and respect for both the Accused Member and the Complainant.

2. If deemed useful and not likely to prejudice the panel, the Hearing Panel Chair may allow the individual(s) who did the review of allegations under Part II to present oral or written documentary and testimony evidence, subject to cross examination by the Accused Member or his or her counsel, for the panel's consideration. This reviewer(s) of the allegations should not participate any further in the hearing or be part of the panel's deliberations or voting.

3. Counsel's participation is subject to the continuing direction and control of the Hearing Panel Chair. The Hearing Panel Chair shall exercise his or her discretion so as to prevent the intimidation or harassment of the Complainant and/or other witnesses given the peer review nature of the proceedings. Panel members may ask questions of the Accused Member.

4. The Accused Member's voluntary waiver of a hearing shall not prevent the Hearing Panel from meeting with, and hearing the evidence of, the Complainant and other witnesses, and reaching a decision in the case. The Accused Member may choose not to be present at the hearing and to present his/her defense through other witnesses and/or Counsel.

5. The Complainant must be present in person at the hearing to testify regarding his/her allegations unless excused by the Hearing Panel Chair, and this should occur only when, in the judgment of the Hearing Panel Chair, participation would be harmful to him/her or extrinsic evidence serves as the Complainant. Complainants may bring a support person to the hearing if approved by the Hearing Panel Chair. Complainants generally do not remain in the hearing once they have presented their testimony and evidence and been cross examined. The Hearing Panel Chair may have them wait outside during the remainder of the hearing in the event further information from the Complainant becomes needed.

B. The Hearing
1. The hearing may consist of:
   a. An oral opening statement by the Complainant, and the Accused Member or his/her Counsel;
   b. Testimony by the Complainant and any witnesses, and any written or oral cross examination by Accused Member or his/her Counsel;
   c. Testimony by the Accused Member;
   d. Questions by the Hearing Panel members; and
   e. Presentation of any evidence determined to be relevant by the Hearing Panel Chair, regardless of its admissibility in a court of law.
2. The Accused Member or his Counsel shall be permitted to make an oral closing statement and/or submit a written statement at the close of the hearing or within a reasonable time thereafter.

Part V: District Branch Decision

After the hearing, the Hearing Panel shall meet and reach a decision based on the information presented at the hearing, including the testimony from the parties and any other witnesses, the documents submitted and any other evidence provided as part of the hearing. The decision shall consist of (A) a determination of whether the Accused Member violated the ethical standards established by the *Principles*, and (B) if so, then what sanction, if any, is appropriate.

A. Determination
1. After the conclusion of the hearing, the panel shall issue a written determination that sets forth the Hearing Panel's findings, recommendations, and reasoning.
2. In making its decision, the Hearing Panel should consider:
   a. The nature and seriousness of the alleged conduct;
   b. Whether or not there is a reasonable belief that an ethics violation occurred.
   c. The credibility of the Accused Member, Complainant and the other witnesses;
   d. Any documents submitted that the panel finds credible; and
3. The DB executive council (or the DB's governing body) must review the panel's determination. The DB executive council can accept or modify the panel's findings. In all cases, the DB shall seek to reach a decision as expeditiously as possible.

4. Before notifying the Complainant and Accused Member, all determinations must be forwarded to the APA Ethics Committee for review pursuant to the procedures set forth in Part VI.
5. Unless the DBEC proceeds under the Education Option, there are two basic findings:
   a. The Accused Member did not act unethically; or b. The Accused Member acted unethically.
6. No Ethical Violation
   a. If the Hearing Panel decides after a hearing that no ethical violation occurred, it shall prepare a written explanation that sets forth the reasons for the determination. This determination shall be submitted to the DB executive council and the APA Ethics Committee for review as set forth in Part VI.
   b. If approved by the DB executive council and the APA Ethics Committee as set forth in Part VI, the DBEC shall notify the Complainant and Accused Member in writing of the determination.
   c. There is no appeal from this determination.
7. Ethical Violation
   a. If the panel decides after a hearing that Accused Member acted unethically, it shall prepare a written explanation that sets forth the reasons for the determination. It shall then proceed to determine the appropriate sanction. This determination shall be submitted to the DB executive committee and the APA Ethics Committee for review as set forth in Part VI.
   b. If approved by both the DB executive committee and APA Ethics Committee, only the Accused Member shall be notified in writing of the determination setting forth the reasons for the determination and the sanction. This Notice should be copied to the APA Ethics Office. This Notice shall also inform the Accused Member of his or her right to appeal the determination to the APA Ethics Committee within 30 days. The appeal right applies to all adverse findings.
   c. The Complainant is not notified of the determination until all appeals have been concluded or the time for the Accused Member to appeal has expired.

B. Sanctions

If the panel finds that an ethical violation has occurred, it must determine the appropriate sanction. This determination may include consideration of any mitigating or aggravating circumstances such as illness or prior findings of unethical conduct that are relevant to the current violation. The three (3) sanctions in increasing order of severity are: (1) Reprimand; (2) Suspension; and (3) Expulsion.
1. Reprimand
   a. A reprimand is an official admonishment by the APA. The reprimand shall identify the conduct considered unethical and the basis of the determination.
   b. The reprimand is confidential and is not published to the general membership of the DB or the APA, or to the general public.

    c. Additional conditions may be included with the reprimand as set forth Part V.C.)

2. Suspension
   a. Suspension is a serious sanction that will be made public. An Accused Member may be suspended for a period not to exceed five (5) years.
   b. A suspended member shall pay dues and is eligible for APA benefits, except that such a member will lose his/her rights to hold office, vote, nominate candidates, propose referenda or amendments to the Bylaws, and serve on any APA committee or component, including the APA Board of Trustees and the APA Assembly. If the suspended member is a Fellow, Life Fellow, Distinguished Fellow or Distinguished Life Fellow, the Fellowship will be suspended for the same period of time.
   c. Each DBEC shall decide which, if any, DB privileges and benefits shall be denied the Accused Member during the period of suspension.
   d. Additional conditions may be included with the suspension as set forth in Part V.C.
   e. The name of any member who is suspended for an ethics violation, along with an explanation of the nature of the violation, shall be reported by the APA Office of Ethics:
      i. In *Psychiatric News*;
      ii. To the DB to be included in the DB newsletter or other usual means of communication with its membership;
      iii. To the medical licensing authority in all states in which the member is licensed;
      iv. To the National Practitioner Data Bank.
   f. The DB should also consult applicable state law to assure that it adheres to any requirements.

3. Expulsion
   a. Expulsion is the most serious sanction. As a result, all determinations to expel an Accused Member must be affirmed by the APA Board of Trustees.
   b. Once a decision to expel a member has been approved by the DB executive council and the APA Ethics Committee, and the appeal process under Part VII has been exhausted or expired the APA Ethics Committee Chair (or his/her designee) shall present the matter and the documentary record to the APA Board of Trustees at the Board's next meeting. The APA Board of Trustees may:
      i. Affirm the sanction;
      ii. Impose a lesser sanction;
      iii. Remand to the APA Ethics Committee or DBEC for further action or consideration in which case these procedures shall apply to those actions; or
      iv. Request further information from the DBEC before voting on the decision to expel.
   c. A decision to affirm an expulsion must be by a vote of two-thirds (2/3) of those Trustees present and voting. A decision to impose a lesser sanction shall be by a majority vote.

d. If the APA Board of Trustees affirms expulsion, the APA Secretary shall notify the DBEC, and the DBEC shall in turn notify the Complainant and Accused Member of the decision and that it is final. The Accused Member shall also be provided copies of the DBEC and/or panel recommendation(s) and reasoning.

e. The name of any member who is expelled from the APA for an ethics violation, along with an explanation of the nature of the violation, shall be reported by the APA Office of Ethics:

    i. In *Psychiatric News*:

    ii. To the DB to be included in the DB newsletter (APA Office of Ethics will provide DBEC with language) or other usual means of communication with its membership;

    iii. To the medical licensing authority in all states in which the member is licensed;

    iv. To the National Practitioner Data Bank.

f. The DB should also consult applicable state law to assure that it adheres to any state requirements.

C. Additional Conditions

Concurrent with the imposition of the sanctions of reprimand and suspension, additional conditions can be imposed. These conditions are designed to reinforce and facilitate ethical behavior.

1. Supervision

    a. The DBEC may impose supervisory requirements on a suspended member. When such conditions are imposed, the following procedures shall apply:

        i. If the DBEC imposes conditions, it shall ensure that the DB monitors compliance;

        ii. If a member fails to satisfy the conditions, the DBEC may decide to recommend a new sanction; and

        iii. If the DBEC determines that a member should be expelled for noncompliance with conditions, the APA Board of Trustees shall review the expulsion in accordance with the provisions set forth in Part VII. E. of these procedures.

    b. In determining whether to require supervision, the Hearing Panel and/or the DBEC should consider the available resources to conduct and monitor such supervision.

2. Education Requirement

    a. The DBEC may impose an Education Requirement as part of the sanctions of reprimand or suspension.

    b. If the DBEC decides to impose an Education Requirement, the DBEC shall identify a specific educational program including courses, reading and/or consultation for the Accused Member to complete within a specified period and shall notify the Accused Member and the APA Ethics Committee of the required program. The DB will monitor the Accused Member's compliance with any such educational requirements. The Accused Member's failure to complete the specified educational requirement(s) may result in the proceedings being reopened (e.g., to determine if a greater sanction is indicated).

3. Personal Treatment

    a. As part of any sanction, personal treatment may be recommended, but not required, and any such recommendation shall be carried out in accordance with the ethical requirements governing confidentiality as set forth in the *Principles*. In appropriate cases, the DBEC may also refer the psychiatrist in question to a program responsible for considering impaired or physically ill physicians.

Part VI: Review by the APA Ethics Committee

A. APA Ethics Committee Review

1. After the DBEC decision is confirmed by its DB executive council (or the DB's governing body), the decision and any pertinent information concerning the procedures followed or relating to the action taken shall be forwarded to the APA Ethics Committee for review. This review applies to all decisions, including those where the DBEC finds that an ethics violation has not occurred.

2. The APA Ethics Committee will appoint a panel composed of at least three (3) voting members of the APA Ethics Committee to undertake these review functions on behalf of the full APA Ethics Committee. The review shall assure that:

    a. The complaint received a comprehensive and fair review;

    b. That the review was in accordance with the applicable procedures; and

    c. The sanction imposed was appropriate.

3. If the APA Ethics subcommittee concludes that these requirements were not satisfied, it shall so advise the DBEC, and the DBEC shall remedy the deficiencies and shall make further reports to the APA Ethics Committee until such time as the APA Ethics Committee is satisfied that these requirements have been met.

4. If the APA Ethics subcommittee concludes that the sanction should be reconsidered by the DBEC, it shall provide a statement of reasons explaining the basis for its opinion, and the DBEC shall reconsider the sanction. After reconsideration, the decision of the DBEC shall be final with the exception that Expulsions must also be approved by the APA Board of Trustees.

5. The Complainant and Accused Member shall not be notified of any decision until this review is completed.

B. Notification of Decision

1. After the APA Ethics Committee or subcommittee completes the review process, the following Notices will be sent:

    a. If the determination is that no ethics violation has occurred, the DB shall provide written Notice to the Complainant and Accused Member of the decision.

    b. If the determination is that an ethical violation did occur, the DBEC shall provide written Notice to the Accused Member of the decision and the sanction. The Accused Member shall be provided: (1) copies of the DBEC and/or panel recommendation(s), (2) the DBEC decision, and (3) notice of his/her right to Appeal the decision within 30 days of receipt of the letter. The Complainant shall not be notified until all appeals or the time for all appeals has expired.

   c. If the decision is to expel the member, the DBEC shall not provide Notice until the APA Board of Trustees has approved the expulsion pursuant to Part V.B.4. Once approved by the Board, the DBEC shall provide written Notice to the Complainant and Accused Member, with a copy to APA, that Expulsion has been approved by the Board of Trustees and that the decision is final.

Part VII: Appeals

A. Appeal Panel

1. All appeals shall be considered and decided by a panel of three (3) members of the APA Ethics Committee who have not been involved in a review of the case pursuant to Part VI.
2. The Chair of the APA Ethics Committee may appoint a replacement if there are not three members of the Committee who have not been involved in the case who are able to serve.

B. Grounds for Appeal

All appeals shall be based on one (1) or more of the following grounds:

1. That there have been significant procedural irregularities or deficiencies in the case;
2. That *The Principles of Medical Ethics with Annotations Especially Applicable to Psychiatry* has been improperly applied;
3. That the findings of or sanction imposed by the DB are not supported by substantial evidence;
4. That substantial new evidence has called into question the findings and conclusions of the district branch.

C. Accused Member's Request for Appeal

1. The Accused Member's request for an appeal must be received within 30 days of the date the Accused Member is notified of the district branch decision. Upon receipt of the Accused Member's request for an appeal, the APA Ethics Committee shall request and the DB shall provide to the APA Ethics Committee a copy of the DB file, including the recording of the hearing. The APA Ethics Committee shall make a copy the DB file available to the Accused Member upon request and compliance with any conditions set by the APA Ethics Committee.
2. In appeals heard by an APA Ethics Committee appeals panel, the panel will review and decide the appeal solely on the basis of the DB's documentary record of its actions and decision and any written appeal statements filed by the Accused Member and the district branch. The Accused Member's statement will be provided to the DB, which may file a written response. Any DB response will be forwarded to the Accused Member, who will have the opportunity to respond in writing prior to the Ethics Committee's consideration of the appeal. Filing

deadlines and other procedures governing the appeal shall be established by the APA Ethics Committee.

D. Decision by APA Ethics Committee Appeal Panel

1. After reviewing all documents, the APA Ethics Committee appeals panel may take any of the following actions: a. Affirm the decision, including the sanction imposed by the district branch; b. Affirm the decision, but alter the sanction imposed by the district branch; c. Reverse the decision of the district branch and terminate the case; or d. Remand the case to the district branch with specific instructions as to what further information or action is necessary. Remands will be employed only in rare cases, such as when new information has been presented on appeal or when there is an indication that important information is available and has not been considered. After the district branch or panel has completed remand proceedings, the case shall be handled in accordance with procedures in Part VI and VII.

2. After the APA Ethics Committee appeals panel reaches a decision, if the decision is anything other than to expel a member or remand, the Chair of the APA Ethics Committee shall provide Notice to the DB of the decision. The DB shall then provide Notice to the Accused Member and the Complainant of the decision and that it is final.

3. If the decision is to expel the member, the decision would be forwarded to the APA Board of Trustees as outlined in Part V.B.4.

Copyright © 2010 American Psychiatric Association
ALL RIGHTS RESERVED
Manufactured in the United States of America
08 07 06 3 2 1

The Principles of Medical Ethics

2013 Edition
(Previous editions 1973, 1978, 1981, 1984, 1985, 1989, 1992, 1993, 1995, 1995 Revised, 1998, 2001, 2001 Revised, 2006, 2008, 2009. 2009 Revised, and 2010

American Psychiatric Association
1000 Wilson Boulevard #1825
Arlington, VA 22209

American Group Psychotherapy Association
AGPA and IBCGP Guidelines for Ethics

Introduction

The American Group Psychotherapy Association is a multi-disciplinary, membership organization dedicated to advancing knowledge, research, and training in group psychotherapy and other group interventions to benefit the client/patient population. The International Board for Certification of Group Psychotherapists advances group psychotherapy by certifying group psychotherapists according to nationally accepted criteria, and promotes these practitioners and principles to other mental health professionals, employers, insurers, educators, and clients for the purpose of maintaining the highest standards for group psychotherapy practice and quality care. Membership in AGPA and/or inclusion in the Certification Board requires adherence to standards of ethical practice as outlined by state licensing boards and/or designated national professional organizations, whichever was applicable in establishing clinical credentials. Those who do not belong to a professional group having a published standard of ethics must follow the principles of ethics established by the American Psychological Association.

Ethical complaints about individuals who are members of AGPA and/or listed in the Certification Board should be directed to the state licensing board or, in the absence of a state license, to the designated primary professional organization of the individual. Should an ethical complaint be received regarding an individual who is a member of AGPA and/or listed in the Certification Board whose state does not have licensure and who does not belong to a primary professional organization, the complainant will be directed to the state or federal legal system to file his or her complaint.

In the event of the revocation, suspension or voluntary relinquishment of a clinical license to practice or membership/certification in the designated national professional organization, membership in AGPA and/or inclusion in the Certification Board will be revoked. In the event an individual referred to the governmental agencies or courts of law is found guilty, his or her AGPA membership and/or his or her inclusion in the Certification Board will be revoked. It is the responsibility of the individual to inform AGPA and/or the Certification Board of any revocation, suspension or voluntary relinquishment of licensure or membership/certification, whichever was used to verify clinical credentials for inclusion in the Certification Board.

Guidelines of Group Psychotherapy Practice

The following guidelines of group psychotherapy practice shall serve as models for group therapists' ethical behavior.

Responsibility to Patient/Client

1. The group psychotherapist provides services with respect for the dignity and uniqueness of each patient/client as well as the rights and autonomy of the individual patient/client.

    1.1 The group psychotherapist shall provide the potential group patient/client with information about the nature of group psychotherapy and apprise him or her of the risks, rights and obligations as a member of a therapy group.

    1.2 The group psychotherapist shall encourage the patient/client's participation in group psychotherapy only so long as it is appropriate to the patient/client's needs.

    1.3 The group psychotherapist shall not practice or condone any form of discrimination on the basis of race, color, sex, sexual orientation, age, religion, national origin or physical handicap, except that this guideline shall not prohibit group therapy practice with population specific or problem specific groups.

2. The group psychotherapist safeguards the patient/client's right to privacy by judiciously protecting information of a confidential nature.

    2.1 The group shall agree that the patient/client as well as the psychotherapist shall protect the identity of its members.

    2.2 The group therapist is knowledgeable about the limits of privileged communication as they apply to group therapy and informs group members of those limits.

    2.3 The group psychotherapist shall not use identifiable information about the group or its members for teaching purposes, publication or professional presentations unless permission has been obtained and all measures have been taken to preserve patient/client anonymity.

    2.4 Except where required by law, the group psychotherapist shall share information about the group members with others only after obtaining appropriate patient/client consent. Specific permission must be requested to permit conferring with the referring therapist or with the individual therapist where the patient/client is in conjoint therapy.

    2.5 When clinical examination suggests that a patient/client may be dangerous to himself/herself or others, it is the group psychotherapist's ethical and legal obligation to take appropriate steps in order to be responsible to society in general, as well as the patient/client.

3. The group psychotherapist acts to safeguard the patient/client and the public from the incompetent, unethical, illegal practice of any group psychotherapist.

3.1 The group psychotherapist must be aware of her/his own individual competencies, and when the needs of the patient/client are beyond the competencies of the psychotherapist, consultation must be sought from other qualified professionals or other appropriate sources.

3.2 The group psychotherapist shall not use her/his professional relationship to advance personal or business interests.

3.3 Sexual intimacy with patients/clients is unethical.

3.4 The group psychotherapist shall protect the patient/client and the public from misinformation and misrepresentation. She/he shall not use false or misleading advertising regarding her/his qualifications or skills as a group psychotherapist.

Professional Standards

The group psychotherapist shall maintain the integrity of the practice of group psychotherapy.

1. It is the personal responsibility of the group psychotherapist to maintain competence in the practice of group psychotherapy through formal educational activities and informal learning experiences.

2. The group psychotherapist has a responsibility to contribute to the ongoing development of the body of knowledge pertaining to group psychotherapy whether involved as an investigator, participant or user of research results.

3. The group psychotherapist shall accept the obligation to attempt to inform and alert other group psychotherapists who are violating ethical principles or to bring those violations to the attention of appropriate professional authorities.

(Revised, February 2002)

AMHCA Code of Ethics

PRINCIPLES FOR AMHCA CODE OF ETHICS

AMHCA Preamble

The American Mental Health Counselors Association (AMHCA) represents mental health counselors. As the professional counseling organization of mental health counselors, AMHCA subscribes to rigorous standards for education, training and clinical practice. Mental health counselors are committed to increasing knowledge of human behavior and understanding of themselves and others. AMHCA members are highly skilled professionals who provide a full range of counseling services in a variety of settings. Members believe in the dignity and worth of the individual and make every reasonable effort to protect human welfare. To this end, AMHCA establishes and promotes the highest professional standards. Mental health counselors subscribe to and pledge to abide by the principles identified in the Code of Ethics.

This code is a document intended as a guide to: assist members to make sound ethical decisions; to define ethical behaviors and best practices for Association members; to support the mission of the Association; and to educate members, students and the public at large regarding the ethical standards of mental health counselors. Mental health counselors are expected to utilize carefully considered ethical-decision making processes when faced with ethical dilemmas.

I. Commitment to Clients

A. Counselor-Client Relationship

1. Primary Responsibility
Mental health counselors value objectivity and integrity in their commitment to understanding human behavior, and they maintain the highest standards in providing mental health counseling services.
   a) The primary responsibility of mental health counselors is to respect client dignity and promote client welfare.
   b) Mental health counselors are clear with clients about the parameters of the counseling relationship. In a professional disclosure statement, they provide information about expectations and responsibilities of both counselor and client in the counseling process, their professional orientation and values regarding the counseling process, emergency procedures, supervision (as applicable) and business practices. Information is also provided regarding client rights and contact information for the state counseling licensure authority.

2. Confidentiality
Mental health counselors have a primary obligation to safeguard information about individuals obtained in the course of practice, teaching, or research. Personal information is communicated to others only with the person's consent, preferably written, or in those circumstances, as dictated by state laws. Disclosure of counseling information is restricted to what is necessary, relevant and verifiable.
   a) Confidentiality is a right granted to all clients of mental health counseling services. From the onset of the counseling relationship, mental health counselors inform clients of these rights including legal limitations and exceptions.

b) The information in client records belongs to the client and shall not be shared without permission granted through a formal release of information. In the event that a client requests that information in his or her record be shared, mental health counselors educate clients to the implications of sharing the materials.

c) The release of information without consent of the client may only take place under the most extreme circumstances: the protection of life (suicidality or homicidality), child abuse, and/ or abuse of incompetent persons and elder abuse. Above all, mental health counselors are required to comply with state and federal statutes concerning mandated reporting.

d) Mental health counselors (or their staff members) do not release information by request unless accompanied by a specific release of information or a valid court order. Mental health counselors make every attempt to release only information necessary to comply with the request or valid court order. Mental health counselors are advised to seek legal advice upon receiving a subpoena in order to respond appropriately.

e) The anonymity of clients served in public and other agencies is preserved, if at all possible, by withholding names and personal identifying data. If external conditions require reporting such information, the client shall be so informed.

f) Information received in confidence by one agency or person shall not be forwarded to another person or agency without the client's written permission.

g) Mental health counselors have the responsibility to ensure the accuracy of, and to indicate the validity of, data shared with other parties.

h) Case reports presented in classes, professional meetings, or publications shall be disguised so that no identification is possible. Permission must be obtained from clients prior to disclosing their identity.

i) Counseling reports and records are maintained under conditions of security, and provisions are made for their destruction after five (5) years post termination or as specified by state regulations. Mental health counselors ensure that all persons in their employ, and volunteers, supervisees and interns, maintain confidentiality of client information.

j) Sessions with clients may be taped or otherwise recorded only with written permission of the client or guardian. Even with a guardian's written consent, mental health counselors should not record a session against the expressed wishes of a client. Such tapes shall be destroyed after five (5) years post termination or as specified by state regulations.

k) The primary client owns the rights to confidentiality; however, in the case where primary clients are minors or are adults who have been legally determined to be incompetent, parents and guardians have legal access to client information. Where appropriate, a parent(s) or guardian(s) may be included in the counseling process; however, mental health counselors must take measures to safeguard client confidentiality within legal limits.

l) In working with families or groups, the rights to confidentiality of each member should be safeguarded. Mental health counselors must make clear that each member of the group has individual rights to confidentiality and that each member of a family, when seen individually, has individual rights to confidentiality within legal limits.

m) When using a computer to store confidential information, mental health counselors take measures to control access to such information. After five (5) years post termination or as specified by state regulations, the information should be deleted from the system.

n) Mental health counselors may justify disclosing information to identifiable third parties if clients disclose that they have a communicable or life threatening illness. However, prior to disclosing such information, mental health counselors must confirm the diagnosis with a medical provider. The intent of clients to inform a third party about their illness and to engage in possible behaviors that could be harmful to an identifiable third party must be assessed as part of the process of determining whether a disclosure should be made to identifiable third parties.

o) Mental health counselors take necessary precautions to ensure client confidentiality of information transmitted electronically through the use of a computer, e-mail, fax, telephone, voice mail, answering machines, or any other electronic means.

p) Mental health counselors protect the confidentiality of deceased clients in accordance with legal requirements and agency or organizational policy.

q) Mental health counselors may disclose information to third-party payers only after clients have authorized such disclosure or as permitted by Federal and/or state statute.

3. Dual/Multiple Relationships

Mental health counselors are aware of their influential position with respect to their clients and avoid exploiting the trust and fostering dependency of the client.

a) Mental health counselors make every effort to avoid dual/multiple relationships with clients that could impair professional judgment or increase the risk of harm. Examples of such relationships may include, but are not limited to: familial, social, financial, business, or close personal relationships with the clients.

b) When deciding whether to enter a dual/multiple relationship with a client, former client or close relationship to the client, mental health counselors will seek consultation and adhere to a credible decision-making process prior to entering this relationship.

c) When a dual/multiple relationship cannot be avoided, mental health counselors take appropriate professional precautions such as informed consent, consultation, supervision and documentation to ensure that judgment is not impaired and no exploitation has occurred.

d) Mental health counselors do not accept as clients, individuals with whom they are involved in an administrative, supervisory or other relationship of an evaluative nature.

4. Exploitive Relationships

Mental health counselors are aware of the intimacy and responsibilities inherent in the counseling relationship. They maintain respect for the client and avoid actions that seek to meet their personal needs at the expense of the client.

a) Romantic or sexual relationships with clients are strictly prohibited. Mental health counselors do not counsel persons with whom they have had a previous sexual relationship.

b) Mental health counselors are strongly discouraged from engaging in romantic or sexual relationships with former clients. Counselors may not enter into an intimate relationship until five years post termination or longer as specified by state regulations. Documentation of supervision or consultation for exploring the risk of exploitation is strongly encouraged.

c) Determining the risk of exploitive relationships includes but is not limited to factors such as duration of counseling, amount of time since counseling, termination circumstances the client's personal history and mental status, and the potential adverse impact on the former client.

d) Mental health counselors are aware of their own values, attitudes, beliefs and behaviors, as well as how these apply in a society with clients from diverse ethnic, social, cultural, religious, and economic backgrounds.

B. Counseling Process

1. Counseling Plans
Mental health counselors use counseling plans to direct their work with clients.

a) Mental health counselors and their clients work jointly in devising integrated, individual counseling plans that offer reasonable promise of success and are consistent with the abilities, ethnic, social, cultural, and values backgrounds, and circumstances of the clients.

b) Mental health counselors and clients regularly review counseling plans to ensure their continued viability and effectiveness, respecting the clients' autonomy.

2. Informed Consent
Clients have the right to know and understand what is expected, how the information divulged will be used, and the freedom to choose whether, and with whom, they will enter into a counseling relationship.

a) Mental health counselors provide information that allows clients to make an informed choice when selecting a provider. Such information includes but is not limited to: counselor credentials, issues of confidentiality, the use of tests and inventories, diagnosis, reports, billing, and therapeutic process. Restrictions that limit clients' autonomy are fully explained.

b) Informed Consent includes the mental health counselor's professional disclosure statement and client bill of rights.

c) When a client is a minor or is unable to give informed consent mental health counselors act in the client's best interest. Parents and legal guardians are informed about the confidential nature of the counseling relationship. Mental health counselors embrace the diversity of the family system and the inherent rights and responsibilities parents/guardians have for the welfare of their children. Mental health counselors therefore strive to establish collaborative relationships with parents/guardians to best serve their minor clients.

d) Informed consent is ongoing and needs to be reassessed throughout the counseling relationship.

e) Mental health counselors inform the client of specific limitations, potential risks, and/or potential benefits relevant to the client's anticipated use of on-line counseling services.

3. Multiple Clients
When working with multiple clients, mental health counselors respect individual client rights and maintain objectivity.
   a) When mental health counselors agree to provide counseling services to two or more persons who have a relationship (such as husband and wife, or parents and children), counselors clarify at the outset, the nature of the relationship they will have with each involved person.
   b) Collateral consent informs family members or significant others involved in counseling, of the parameters and limitations of confidentiality.
   c) If it becomes apparent that mental health counselors are unable to maintain objectivity resulting in conflicting roles, they must appropriately clarify, adjust, or withdraw from roles.
   d) Rules of confidentiality extend to all clients who receive services, not just those identified as primary clients.
   e) When working in groups, mental health counselors screen prospective group counseling/therapy participants. Every effort is made to select members whose needs and goals are compatible with goals of the group, who will not impede the group process, and whose well-being will not be jeopardized by the group experience.
   f) In the group setting, mental health counselors take reasonable precautions to protect clients from physical, emotional, and psychological harm or trauma.

4. Clients Served By Others
Mental health counselors do not enter into counseling relationships with a person being served by another mental health professional unless all parties have been informed and agree.
   a) When clients choose to change professionals but have not terminated services with the former professional, it is important to encourage the individual to first deal with that termination prior to entering into a new therapeutic relationship.
   b) When clients work with multiple providers, it is important to secure permission to work collaboratively with the other professional involved.

5. Termination and Referral
Mental health counselors do not abandon or neglect their clients in counseling.
   a) Assistance is given in making appropriate arrangements for the continuation of treatment, when necessary, during interruptions such as vacation and following termination.
   b) Mental health counselors terminate a counseling relationship when it is reasonably clear that the client is no longer benefiting, when services are no longer required, when counseling no longer serves the needs and/or interests of the client, or when agency or institution limits do not allow provision of further counseling services.
   c) Mental health counselors may terminate a counseling relationship when clients do not pay fees charged or when insurance denies treatment. In such cases, appropriate referrals are offered to the clients.

d) If mental health counselors determine that services are not beneficial to the client, they avoid entering or terminate immediately the counseling relationship. In such situations, appropriate referrals are made. If clients decline the suggested referral, mental health counselors discontinue the relationship.

e) When mental health counselors refer clients to other professionals, open and collaborative communication is important to ensure an appropriate transition.

f) If clients are in danger, such as domestic violence or suicidality, mental health counselors take steps to secure a safety plan, refer to appropriate resources, and if necessary contact appropriate support.

6. Technology-Assisted Counseling

Technology-assisted counseling includes but is not limited to computer, telephone, internet and other communication devices.

Mental health counselors take reasonable steps to protect patients, clients, students, research participants and others from harm. Mental health counselors performing technology-assisted counseling comply with all other provisions of this Ethics Code. Mental health counselors:

a) Establish methods to ascertain the client's identity and obtain alternative methods of contacting the client in an electronic emergency.

b) Electronically transfer client confidential information to authorized third-party recipients only when both the mental health counselor and the authorized recipient have secure transfer and acceptance capabilities as state and federal laws regulate.

c) Ensure that clients are intellectually, emotionally, and physically capable of using technology-assisted counseling services, and of understanding the potential risks and/or limitations of such services.

d) Provide technology-assisted counseling services only in practice areas within their expertise. Mental health counselors do not provide services to clients in states where doing so would violate local licensure laws or regulations.

e) Confirm that the provision of technology-assisted counseling services are not prohibited by or otherwise violate any applicable state or local statutes, rules, regulations or ordinances, codes of professional membership organizations and certifying boards, and/or codes of state licensing boards.

7. Clients' Rights

In all mental health services, wherever and however they are delivered, clients have the right to be treated with dignity, consideration and respect at all times. Clients have the right:

a) To expect quality service provided by concerned, trained, professional and competent staff.

b) To expect complete confidentiality within the limits of both Federal and state law, and to be informed about the legal exceptions to confidentiality; and to expect that no information will be released without the client's knowledge and written consent.

c) To a clear working contract in which business items, such as time of sessions, payment plans/fees, absences, access, emergency procedures, third-party reimbursement procedures, termination and referral procedures, and advanced notice of the use of collection agencies, are discussed.

d) To a clear statement of the purposes, goals, techniques, rules limitations, and all other pertinent information that may affect the ongoing mental health counseling relationship.

e) To appropriate information regarding the mental health counselor's education, training, skills, license and practice limitations and to request and receive referrals to other clinicians when appropriate.

f) To full, knowledgeable, and responsible participation in the ongoing treatment plan to the maximum extent feasible.

g) To obtain information about their case record and to have this information explained clearly and directly.

h) To request information and/or consultation regarding the conduct and progress of their therapy.

i) To refuse any recommended services and to be advised of the consequences of this action.

j) To a safe environment for counseling free of emotional, physical, or sexual abuse.

k) To a client grievance procedure, including requests for consultation and/or mediation; and to file a complaint with the mental health counselor's supervisor (where relevant), and/or the appropriate credentialing body.

l) To a clearly defined ending process, and to discontinue therapy at any time.

8. End-of-Life Care for Terminally Ill Clients

a) Mental health counselors ensure that clients receive quality end-of-life care for their physical, emotional, social, and spiritual needs. This includes providing clients with an opportunity to participate in informed decision making regarding their end-of-life care, and a thorough assessment, from a qualified end-of-life care professional, of clients' ability to make competent decisions on their behalf.

b) Mental health counselors are aware of their own personal, moral, and competency issues as it relates to end-of-life decisions. When mental health counselors assess that they are unable to work with clients on the exploration of end-of-life options, they make appropriate referrals to ensure clients receive appropriate help.

c) Depending upon the applicable state laws, the circumstances of the situation, and after seeking consultation and supervision from competent professional and legal entities, mental health counselors have the options of breaking or not breaking confidentiality of terminally ill clients who plan on hastening their deaths.

C. Counselor Responsibility and Integrity

1. Competence

The maintenance of high standards of professional competence is a responsibility shared by all mental health counselors in the best interests of the client, the public, and the profession. Mental health counselors:

a) Recognize the boundaries of their particular competencies and the limitations of their expertise.

b) Provide only those services and use only those techniques for which they are qualified by education, training, or experience.

c) Maintain knowledge of relevant scientific and professional information related to the services rendered, and recognizes the need for on-going education.

d) Represent accurately their competence, education, training, and experience including licenses and certifications.

e) Perform their duties, as teaching professionals, based on careful preparation in order that their instruction is accurate, up-to-date and educational.

f) Recognize the importance of continuing education and remain open to new counseling approaches and procedures documented by peer-reviewed scientific and professional literature.

g) Recognize the important need to be competent in regard to cultural diversity and are sensitive to the diversity of varying populations as well as to changes in cultural expectations and values over time.

h) Recognize that their effectiveness is dependent on their own mental and physical health. Should their involvement in any activity, or any mental, emotional, or physical health problem, compromise sound professional judgment and competency, they seek capable professional assistance to determine whether to limit, suspend, or terminate services to their clients.

i) Have a responsibility to maintain high standards of professional conduct at all times.

j) Take appropriate steps to rectify ethical issues with colleagues by using procedures developed by employers and/or state licensure boards.

k) Are aware of the intimacy of the counseling relationship, maintain a healthy respect for the integrity of the client, and avoid engaging in activities that seek to meet the mental health counselor's personal needs at the expense of the client.

l) Will actively attempt to understand the diverse cultural backgrounds of the clients with whom they work. This includes learning how the mental health counselor's own cultural/ethical/racial/religious identity impacts his or her own values and beliefs about the counseling process.

m) Are responsible for continuing education and remaining abreast of current trends and changes in the field including the professional literature on best practices.

n) Develop a plan for termination of practice, death or incapacitation by assigning a colleague or records custodian to handle transfer of clients and files.

2. Non-discrimination

Mental health counselors do not condone or engage in any discrimination based on age, color, culture, disability, ethnic group, gender, race, religion, sexual orientation, marital status, or socioeconomic status.

Mental health counselors do not condone or engage in sexual harassment. Sexual harassment is defined as any solicitation, physical, or verbal or nonverbal conduct that is sexual in nature that occurs in connection with professional activities or roles, and that is either unwelcome or offensive, or creates a hostile workplace or learning environment, or is sufficiently severe or intense to be perceived as harassment to a reasonable person in the context in which the behavior occurred. Sexual harassment can consist of a single intense or severe act or multiple persistent or pervasive acts.

3. Conflict of Interest

Mental health counselors are aware of possible conflicts of interests that may arise between the counselor and the client, the employer, consultant and other professionals.

Mental health counselors may choose to consult with any other professionally competent person about a client assuring that no conflict of interest exists. When conflicts occur, mental health counselors clarify the nature of the conflict and inform all parties of the nature and direction of their loyalties and responsibilities, and keep all parties informed of their commitments.

D. Assessment and Diagnosis

1. Selection and Administration

Mental health counselors utilize tests (herein references educational, psychological, and career assessment instruments), interviews, and other assessment techniques and diagnostic tools in the counseling process for the purpose of determining the client's particular needs in the context of his/her situation.

a) Mental health counselors choose assessment methods that are reliable, valid and appropriate based on the age, gender, race, ability and other client characteristics. If tests must be used in the absence of information regarding the aforementioned factors, the limitations of generalizability should be duly noted.

b) In selecting assessment tools, mental health counselors justify the logic of their choices in relation to the client's needs and the clinical context in which the assessment occurs.

c) Mental health counselors avoid using outdated or obsolete tests, and remain current regarding test publication and revision.

d) Mental health counselors use assessments only in the context of professional, academic, or training relationships.

e) Mental health counselors provide the client with appropriate information regarding the reason for assessment, the approximate length of time required, and to whom the report will be distributed.

f) Mental health counselors provide an appropriate assessment environment with regard to temperature, privacy, comfort, and freedom from distractions.

2. Interpretation and Reporting

Mental health counselors respects the rights and dignity of the client in assessment, interpretation, and diagnosis of mental disorders and makes every effort to assure that the client receives the appropriate treatment.

a) Mental health counselors base diagnoses and other assessment summaries on multiple sources of data whenever possible.

b) Mental health counselors are careful not to draw conclusions unless empirical evidence is present.

c) Mental health counselors consider multicultural factors (including but not limited to gender, race, religion, age, ability, culture, class, ethnicity, sexual orientation) in test interpretation, in diagnosis, and in the formulation of prognosis and treatment recommendations.

d) Mental health counselors are responsible for evaluating the quality of computer software interpretations of test data. Mental health counselors should obtain information regarding validity of computerized test interpretation before utilizing such an approach.

e) Mental health counselors clearly explain computerized test results in their summaries and reports.

f) Mental health counselors write reports in a style that is clear, concise and easily understandable for the lay reader.

g) To the extent possible mental health counselors provide test results in a neutral and nonjudgmental manner.

h) Mental health counselors are responsible for ensuring the confidentiality and security of assessment reports, test data, and test materials regardless of how the material is maintained or transmitted.

i) Mental health counselors train their staff to respect the confidentiality of test reports in the context of typing, filing, or mailing them.

j) Mental health counselors (or their staff members) do not release an assessment or evaluation report by request unless accompanied by a specific release of information or a valid court order. A subpoena is insufficient to release a report. In such a case, the counselor must inform his or her client of the situation. If the client refuses release, the mental health counselor coordinates between the client's attorney and the requesting attorney to protect client confidentiality and the counselor's legal welfare.

3. Competence

Mental health counselors employ only those diagnostic tools and assessment instruments they are trained to use by education, or supervised training and clinical experience.

a) Mental health counselors seek appropriate workshops, supervision and training to familiarize themselves with assessment techniques and the use of specific assessment instruments.

b) Mental health counselor supervisors ensure that their supervisees have adequate training in interpretation before allowing them to evaluate tests independently.

4. Forensic Activity

Mental health counselors who are requested or required to perform forensic functions, such as assessments, interviews, consultations, report writing, responding to subpoenas, or offering expert testimony, comply with all provisions of this Ethics Code and act in accordance with applicable state law.

a) Mental health counselors who engage in forensic activity must possess appropriate knowledge and competence, including specialized knowledge about special populations, specialized testing and specialized interview techniques.

b) When conducting interviews, writing reports or offering testimony mental health counselors objectively offers their findings without bias, personal opinion or investment in the ultimate outcome.

c) The client, in a forensic evaluation will be informed about the limits of confidentiality, the role of the mental health counselor, the purpose of the assessment and potential for unfavorable findings.

d) Mental health counselors' forensic written reports and recommendations are based upon information and techniques appropriate to the evaluation.
e) Mental health counselors do not provide written conclusions or forensic testimony regarding any individual without assessment of that individual adequate to support any statements or conclusions offered in the forensic setting.
f) When testifying, the mental health counselors clearly present their qualifications and specialized training. They describe fairly the basis for their professional judgment, conclusions, and testimony. Counselors remain cognizant of the social responsibility they bear.
g) In general, mental health counselors do not evaluate, for forensic purposes, individuals whom they are currently counseling or have counseled in the past. In addition, in general, mental health counselors do not counsel individuals they are currently evaluating, or have evaluated in the past, for forensic purposes.
h) Forensic mental health counselors do not act as an advocate for the legal system, perpetrators, or victims of criminal activity.

E. Record-Keeping, Fee Arrangements, and Bartering

1. Recordkeeping
Mental health counselors create and maintain accurate and adequate clinical and financial records.
a) Mental health counselors create, maintain, store, transfer, and dispose of client records in ways that protect confidentiality and are in accordance with applicable regulations or laws.
b) Mental health counselors establish a plan for the transfer, storage, and disposal of client records in the event of withdrawal from practice or death of the counselor that maintains confidentiality and protects the welfare of the client.

2. Fee Arrangements, Bartering, and Gifts
Mental health counselors are cognizant of cultural norms in relation to fee arrangements, bartering, and gifts. Mental health counselors clearly explain to clients, early in the counseling relationship, all financial arrangements related to counseling.
a) In establishing professional counseling fees, mental health counselors take into consideration the financial situation of clients and locality. If the usual fees create undue hardship for the client, the counselor may adjust fees or assist the client to locate comparable, affordable services.
b) Mental health counselors usually refrain from accepting goods or services from clients in return for counseling services because such arrangements may create the potential for conflicts, exploitation and distortion of the professional relationship. However, bartering may occur if the client requests it, there is no exploitation, and the cultural implications and other concerns of such practice are discussed with the client and agreed upon in writing.
c) Mental health counselors contribute to society by providing pro bono services.
d) When accepting gifts, mental health counselors take into consideration the therapeutic relationship, motivation of giving, the counselor's motivation for receiving or declining, cultural norms, and the value of the gift.

F. Other Roles

1. Consultant
Mental health counselors acting as consultants have a high degree of self-awareness of their own values, knowledge, skills and needs in entering a helping relationship that involves human and/or organizational change.
  a) The focus of the consulting relationship is on the issues to be resolved and not on the personal characteristics of those presenting the consulting issues.
  b) Mental health counselors develop an understanding of the problem presented by the client and secure an agreement with the client, specifying the terms and nature of the consulting relationship.
  c) Mental health counselors are reasonably certain that they and their clients have the competencies and resources necessary to follow the consultation plan.
  d) Mental health counselors encourage adaptability and growth toward self-direction.
  e) Mental health counselors keep all proprietary information confidential.
  f) Mental health counselors avoid conflicts of interest in selecting consultation clients.

2. Advocate
Mental health counselors may serve as advocates at the individual, institutional, and/or societal level in an effort to foster sociopolitical change that meets the needs of the client or the community.
  a) Mental health counselors are aware of and make every effort to avoid pitfalls of advocacy including conflicts of interest, inappropriate relationships and other negative consequences. Mental health counselors remain sensitive to the potential personal and cultural impact on clients of their advocacy efforts.
  b) Mental health counselors may encourage clients to challenge familial, institutional, and societal obstacles to their growth and development and they may advocate on the clients' behalf. Mental health counselors remain aware of the potential dangers of becoming overly involved as an advocate.

II. Commitment to Other Professionals

A. Relationship With Colleagues
Mental health counselors act with due regard for the needs and feelings of their colleagues in counseling and other professions. Mental health counselors respect the rights and obligations of the institutions or organizations with which they associate.
  1. Mental health counselors understand how related professions complement their work and make full use of other professional, technical, and administrative resources that best serve the interests of clients.
  2. Mental health counselors know and take into account the traditions and practices of other professional groups with which they work and cooperate fully in working for the benefit of public welfare.
  3. Mental health counselors treat professional colleagues with the same dignity and respect afforded to clients. Professional discourse should be free of personal attacks.

4. Mental health counselors respect the viability, reputation, and proprietary rights of organizations that they serve.
5. Credit is assigned to those who have contributed to a publication, in proportion to their contribution.
6. Mental health counselors do not accept or offer referral fees from other professionals.
7. When mental health counselors have knowledge of the impairment, incompetence, or unethical conduct of a mental health professional, they are obliged to attempt to rectify the situation. Failing an informal solution, mental health counselors should bring such unethical activities to the attention of the appropriate state licensure board and/or the ethics committee of the professional association.

B. Clinical Consultation

Mental health counselors may offer or seek clinical consultation from another mental health professional. In clinical consulting mental health counselors provide critical and supportive feedback. Clinical consultation does not imply hierarchy or responsibility for client outcome.

III. Commitment to Students, Supervisees and Employee Relationships

Mental health counselors have an ethical concern for the integrity and welfare of supervisees, students, and employees. These relationships typically include an evaluative component and therefore need to be maintained on a professional and confidential basis. Mental health counselors recognize the influential position they have with regard to both current and former supervisees, students and employees and avoid exploiting their trust and dependency.
1. Mental health counselors do not engage in ongoing counseling relationships with current supervisees, students and employees.
2. All forms of sexual behavior with supervisees, students and employees are unethical.
3. Mental health counselors do not engage in any form of harassment of supervisees, students, employees or colleagues.
4. Mental health counselor supervisors advise their supervisees, students and employees against holding themselves out to be competent to engage in professional services beyond their training, experience, or credentials.
5. With supervisees, students and employees, mental health counselors make every effort to avoid dual/multiple relationships that could bias their judgment or increase the risk of personal or financial exploitation. When a dual/multiple relationship cannot be avoided, mental health counselors take appropriate professional precautions to make sure that detrimental effects are minimized. Examples of such dual/multiple relationships include, but are not limited to, a supervisee who receives supervision as a benefit of employment.

166

6. Mental health counselors do not disclose supervisee confidences regarding client information except:
   a) to prevent clear and imminent danger to a person or persons
   b) as mandated by law
       i) as in mandated child or senior abuse reporting or
       ii) where the counselor is a defendant in a civil, criminal, or disciplinary action or
       iii) where there is a waiver of confidentiality obtained, in writing, prior to such a release of information
   c) in educational or training settings where only other professionals who will share responsibility for the training of the supervisee are present and formal written client consent has been obtained for such disclosures for training purposes.
7. In the informed consent statement, students and mandated supervisees notify the client they are in supervision and provide their clients with the name and credentials of their supervisor, if requested.
8. Students and supervisees have the same ethical obligations to clients as those required of mental health counselors.
9. The primary obligation of supervisors is to monitor services provided by supervisees to ensure client welfare.
10. Supervisors are expected to monitor clinical performance of supervisees; including but not limited to regular meetings, review of case notes and records, direct observation of supervisee's clinical work via audio/video records, or live supervision.
11. Supervisors provide written informed consent prior to beginning a supervision relationship that documents business address and telephone number; list of degrees, license, and credentials/certifications held; areas of competence in clinical mental health counseling; training in supervision and experience providing supervision; model of or approach to supervision, including the role, objectives and goals of supervision, and modalities; evaluation procedures in the supervisory relationship; the limits and scope of confidentiality and privileged communication within the supervisory relationship; procedures for supervisory emergencies and supervisor absences; use of supervision agreements; and procedures for supervisee endorsement for certification and/or licensure, or employment to those whom are competent, ethical, and qualified.

IV. Commitment to the Profession

Mental health counselors promote the mission, goals, values, and knowledge of the profession. They engage in activities that maintain and increase the respect, integrity, and knowledge base of the counseling profession and human welfare. Such activities include but are not limited to teaching, research, serving on professional boards and membership in professional associations.

A. Teaching

As teaching professionals, mental health counselors perform their duties based on careful preparation to provide instruction that is accurate, current, and educational.

B. Research and Publications

Mental health counselors, as researchers, conduct investigations and publish findings with respect for dignity and welfare of the participants and integrity of the profession.

1. The ethical researcher seeks advice from other professionals if any plan of research suggests a deviation from any ethical principle of research with human subjects. Such deviation protects the dignity and welfare of the client and places on the researcher a special burden to act in the subject's interest.
2. The ethical researcher is open and honest in the relationship with research participants.
3. The ethical researcher protects participants from physical and mental discomfort, harm, and danger. If the risks of such consequences exist, the investigator is required to inform participants of that fact, secure consent before proceeding, and take all possible measures to minimize the distress.
4. The ethical researcher instructs research participants that they are free to withdraw from participation at any time.
5. The ethical researcher understands that information obtained about research participants during the course of an investigation is confidential. When the possibility exists that others may obtain access to such information, participants are made aware of the possibility and the plan for protecting confidentiality and for storage and disposal of research records.
6. The ethical researcher gives sponsoring agencies, host institutions, and publication channels the same respect and opportunity for informed consent that they accord to individual research participants.
7. The ethical researcher is aware of his or her obligation to future research and ensures that host institutions are given feedback information and proper acknowledgement.

C. Service on Public or Private Boards and Other Organizations

When serving as members of governmental or other organizational bodies, mental health counselors represent the mental health counseling profession and are accountable as individuals to the Code of Ethics of the American Mental Health Counselors Association.

V. Commitment to the Public

Mental health counselors recognize they have a moral, legal, and ethical responsibility to the community and to the general public. Mental health counselors are aware of the prevailing community and cultural values, and the impact of professional standards on the community.

A. Public Statements

Mental health counselors in their professional roles may be expected or required to make public statements providing counseling information or professional opinions, or supply information about the availability of counseling products and services. In making such statements, mental health counselors accurately represent their education, professional qualifications, licenses and credentials, expertise, affiliations, and functions, as well as those of the institutions or organizations with which the statements may be associated. Public statements serve the purpose of providing information to aid the public in making informed judgments and choices. All public statements will be consistent with this Code of Ethics.

B. Advertising

Mental health counselors advertise the following: highest counseling-related degree, type and level of certification or license, and type and/or description of services or other relevant information concerning areas of clinical competence. These statements will not be false, inaccurate, misleading, or out of context.

C. Resolution of Ethical Problems

Members are encouraged to consult with the AMHCA Ethics Committee regarding processes to resolve ethical dilemmas which may arise in clinical practice. Members are also encouraged to use commonly recognized procedures for ethical decision-making to resolve ethical conflicts.

The American Mental Health Counselors Association, its Board of Directors, and its National Committee on Ethics do not investigate or adjudicate ethical complaints. In the event a member has his or her license suspended or revoked by an appropriate state licensure board, the AMHCA Board of Directors may then act in accordance with AMHCA's National By-Laws to suspend or revoke his or her membership. Any member so suspended may apply for reinstatement upon the reinstatement of his or her licensure.

American Mental Health Counselors Association
801 N. Fairfax Street, Ste. 304
Alexandria, VA 22314
V: 800-326-2642   F: 703-548-4775
www.amhca.org

American Association for Marriage and Family Therapy
Code of Ethics
Effective July 1, 2012

Preamble

The Board of Directors of the American Association for Marriage and Family Therapy (AAMFT) hereby promulgates, pursuant to Article 2, Section 2.01.3 of the Association's Bylaws, the Revised AAMFT Code of Ethics, effective July 1, 2012.

The AAMFT strives to honor the public trust in marriage and family therapists by setting standards for ethical practice as described in this Code. The ethical standards define professional expectations and are enforced by the AAMFT Ethics Committee. The absence of an explicit reference to a specific behavior or situation in the Code does not mean that the behavior is ethical or unethical. The standards are not exhaustive. Marriage and family therapists who are uncertain about the ethics of a particular course of action are encouraged to seek counsel from consultants, attorneys, supervisors, colleagues, or other appropriate authorities.

Both law and ethics govern the practice of marriage and family therapy. When making decisions regarding professional behavior, marriage and family therapists must consider the AAMFT Code of Ethics and applicable laws and regulations. If the AAMFT Code of Ethics prescribes a standard higher than that required by law, marriage and family therapists must meet the higher standard of the AAMFT Code of Ethics. Marriage and family therapists comply with the mandates of law, but make known their commitment to the AAMFT Code of Ethics and take steps to resolve the conflict in a responsible manner. The AAMFT supports legal mandates for reporting of alleged unethical conduct.

The AAMFT Code of Ethics is binding on members of AAMFT in all membership categories, all AAMFT Approved Supervisors and all applicants for membership or the Approved Supervisor designation. AAMFT members have an obligation to be familiar with the AAMFT Code of Ethics and its application to their professional services. Lack of awareness or misunderstanding of an ethical standard is not a defense to a charge of unethical conduct.

The process for filing, investigating, and resolving complaints of unethical conduct is described in the current AAMFT Procedures for Handling Ethical Matters. Persons accused are considered innocent by the Ethics Committee until proven guilty, except as otherwise provided, and are entitled to due process. If an AAMFT member resigns in anticipation of, or during the course of, an ethics investigation, the Ethics Committee will complete its investigation. Any publication of action taken by the Association will include the fact that the member attempted to resign during the investigation.

Principle I: Responsibility to Clients

Marriage and family therapists advance the welfare of families and individuals. They respect the rights of those persons seeking their assistance, and make reasonable efforts to ensure that their services are used appropriately.

1.1   **Non-Discrimination**. Marriage and family therapists provide professional assistance to persons without discrimination on the basis of race, age, ethnicity, socioeconomic status, disability, gender, health status, religion, national origin, sexual orientation, gender identity or relationship status.

1.2   **Informed Consent**. Marriage and family therapists obtain appropriate informed consent to therapy or related procedures and use language that is reasonably understandable to clients. The content of informed consent may vary depending upon the client and treatment plan; however, informed consent generally necessitates that the client: (a) has the capacity to consent; (b) has been adequately informed of significant information concerning treatment processes and procedures; (c) has been adequately informed of potential risks and benefits of treatments for which generally recognized standards do not yet exist; (d) has freely and without undue influence expressed consent; and (e) has provided consent that is appropriately documented. When persons, due to age or mental status, are legally incapable of giving informed consent, marriage and family therapists obtain informed permission from a legally authorized person, if such substitute consent is legally permissible.

1.3   **Multiple Relationships**. Marriage and family therapists are aware of their influential positions with respect to clients, and they avoid exploiting the trust and dependency of such persons. Therapists, therefore, make every effort to avoid conditions and multiple relationships with clients that could impair professional judgment or increase the risk of exploitation. Such relationships include, but are not limited to, business or close personal relationships with a client or the client's immediate family. When the risk of impairment or exploitation exists due to conditions or multiple roles, therapists document the appropriate precautions taken.

1.4   **Sexual Intimacy with Current Clients and Others**. Sexual intimacy with current clients, or their spouses or partners is prohibited. Engaging in sexual intimacy with individuals who are known to be close relatives, guardians or significant others of current clients is prohibited.

1.5   **Sexual Intimacy with Former Clients and Others**. Sexual intimacy with former clients, their spouses or partners, or individuals who are known to be close relatives, guardians or significant others of clients is likely to be harmful and is therefore prohibited for two years following the termination of therapy or last professional contact. After the two years following the last professional contact or termination, in an effort to avoid exploiting the trust and dependency of clients, marriage and family therapists should not engage in sexual intimacy with former clients, or their spouses or partners. If therapists engage in sexual intimacy with former clients, or their spouses or partners, more than two years after termination or last professional contact, the burden shifts to the therapist to demonstrate that there has been no exploitation or injury to the former client, or their spouse or partner.

1.6 Reports of Unethical Conduct. Marriage and family therapists comply with applicable laws regarding the reporting of alleged unethical conduct.

1.7 No Furthering of Own Interests. Marriage and family therapists do not use their professional relationships with clients to further their own interests.

1.8 Client Autonomy in Decision Making. Marriage and family therapists respect the rights of clients to make decisions and help them to understand the consequences of these decisions. Therapists clearly advise clients that clients have the responsibility to make decisions regarding relationships such as cohabitation, marriage, divorce, separation, reconciliation, custody, and visitation.

1.9 Relationship Beneficial to Client. Marriage and family therapists continue therapeutic relationships only so long as it is reasonably clear that clients are benefiting from the relationship.

1.10 Referrals. Marriage and family therapists assist persons in obtaining other therapeutic services if the therapist is unable or unwilling, for appropriate reasons, to provide professional help.

1.11 Non-Abandonment. Marriage and family therapists do not abandon or neglect clients in treatment without making reasonable arrangements for the continuation of treatment.

1.12 Written Consent to Record. Marriage and family therapists obtain written informed consent from clients before videotaping, audio recording, or permitting third-party observation.

1.13 Relationships with Third Parties. Marriage and family therapists, upon agreeing to provide services to a person or entity at the request of a third party, clarify, to the extent feasible and at the outset of the service, the nature of the relationship with each party and the limits of confidentiality.

1.14 Electronic Therapy. Prior to commencing therapy services through electronic means (including but not limited to phone and Internet), marriage and family therapists ensure that they are compliant with all relevant laws for the delivery of such services. Additionally, marriage and family therapists must: (a) determine that electronic therapy is appropriate for clients, taking into account the clients' intellectual, emotional, and physical needs; (b) inform clients of the potential risks and benefits associated with electronic therapy; (c) ensure the security of their communication medium; and (d) only commence electronic therapy after appropriate education, training, or supervised experience using the relevant technology.

Principle II: Confidentiality

Marriage and family therapists have unique confidentiality concerns because the client in a therapeutic relationship may be more than one person. Therapists respect and guard the confidences of each individual client.

2.1 **Disclosing Limits of Confidentiality**. Marriage and family therapists disclose to clients and other interested parties, as early as feasible in their professional contacts, the nature of confidentiality and possible limitations of the clients' right to confidentiality. Therapists review with clients the circumstances where confidential information may be requested and where disclosure of confidential information may be legally required. Circumstances may necessitate repeated disclosures.

2.2 **Written Authorization to Release Client Information**. Marriage and family therapists do not disclose client confidences except by written authorization or waiver, or where mandated or permitted by law. Verbal authorization will not be sufficient except in emergency situations, unless prohibited by law. When providing couple, family or group treatment, the therapist does not disclose information outside the treatment context without a written authorization from each individual competent to execute a waiver. In the context of couple, family or group treatment, the therapist may not reveal any individual's confidences to others in the client unit without the prior written permission of that individual.

2.3 **Confidentiality in Non-Clinical Activities**. Marriage and family therapists use client and/or clinical materials in teaching, writing, consulting, research, and public presentations only if a written waiver has been obtained in accordance with Subprinciple 2.2, or when appropriate steps have been taken to protect client identity and confidentiality.

2.4 **Protection of Records**. Marriage and family therapists store, safeguard, and dispose of client records in ways that maintain confidentiality and in accord with applicable laws and professional standards.

2.5 **Preparation for Practice Changes**. In preparation for moving from the area, closing a practice, or death, marriage and family therapists arrange for the storage, transfer, or disposal of client records in conformance with applicable laws and in ways that maintain confidentiality and safeguard the welfare of clients.

2.6 **Confidentiality in Consultations**. Marriage and family therapists, when consulting with colleagues or referral sources, do not share confidential information that could reasonably lead to the identification of a client, research participant, supervisee, or other person with whom they have a confidential relationship unless they have obtained the prior written consent of the client, research participant, supervisee, or other person with whom they have a confidential relationship. Information may be shared only to the extent necessary to achieve the purposes of the consultation.

2.7 **Protection of Electronic Information**. When using electronic methods for communication, billing, recordkeeping, or other elements of client care, marriage and family therapists ensure that their electronic data storage and communications are privacy protected consistent with all applicable law.

Principle III: Professional Competence and Integrity

Marriage and family therapists maintain high standards of professional competence and integrity.

3.1 **Maintenance of Competency**. Marriage and family therapists pursue knowledge of new developments and maintain their competence in marriage and family therapy through education, training, or supervised experience.

3.2 **Knowledge of Regulatory Standards**. Marriage and family therapists maintain adequate knowledge of and adhere to applicable laws, ethics, and professional standards.

3.3 **Seek Assistance**. Marriage and family therapists seek appropriate professional assistance for their personal problems or conflicts that may impair work performance or clinical judgment.

3.4 **Conflicts of Interest**. Marriage and family therapists do not provide services that create a conflict of interest that may impair work performance or clinical judgment.

3.5 **Veracity of Scholarship**. Marriage and family therapists, as presenters, teachers, supervisors, consultants and researchers, are dedicated to high standards of scholarship, present accurate information, and disclose potential conflicts of interest.

3.6 **Maintenance of Records**. Marriage and family therapists maintain accurate and adequate clinical and financial records in accordance with applicable law.

3.7 **Development of New Skills**. While developing new skills in specialty areas, marriage and family therapists take steps to ensure the competence of their work and to protect clients from possible harm. Marriage and family therapists practice in specialty areas new to them only after appropriate education, training, or supervised experience.

3.8 **Harassment**. Marriage and family therapists do not engage in sexual or other forms of harassment of clients, students, trainees, supervisees, employees, colleagues, or research subjects.

3.9 **Exploitation**. Marriage and family therapists do not engage in the exploitation of clients, students, trainees, supervisees, employees, colleagues, or research subjects.

3.10 **Gifts**. Marriage and family therapists do not give to or receive from clients (a) gifts of substantial value or (b) gifts that impair the integrity or efficacy of the therapeutic relationship.

3.11 Scope of Competence. Marriage and family therapists do not diagnose, treat, or advise on problems outside the recognized boundaries of their competencies.

3.12 Accurate Presentation of Findings. Marriage and family therapists make efforts to prevent the distortion or misuse of their clinical and research findings.

3.13 Public Statements. Marriage and family therapists, because of their ability to influence and alter the lives of others, exercise special care when making public their professional recommendations and opinions through testimony or other public statements.

3.14 Separation of Custody Evaluation from Therapy. To avoid a conflict of interest, marriage and family therapists who treat minors or adults involved in custody or visitation actions may not also perform forensic evaluations for custody, residence, or visitation of the minor. Marriage and family therapists who treat minors may provide the court or mental health professional performing the evaluation with information about the minor from the marriage and family therapist's perspective as a treating marriage and family therapist, so long as the marriage and family therapist does not violate confidentiality.

3.15 Professional Misconduct. Marriage and family therapists are in violation of this Code and subject to termination of membership or other appropriate action if they: (a) are convicted of any felony; (b) are convicted of a misdemeanor related to their qualifications or functions; (c) engage in conduct which could lead to conviction of a felony, or a misdemeanor related to their qualifications or functions; (d) are expelled from or disciplined by other professional organizations; (e) have their licenses or certificates suspended or revoked or are otherwise disciplined by regulatory bodies; (f) continue to practice marriage and family therapy while no longer competent to do so because they are impaired by physical or mental causes or the abuse of alcohol or other substances; or (g) fail to cooperate with the Association at any point from the inception of an ethical complaint through the completion of all proceedings regarding that complaint.

Principle IV: Responsibility to Students and Supervisees

Marriage and family therapists do not exploit the trust and dependency of students and supervisees.

4.1 Exploitation. Marriage and family therapists who are in a supervisory role are aware of their influential positions with respect to students and supervisees, and they avoid exploiting the trust and dependency of such persons. Therapists, therefore, make every effort to avoid conditions and multiple relationships that could impair professional objectivity or increase the risk of exploitation. When the risk of impairment or exploitation exists due to conditions or multiple roles, therapists take appropriate precautions.

4.2 Therapy with Students or Supervisees. Marriage and family therapists do not provide therapy to current students or supervisees.

4.3 Sexual Intimacy with Students or Supervisees. Marriage and family therapists do not engage in sexual intimacy with students or supervisees during the evaluative or training relationship between the therapist and student or supervisee. If a supervisor engages in sexual activity with a former supervisee, the burden of proof shifts to the supervisor to demonstrate that there has been no exploitation or injury to the supervisee.

4.4 Oversight of Supervisee Competence. Marriage and family therapists do not permit students or supervisees to perform or to hold themselves out as competent to perform professional services beyond their training, level of experience, and competence.

4.5 Oversight of Supervisee Professionalism. Marriage and family therapists take reasonable measures to ensure that services provided by supervisees are professional.

4.6 Existing Relationship with Students or Supervisees. Marriage and family therapists avoid accepting as supervisees or students those individuals with whom a prior or existing relationship could compromise the therapist's objectivity. When such situations cannot be avoided, therapists take appropriate precautions to maintain objectivity. Examples of such relationships include, but are not limited to, those individuals with whom the therapist has a current or prior sexual, close personal, immediate familial, or therapeutic relationship.

4.7 Confidentiality with Supervisees. Marriage and family therapists do not disclose supervisee confidences except by written authorization or waiver, or when mandated or permitted by law. In educational or training settings where there are multiple supervisors, disclosures are permitted only to other professional colleagues, administrators, or employers who share responsibility for training of the supervisee. Verbal authorization will not be sufficient except in emergency situations, unless prohibited by law.

Principle V: Responsibility to Research Participants

Investigators respect the dignity and protect the welfare of research participants, and are aware of applicable laws, regulations, and professional standards governing the conduct of research.

5.1 Protection of Research Participants. Investigators are responsible for making careful examinations of ethical acceptability in planning studies. To the extent that services to research participants may be compromised by participation in research, investigators seek the ethical advice of qualified professionals not directly involved in the investigation and observe safeguards to protect the rights of research participants.

5.2 Informed Consent. Investigators requesting participant involvement in research inform participants of the aspects of the research that might reasonably be expected to influence willingness to participate. Investigators are especially sensitive to the possibility of diminished consent when participants are also receiving clinical services, or have impairments which limit understanding and/or communication, or when participants are children.

5.3 Right to Decline or Withdraw Participation. Investigators respect each participant's freedom to decline participation in or to withdraw from a research study at any time. This obligation requires special thought and consideration when investigators or other members of the research team are in positions of authority or influence over participants. Marriage and family therapists, therefore, make every effort to avoid multiple relationships with research participants that could impair professional judgment or increase the risk of exploitation.

5.4 Confidentiality of Research Data. Information obtained about a research participant during the course of an investigation is confidential unless there is a waiver previously obtained in writing. When the possibility exists that others, including family members, may obtain access to such information, this possibility, together with the plan for protecting confidentiality, is explained as part of the procedure for obtaining informed consent.

Principle VI: Responsibility to the Profession

Marriage and family therapists respect the rights and responsibilities of professional colleagues and participate in activities that advance the goals of the profession.

6.1 Conflicts Between Code and Organizational Policies. Marriage and family therapists remain accountable to the AAMFT Code of Ethics when acting as members or employees of organizations. If the mandates of an organization with which a marriage and family therapist is affiliated, through employment, contract or otherwise, conflict with the AAMFT Code of Ethics, marriage and family therapists make known to the organization their commitment to the AAMFT Code of Ethics and attempt to resolve the conflict in a way that allows the fullest adherence to the Code of Ethics.

6.2 Publication Authorship. Marriage and family therapists assign publication credit to those who have contributed to a publication in proportion to their contributions and in accordance with customary professional publication practices.

6.3 Authorship of Student Work. Marriage and family therapists do not accept or require authorship credit for a publication based on research from a student's program, unless the therapist made a substantial contribution beyond being a faculty advisor or research committee member. Co-authorship on a student thesis, dissertation, or project should be determined in accordance with principles of fairness and justice.

6.4 Plagiarism. Marriage and family therapists who are the authors of books or other materials that are published or distributed do not plagiarize or fail to cite persons to whom credit for original ideas or work is due.

6.5 Accuracy in Publication and Advertising. Marriage and family therapists who are the authors of books or other materials published or distributed by an organization take reasonable precautions to ensure that the organization promotes and advertises the materials accurately and factually.

6.6 Pro Bono. Marriage and family therapists participate in activities that contribute to a better community and society, including devoting a portion of their professional activity to services for which there is little or no financial return.

6.7 Advocacy. Marriage and family therapists are concerned with developing laws and regulations pertaining to marriage and family therapy that serve the public interest, and with altering such laws and regulations that are not in the public interest.

6.8 Public Participation. Marriage and family therapists encourage public participation in the design and delivery of professional services and in the regulation of practitioners.

Principle VII: Financial Arrangements

Marriage and family therapists make financial arrangements with clients, third-party payors, and supervisees that are reasonably understandable and conform to accepted professional practices.

7.1 Financial Integrity. Marriage and family therapists do not offer or accept kickbacks, rebates, bonuses, or other remuneration for referrals; fee-for-service arrangements are not prohibited.

7.2 Disclosure of Financial Policies. Prior to entering into the therapeutic or supervisory relationship, marriage and family therapists clearly disclose and explain to clients and supervisees: (a) all financial arrangements and fees related to professional services, including charges for canceled or missed appointments; (b) the use of collection agencies or legal measures for nonpayment; and (c) the procedure for obtaining payment from the client, to the extent allowed by law, if payment is denied by the third-party payor. Once services have begun, therapists provide reasonable notice of any changes in fees or other charges.

7.3 Notice of Payment Recovery Procedures. Marriage and family therapists give reasonable notice to clients with unpaid balances of their intent to seek collection by agency or legal recourse. When such action is taken, therapists will not disclose clinical information.

7.4 Truthful Representation of Services. Marriage and family therapists represent facts truthfully to clients, third-party payors, and supervisees regarding services rendered.

7.5 Bartering. Marriage and family therapists ordinarily refrain from accepting goods and services from clients in return for services rendered. Bartering for professional services may be conducted only if: (a) the supervisee or client requests it; (b) the relationship is not exploitative; (c) the professional relationship is not distorted; and (d) a clear written contract is established.

7.6 Withholding Records for Non-Payment. Marriage and family therapists may not withhold records under their immediate control that are requested and needed for a client's treatment solely because payment has not been received for past services, except as otherwise provided by law.

Principle VIII: Advertising

Marriage and family therapists engage in appropriate informational activities, including those that enable the public, referral sources, or others to choose professional services on an informed basis.

8.1 Accurate Professional Representation. Marriage and family therapists accurately represent their competencies, education, training, and experience relevant to their practice of marriage and family therapy.

8.2 Promotional Materials. Marriage and family therapists ensure that advertisements and publications in any media (such as directories, announcements, business cards, newspapers, radio, television, Internet, and facsimiles) convey information that is necessary for the public to make an appropriate selection of professional services and consistent with applicable law.

8.3 Professional Affiliations. Marriage and family therapists do not use names that could mislead the public concerning the identity, responsibility, source, and status of those practicing under that name, and do not hold themselves out as being partners or associates of a firm if they are not.

8.4 Professional Identification. Marriage and family therapists do not use any professional identification (such as a business card, office sign, letterhead, Internet, or telephone or association directory listing) if it includes a statement or claim that is false, fraudulent, misleading, or deceptive.

8.5 Educational Credentials. In representing their educational qualifications, marriage and family therapists list and claim as evidence only those earned degrees: (a) from institutions accredited by regional accreditation sources; (b) from institutions recognized by states or provinces that license or certify marriage and family therapists; or (c) from equivalent foreign institutions.

8.6 Correction of Misinformation. Marriage and family therapists correct, wherever possible, false, misleading, or inaccurate information and representations made by others concerning the therapist's qualifications, services, or products.

8.7 Employee or Supervisee Qualifications. Marriage and family therapists make certain that the qualifications of their employees or supervisees are represented in a manner that is not false, misleading, or deceptive.

8.8 Specialization. Marriage and family therapists do not represent themselves as providing specialized services unless they have the appropriate education, training, or supervised experience.

Code of Ethics pdf version
Violations of this Code should be submitted in writing to the attention of:
AAMFT Ethics Committee
112 South Alfred Street, Alexandria, VA 22314
Phone: (703) 838-9808
Fax: (703) 838-9805
email: *ethics@aamft.org*

Ethical Code for the International Association of Marriage and Family Counselors

Abstract

The Board of Directors of the International Association of Marriage and Family Counselors requested the IAMFC Ethics Committee to revise the IAMFC Ethical Code (2006). The revised Ethical Code of the IAMFC focuses on current issues in marriage and family counseling. The Ethical Code of IAMFC (2011), which appears in the following article, has been approved by the Board of Directors of IAMFC and the American Counseling Association and is consistent with the current Code of Ethics of the American Counseling Association (2005).

Preamble

The International Association of Marriage and Family Counselors (IAMFC) is an organization dedicated to advancing practice, training, and research in couple and family counseling. Members may specialize in areas such as premarital counseling, couple counseling, family counseling, sex counseling, intergenerational counseling, separation and divorce counseling, relocation counseling, custody evaluation, and parenting training. Couple and family counselors may work with special populations, including stepfamilies, nontraditional couples and family systems, multicultural couples and families, disadvantaged families, and dual-career couples. In conducting their professional activities, members commit themselves to protect family relationships and advocate for the healthy growth and development of the family as a whole and each member's unique needs, while advocating for the counseling profession and the professionalism of counselors. IAMFC members recognize that the relationship between the provider and consumer of services is characterized as professional. However, IAMFC members should remain informed of social and cultural trends as well as scientific and technological changes affecting the foundation of the professional counseling relationship.

This code of ethics provides a framework for ethical practices by IAMFC members and other professionals engaged in couple and family counseling. It is divided into the following nine sections: the counseling relationship and client well-being, confidentiality and privacy, competence and professional responsibilities, collaboration and professional relationships, assessment and evaluation, counselor education and supervision, research and publication, ethical decision making and resolution, and diversity. The observations and recommendations presented within these nine areas above are meant to supplement the current ethical standards of the American Counseling Association. Although an ethical code cannot anticipate every possible situation or dilemma, the IAMFC ethical guidelines can assist members in insuring the welfare and dignity of the couples and families who seek services.

The ethical code of the IAMFC incorporates the ethics of principles and virtues. The IAMFC Ethical code articulates some specific principles and guidelines which protect consumers from potentially harmful practices, thereby empowering professionals to maintain high standards for effective practice.

The IAMFC Ethical Code also addresses the character of the professional couple and family counselor. Ethics of character or virtue contribute to professional aspirations and values. Each of the nine sections includes aspirations and principles.

Section A: The Counseling Relationship and Client Well-Being

Couple and family counselors contribute to the healthy development and evolution of family systems. They are committed to understanding problems and learning needs from multiple contexts. Couple and family counselors, in particular, embrace models of practice based on family dynamics and systems. Professional counselors realize that their perspectives influence the conceptualization of problems, identification of clients, and implementation of possible solutions. Couple and family counselors examine personal biases and values. They actively attempt to understand and serve couples and families from diverse cultural backgrounds. Professional couple and family counselors are willing to remove barriers to the counseling relationship, act as responsible public servants, and become involved in advocacy in the best interests of couples and families.

1. Couple and family counselors demonstrate caring, empathy, and respect for client well-being. They promote safety, security, and sense of community for couples and families. Due to potential risks involved, couple and family counselors should not use intrusive interventions without sound theoretical rationale, research support, and clinical consultation or supervision.
2. Couple and family counselors recognize that each family is unique. Couple and family counselors do not promote bias and stereotyping regarding family roles and functions.
3. Couple and family counselors respect the autonomy of the families with whom they work. They do not make decisions that rightfully belong to family members. When indicated and possible, couple and family counselors share client's clinical impressions and recommendations, decision-making processes, problem-solving strategies, and intervention outcomes with clients.
4. Couple and family counselors respect cultural diversity. They do not discriminate or condone discrimination on the basis of race, gender, disability, religion, age, sexual orientation, cultural background, national origin, marital status, political affiliation, or socioeconomic status.
5. Couple and family counselors promote open, honest, and direct relationships with consumers of professional services. Couple and family counselors inform clients about the goals of counseling, qualifications of the counselor(s), limits of confidentiality, potential risks, and benefits associated with specific techniques, duration of treatment, costs of services, appropriate alternatives to couple and family counseling, and reasonable expectations for outcomes.

6. Couple and family counselors promote primary prevention. They advocate for the development of clients' cognitive, moral, social, emotional, spiritual, physical, educational, relational, and vocational skills. Couple and family counselors promote effective couple and family communication and facilitate problem-solving skills needed to prevent future problems.

7. Couple and family counselors have an obligation to determine and inform counseling participants who are identified as the primary client. The couple and family counselor should make clear to clients if they have any obligations to an individual, a couple, a family, a third party, or an institution.

8. Couple and family counselors who are IAMFC members have a professional duty to monitor their places of employment, making recommendations so that the environment is conducive to the positive growth and development of clients. When there is a conflict of interest between the needs of the client and counselor's employing institution, the IAMFC member works to clarify his or her commitment to all parties. IAMFC members recognize that the acceptance of employment implies agreement with the policies and practices of the agency or institution.

9. Couple and family counselors do not harass, exploit, coerce, or manipulate clients for personal gain. Couple and family counselors avoid, whenever possible, multiple relationships such as business, social, or sexual contacts with any current clients or their family members. Couple and family counselors should refrain generally front nonprofessional relationships with former clients and their family members because termination of counseling is a complex process.

10. Couple and family counselors are responsible for demonstrating there is no harm front any relationship with a client or family member. The key element in this ethical principle is the avoidance of exploitation of vulnerable clients.

11. Couple and family counselors have an obligation to withdraw from a counseling relationship ifthe continuation of services would not be in the best interest of the client or would result in a violation of ethical standards. If the counseling relationship is no longer helpful or productive, couple and family counselors have an obligation to assist in locating alternative services and making referrals as needed.

12. Couple and family counselors do not abandon clients. They arrange for appropriate termination of counseling relationships and transfer of services as indicated.

13. Couple and family counselors maintain accurate and up-to-date records. They make all file information available to clients unless there is compelling evidence that such access would be harmful to the client. In situations involving multiple clients, couple and family counselors provide individual clients with parts of records related directly to them, protecting confidential information related to other clients who have not authorized release. Couple and family counselors include sufficient and timely documentation in client records to facilitate delivery of services and referral to other professionals as needed.

14. Couple and family counselors establish fees that are reasonable and customary depending upon the scope and location of their practices. Couple and family counselors in community agencies, schools, and other public settings do not solicit gifts or charge fees for services that are available in the counselor's employing agency or institution.

15. Culturally sensitive couple and family counselors recognize that gifts are tokens of respect and gratitude in some cultures. Couple and family counselors may receive gifts or participate in family rituals that promote healthy interaction and do not exploit clients.
16. Couple and family counselors maintain ethical and effective practices as they address the benefits and limitations of technological innovations and cultural changes. Counseling may be conducted or assisted by telephones, computer hardware and software, and other communication technologies. Technology-assisted distance counseling services may expand the scope and influence of couple and family counseling. However, counselors are responsible for developing competencies in the use of new technologies and safeguarding private and confidential information.
17. When a conflict of values arises which inhibits the couples and family counselor's professionalism and/or objectivity in the counseling relationship, the couples and family counselor should refer the couple or family being served to another qualified counselor. Additionally, it is recommended that the counselor obtain supervision or counseling to address any issue that may inhibit the counselor's effective practice.

Section B: Confidentiality and Privacy

Couple and family counselors recognize that trust is the foundation of an effective counseling relationship. Professional counselors maintain appropriate boundaries so that clients reasonably expect that information shared will not be disclosed to others without prior written consent. Due to the nature of couple and family counseling, safeguards must be established in the counseling process to insure privacy of client disclosures without contributing to dysfunctional family secrets. Clients have the right to know the limits of confidentiality, privacy, and privileged communication, including the fact that family members may themselves disclose counseling-related information outside counseling. Thus, couples and family counselors should inform clients that while confidentiality may be maintained by the counselor, the counselor has no control over information that family members may share with one another. Therefore, in these instances, confidentiality, while desired, may not be guaranteed.

1. Couple and family counselors may disclose private information to others under specific circumstances known to the individual client or client family members. Ideally, the client consents to disclosure by signing an authorization to release information. Each person receiving counseling who is legally competent to sign a waiver of right to confidentiality should execute an authorization. The authorization should be time limited, consistent with legal statutes, and limited to the scope agreed to by the counselor and client. The client may rescind or withdraw the authorization.
2. Couple and family counselors inform parents and legal guardians about the confidential nature of the counseling relationship. When working with minor or juvenile clients, as well as adult clients who lack the capacity to authorize release of confidential information, couple and family counselors seek consent from the appropriate custodial parent or guardian to disclose information.

3. Couple and family counselors inform clients of exceptions to the general principle that information will be kept confidential or released only upon written client authorization. Disclosure of private information may be mandated by state law. For example, states require reporting of suspected abuse of children or other vulnerable populations. Couple and family counselors may have sound legal or ethical justification for disclosing information if someone is in imminent danger. A court may have jurisdiction to order release of confidential information without a client's permission. However, all releases of information not authorized by clients should be minimal or narrow as possible to limit potential harm to the counseling relationship.
4. Couple and family counselors inform clients who may have access to their counseling records, as well as any information that may be released for third-party payment or insurance reimbursement. State and federal laws may affect record keeping and release of information from client records.
5. Couple and family counselors store records in a way that protects confidentiality. Written records should be kept in a locked file drawer or cabinet and computerized record systems should have appropriate passwords and safeguards to prevent unauthorized entry.
6. Couple and family counselors inform clients if sessions are to be recorded on tape or digital media and obtain written consent authorizing recording for particular purposes. When more than one person is receiving counseling, all persons who are legally competent must give informed consent in writing for the recording.

Couple and family counselors inform clients that statements made by a family member to the counselor during an individual counseling, consultation, or collateral contact are to be treated as confidential. Such statements are not disclosed to other family members without the individual's permission However, the couple and family counselor should clearly identify the client of counseling, which may be the couple or family system, and inform clients in writing who(m) the identified client is. Couple and family counselors should inform clients that they do not maintain family secrets, collude with some family members against others, or otherwise contribute to dysfunctional family system dynamics. If a client's refusal to share information from individual contacts interferes with the agreed goals of counseling, the counselor may terminate treatment and refer the clients to another counselor. Some couple and family counselors choose to not meet with individuals, preferring to serve family systems.

1. Couple and family counselors provide reasonable access to counseling records when requested by competent clients. In situations involving multiple clients, counselors provide only the records directly related to a particular individual, protecting confidential information related to any other client.
2. Couple and family counselors provide reasonable access to counseling records of minor children when requested by parents or guardians having legal rights to custody and health decision making. However, counselors do not become embroiled in custody disputes or parent and child conflicts occasioned by records release. Professional counselors attempt to protect the counseling relationship with children by suggesting limits to disclosure appropriate to the particular situation.
3. Couples and family counselors keep counseling records following the termination of counseling services so that there is reasonable access to the records in the

future, maintaining the records in accordance with state and federal statutes and applicable accreditation standards. Couples and family counselors should also follow the recommended procedures for records access and retention outlined by the American Counseling Association Code of Ethics.

4. Couples and family counselors take reasonable precautions to ensure clients' access to records and client confidentiality in the event of a counselor's death or incapacitation. Additionally, couples and family counselors are encouraged to have a written plan, such as a professional will, specifying individuals who take charge of client records if the couples and family counselor terminates his/her practice for any reason.

5. Couple and family counselors maintain privacy and confidentiality in research, publication, case consultation, teaching, supervision, and other professional activities. Ideally, counselors secure informed consent and authorization to release information in all professional activities.

Section C: Competence and Professional Responsibilities

Couple and family counselors aspire to maintain competency through initial training, ongoing supervision and consultation, and continuing education. They have responsibilities to abide by this ethical code as well as other professional codes related to professional identity and group membership. In particular, couple and family counselors should become active in professional associations such as the IAMFC and the American Counseling Association and encourage beneficial changes in professionals and the counseling profession.

1. Couple and family counselors have the responsibility to develop and maintain basic skills in couple and family counseling through graduate training, supervision, and consultation. An outline of these skills is provided by the current Council for Accreditation of Counseling and Related Educational Programs (CACREP) *Standards for Marital, Couple, and Family Counseling*.

2. Couple and family counselors recognize the need for familiarizing themselves with new developments in the field of couple and family counseling. They pursue continuing education afforded by books, journals, courses, workshops, conferences, and conventions.

3. Couple and family counselors accurately represent their education, expertise, training, and experience. Professional counselors objectively represent their professional qualifications, skills, and specialties to the public. Membership in a professional organization, including IAMFC, is not used to suggest competency.

4. Couple and family counselors insure that announcements or advertisements of professional services focus on objective information that enables the client to make informed decisions. Providing information, such as highest relevant academic degree, licenses or certifications, office hours, types of services offered, fee structure, and languages spoken, can help clients select couple and family counselors.

5. Couple and family counselors do not attempt to diagnose or treat problems beyond the scope of their training and abilities. They do not engage in specialized counseling interventions or techniques unless they have received appropriate training and preparation in the methods.

6. Couple and family counselors do not undertake any professional activity in which their personal problems might adversely affect their performance. Instead, they focus on obtaining appropriate professional assistance to help them resolve the problem.
7. Couple and family counselors do not engage in actions that violate the legal standards of their community. They do not encourage clients or others to engage in unlawful activities.
8. Couple and family counselors have the responsibility to provide public information that enhances couple and family life. Such statements should be based on sound, scientifically acceptable theories, techniques, and approaches. Due to the inability to complete a comprehensive assessment and provide follow-up, members should not give specific advice to an individual through the media.
9. Couple and family counselors produce advertisements about workshops or seminars that contain descriptions of the audiences for which the programs are intended. Due to their subjective nature, statements either from clients or from the counselor about the uniqueness, effectiveness, or efficiency of services should be avoided Announcements and advertisements should never contain false, misleading, or fraudulent statements.
10. Couple and family counselors promoting tapes, books, or other products for commercial sale make every effort to insure that announcements and advertisements are presented in a professional and factual manner.

Section D: Collaboration and Professional Relationships

Couple and family counselors work to maintain good relationships with professional peers within and outside the field of counseling. Consultation and collaboration represent means by which couple and family counselors can remove barriers to underserved populations. Interdisciplinary teamwork may be required to best serve clients.

Couple and family counselors aspire to maintain competency through initial training, ongoing supervision and consultation, and continuing education. They have responsibilities to abide by this ethical code as well as other professional codes related to professional identity and group membership. In particular, couple and family counselors should become active in professional associations such as the IAMFC and the American Counseling Association.
1. Couple and family counselors are knowledgeable about the roles and functions of other disciplines, especially in the helping professions such as psychiatry, psychology, social work, and mental health counseling. Counselors work to strengthen interdisciplinary relations with colleagues.
2. Couple and family counselors enter into professional partnerships in which each partner adheres to the ethical standards of their professions. Couple and family counselors should not charge a fee for offering or accepting referrals.
3. Couple and family counselors do not engage in harmful relationships with individuals over whom they have supervisory, evaluative, or instructional control. They do not engage in harassment or other abuses of power or authority.

4. Couple and family counselors work to insure the ethical delivery of effective services in any agency or institution in which they are employed. Couple and family counselors engaging in consultation and collaboration take responsibility for the well-being and ethical treatment of clients. Counselors alert administrators about inappropriate policies and practices in institutions they serve.
5. Couple and family counselors working as subcontractors of counseling services for a third party have a duty to inform clients of limitations that the organization may place on the counseling or consulting relationship.
6. Couple and family counselors maintain good working relationships with team members and collaborators. They promote healthy boundaries and organizational climate. Couple and family counselors refrain from becoming involved in splitting, triangulation, and indirect forms of communication that could be harmful to colleagues or the organization they share.
7. Couple and family counselors do not offer services to clients served by other professionals without securing a referral or release. The counselor should be authorized by the client to contact the other professional to coordinate or transfer care. There may be special considerations regarding transfer of care in the termination of an abusive counseling relationship.

Section E: Assessment and Evaluation

Couple and family counselors are highly skilled in relational and interpersonal assessment. They recognize the potential values to clients from appropriate educational, psychological, and vocational evaluation. However, couple and family counselors are sensitive to misuse and abuse of assessment results. Counselors avoid, whenever possible, evaluation, assessment, or diagnosis that restricts the overall development and freedom of choice of individuals, couples, and families.

Recognizing the origins of couple and family counseling in systems thinking, they avoid, whenever possible, assigning problems to individuals. Instead, professional counselors aspire to identify solutions that promote the well-being of family systems.
1. Couple and family counselors use assessment procedures to promote the best interests and well-being of the client in clarifying concerns, establishing treatment goals, evaluating therapeutic progress, and promoting objective decision making.
2. Couple and family counselors recognize that clients have the right to know the results, interpretations, and conclusions drawn from assessment interviews and instruments, as well as how this information will be used Couple and family counselors safeguard assessment data and maintain the confidentiality of evaluation records and reports.
3. Couple and family counselors use assessment methods that are reliable, valid, and relevant to the goals of the client. Couple and family counselors using tests or inventories should have a thorough understanding of measurement concepts, including relevant psychometric and normative data. When using computer-assisted scoring, counselors obtain empirical evidence for the reliability and validity of the methods and procedures.

4. Couple and family counselors do not use inventories and tests that have outdated items or normative data. They refrain from using assessment instruments and techniques likely to be biased or prejudiced.
5. Couple and family counselors do not use assessment methods that are outside the scope of their qualifications, training, or statutory limitations. They consult with psychologists, mental health counselors, or other professional colleagues in interpreting and understanding particular test results.
6. Couple and family counselors conducting custody evaluations recognize the potential impact that their reports can have on family members. They are committed to a thorough assessment of both parents. Therefore, custody recommendations should not be made on the basis of information from only one parent. Couple and family counselors only use instruments that have demonstrated reliability, validity, and utility in custody evaluations. They do not make recommendations based solely on test and inventory scores.
7. Couple and family counselors clarify the differences between forensic examination and counseling. When couples and family counselors are conducting forensic examination, they inform clients who may have access to the results of the examination and the circumstances under which information may be released.
8. Members strive to follow current guidelines and standards for testing published or disseminated by the American Counseling Association, American Educational Research Association, American Psychological Association, Association for Assessment in Counseling and Education, National Council on Measurement in Evaluation, and other groups dedicated to professional expertise in assessment.

Section F: Counselor Education and Supervision

Couple and family counselors are likely to engage in some training and supervision activities, including peer consultation and supervision. Couple and family counselors recognize potential power imbalances in teacher and student, supervisor and supervisee, and consultant and consultee relationships. They do not abuse power or influence and instead, work to protect students, supervisees, and consultees from exploitation. Couple and family counselors maintain appropriate boundaries that promote growth and development for all parties. They recognize and respect cultural differences, adjusting their professional efforts to fit the learning needs of trainees.

1. Couple and family counselors who provide supervision acquire and maintain skills pertaining to the supervision process. They are able to demonstrate for supervisees the application of counseling theory and process to client issues. Supervisors are knowledgeable about different methods and conceptual approaches to supervision.
2. Couple and family counselors who provide supervision respect the inherent imbalance of power in the supervisory relationship. They do not use their potentially influential positions to exploit students, supervisees, or employees. Supervisors do not ask supervisees to engage in behaviors not directly related to the supervision process, and they clearly separate supervision and evaluation. Supervisors also avoid multiple relationships that might impair their professional judgment or increase the possibility of exploitation.

3. Sexual intimacy with students or supervisees is prohibited.
4. Couple and family counselors who provide supervision are responsible for both the promotion of supervisee learning and development and the advancement of couple and family counseling. Supervisors recruit students into professional organizations, educate students about professional ethics and standards, provide service to professional organizations, strive to educate new professionals, and work to improve professional practices.
5. Couple and family counselors who provide supervision have the responsibility to inform students of the specific expectations regarding skill building, knowledge acquisition, and development of competencies. Supervisors also provide ongoing and timely feedback to their supervisees.
6. Couple and family counselors who provide supervision are responsible for protecting the rights and well-being of their supervisees' clients. They monitor their supervisees' counseling on an ongoing basis and maintain policies and procedures to protect the confidentiality of clients whose sessions have been electronically recorded.
7. Couple and family counselors who provide supervision maintain ethical standards for counselor supervision. Counselor educators and supervisors may consult publications of the Association for Counselor Education and Supervision to clarify ethical issues in supervisory relationships.
8. Couple and family counselors serving as supervisors utilize sound supervision and counseling theory in supervision practice. Additionally, couple and family counselors infuse their supervision with the Advocacy Competencies and the Multicultural Counseling Competencies endorsed by the American Counseling Association.
9. Couple and family counselors who are counselor educators encourage their programs to maintain the current guidelines provided in the CACREP *Standards for Marital, Couple, and Family Counseling*. They also encourage training programs to offer coursework and supervision indicated by particular accreditation boards.
10. Couple and family counselors involved in training and supervision, especially educators and students, should encourage, teach, and implement advocacy awareness for supervisees, as well as explore ethical principles and aspirational goals. Counselor educators must infuse ethical studies throughout the curriculum.
11. Couples and family counselors who serve as supervisors must promote ethical practice throughout their supervision.
12. Couple and family counselors refer to the current American Counseling Association *Code of Ethics* and ACES *Code of Ethics* as sources document or training and supervision in professional counseling.

Section G: Research and Publication

Couple and family counselors should engage in research and publication that advances the profession of couple and family counseling. They act to proactively prevent harm to research participants and produce results that are beneficial to couples and families. Couple and family counselors maintain high ethical standards of informed consent and protection of confidentiality when conducting research projects or producing publications. They solicit input from peers, institutional review boards, and other stakeholders to minimize risks and enhance outcomes.

1. Couple and family counselors shall be fully responsible for their choice of research topics and the methods used for investigation, analysis, and reporting. They must be particularly careful that findings do not appear misleading, that the research is planned to allow for the inclusion of alternative hypotheses, and that provision is made for discussion of the limitations of the study.

2. Couple and family counselors safeguard the privacy of their research participants. Data about individual participants are not released unless the individual is informed about the exact nature of the information to be released and gives written permission for disclosure.

3. Couple and family counselors protect the safety of their research participants. Researchers follow guidelines of a peer review committee or institutional research board. Prospective participants are informed in writing about any potential risk associated with a study and are notified before and during any study that they can withdraw at any time.

4. Couple and family counselors make their original data available to other researchers. They contribute to the advancement of the field by encouraging the research and publication efforts of colleagues.

5. Couple and family counselors only take credit for research in which they make a substantial contribution and give credit to all contributors. Authors are listed from greatest to least amount of contribution.

6. Couple and family counselors do not plagiarize. Ideas or data that did not originate with the author and are not common knowledge are clearly credited to the original source.

7. Couple and family counselors are aware of their obligation to be role models for graduate students and other future researchers. Thus, they act in accordance with the highest standards possible while engaged in research and publication.

8. Couple and family counselors review materials submitted for research, publication, and other scholarly purposes. They respect the confidentiality and proprietary rights of those who submit their products for review. Counselors engaged in reviews of manuscripts and presentation proposals use valid and defensible standards, act within the limits of their competencies, and refrain from personal biases. In this manner, authors and researchers are supported and the field of couple and family counseling is advanced.

Section H: Ethical Decision Making and Resolution

Couple and family counselors incorporate ethical practices in their daily work. They discuss ethical dilemmas with colleagues and engage in ethical decision making in all aspects of couple and family counseling. They hold other counselors to sound ethical principles and encourage professional virtues and aspirations in themselves and other counselors. Couple and family counselors work with other professionals to resolve ethical issues.

1. Couple and family counselors are responsible for understanding the American Counseling Association *Code of Ethics,* the *Ethical Code of the International*

Association of Couple and Family Counselors, and other applicable ethics codes from professional associations, certification and licensure boards, and other credentialing organizations by which they are regulated.

2. Couple and family counselors have the responsibility to confront unethical behavior of other counselors or therapists. The first step must be discussing the violation directly with the caregiver, unless the confrontation would put a client at risk. If the problem continues, the couple and family counselor may contact the professional organization or licensure board of the counselor or therapist in question.

3. Couple and family counselors specify the nature of conflicts between work requirements and other demands of an employing organization and the relevant codes of ethics. Employment and consultation of couple and family counselors should not compromise ethical standards. They work toward beneficial changes in the organizations of which they are members.

4. Couple and family counselors do not engage in unwarranted or invalid complaints. Ethics violations are reported when informal attempts at resolution have failed or violations are likely to substantially harm an individual or organization. Couple and family counselors should follow the reporting requirements specified by laws and regulations in their jurisdictions.

5. Couple and family counselors cooperate with ethics committees and other duly constituted organizations having jurisdiction over the professional charged with an ethics violation. Counselors assist professional associations in promoting ethical behavior and professional conduct.

Section I: Diversity

Couples and family counselors respect the dignity, potential and uniqueness of couples and families within their cultural context. They infuse their counseling and supervision with advocacy strategies which facilitate client wellness. Furthermore, couples and family counselors advocate systems which facilitate wellness and positive human growth. They actively seek to eliminate oppression of human rights, understanding that advocacy enables client empowerment.

1. Couples and family counselors perform advocacy at multiple levels, including advocacy for clients, communities, and social systems. Further, couples and family counselors make efforts to remove barriers that oppress clients at all levels. Couples and family counselors must be aware and understand how to implement the Advocacy Competencies endorsed by the American Counseling Association.

2. Couples and family counselors recognize diversity and its influence on themselves and their clients. Couples and family counselors are cognizant of the impact of world views, values, and cultural influences. Couples and family counselors must be aware of and understand how to implement the Multicultural Counseling Competencies endorsed by the American Counseling Association.

Association for Specialists in Group Work: Best Practice Guidelines 2007 Revisions

R. Valorie Thomas
Rollins College
Debra A. Pender
Northern Illinois University

The Association for Specialists in Group Work (ASGW) supports the practice of ethical and effective group work through the publication of guiding principles in planning, performing and processing group work. Originally prepared, approved and published in 1998 (ASGW; Rapin and Keel), the current revision addresses changes in the American Counseling Association Code of Ethics (ACA, 2005). The revisions were reviewed and approved by the ASGW Executive Board on March 23, 2007.

The Association for Specialists in Group Work (ASGW) is a division of the American Counseling Association whose members are interested in and specialize in group work. Group Workers are defined as mental health professionals who use a group modality as an intervention when working with diverse populations. We value the creation of community while recognizing diverse perspectives; service to our members, clients, and the profession; and value leadership as a process to facilitate the growth and development of individuals and groups within their social and cultural contexts.

Preamble

The Association for Specialists in Group Work recognizes the commitment of its members to the Code of Ethics (as revised in 2005) of its parent organization, the American Counseling Association, and nothing in this document shall be construed to supplant that code. These Best Practice Guidelines are intended to clarify the application of the ACA Code of Ethics to the field of group work by defining Group Workers' responsibility and scope of practice involving those activities, strategies and interventions that are consistent and current with effective and appropriate professional ethical and community standards. ASGW views ethical process as being integral to group work and views Group Workers as ethical agents. Group Workers, by their very nature in being responsible and responsive to their group members, necessarily embrace a certain potential for ethical vulnerability. It is incumbent upon Group Workers to give considerable attention to the intent and context of their actions because the attempts of Group Workers to influence human behavior through group work always have ethical implications. These Best Practice Guidelines address Group Workers' responsibilities in planning, performing and processing groups.

Section A: Best Practice in Planning

A.1. Professional Context and Regulatory Requirements

Group Workers actively know, understand and apply the ACA Code of Ethics (2005), the ASGW Professional Standards for the Training of Group Workers, these ASGW Best Practice Guidelines, the ASGW diversity competencies, and the AMCD Multicultural Counseling Competencies and Standards, relevant state laws, accreditation requirements, relevant National Board for Certified Counselors Codes and Standards, their organization's standards, and insurance requirements impacting the practice of group work.

A.2. Scope of Practice and Conceptual Framework

Group Workers define the scope of practice related to the core and specialization competencies defined in the ASGW Training Standards. Group Workers are aware of personal strengths and weaknesses in leading groups. Group Workers develop and are able to articulate a general conceptual framework to guide practice and a rationale for use of techniques that are to be used. Group Workers limit their practice to those areas for which they meet the training criteria established by the ASGW Training Standards.

A.3. Assessment

a. Assessment of self. Group Workers actively assess their knowledge and skills related to the specific group(s) offered. Group Workers assess their values, beliefs and theoretical orientation and how these impact upon the group, particularly when working with a diverse and multicultural population.
b. Ecological assessment. Group Workers assess community needs, agency or organization resources, sponsoring organization mission, staff competency, attitudes regarding group work, professional training levels of potential group leaders regarding group work; client attitudes regarding group work, and multicultural and diversity considerations. Group Workers use this information as the basis for making decisions related to their group practice, or to the implementation of groups for which they have supervisory, evaluation, or oversight responsibilities.

A.4. Program Development and Evaluation

a. Group Workers identify the type(s) of group(s) to be offered and how they relate to community needs.
b. Group Workers concisely state in writing the purpose and goals of the group. Group Workers also identify the role of the group members in influencing or determining the group goals.
c. Group Workers set fees consistent with the organization's fee schedule, taking into consideration the financial status and locality of prospective group members.
d. Group Workers choose techniques and a leadership style appropriate to the type(s) of group(s) being offered.
e. Group Workers have an evaluation plan consistent with regulatory, organization and insurance requirements, where appropriate.

f. Group Workers take into consideration current professional guidelines when using technology, including but not limited to Internet communication.

A.5. Resources

Group Workers coordinate resources related to the kind of group(s) and group activities to be provided, such as: adequate funding; the appropriateness and availability of a trained co-leader; space and privacy requirements for the type(s) of group(s) being offered; marketing and recruiting; and appropriate collaboration with other community agencies and organizations.

A.6. Professional Disclosure Statement

Group Workers maintain awareness and sensitivity regarding cultural meaning of confidentiality and privacy. Group Workers respect differing views towards disclosure of information. They have a professional disclosure statement which includes information on confidentiality and exceptions to confidentiality, theoretical orientation, information on the nature, purpose(s) and goals of the group, the group services that can be provided, the role and responsibility of group members and leaders, Group Workers qualifications to conduct the specific group(s), specific licenses, certifications and professional affiliations, and address of licensing=credentialing body.

A.7. Group and Member Preparation

a. Group Workers screen prospective group members if appropriate to the type of group being offered. When selection of group members is appropriate, Group Workers identify group members whose needs and goals are compatible with the goals of the group.
b. Group Workers facilitate informed consent. They communicate information in ways that are both developmentally and culturally appropriate. Group Workers provide in oral and written form to prospective members (when appropriate to group type): the professional disclosure statement; group purpose and goals; group participation expectations including voluntary and involuntary membership; role expectations of members and leader(s); policies related to entering and exiting the group; policies governing substance use; policies and procedures governing mandated groups (where relevant); documentation requirements; disclosure of information to others; implications of out-of-group contact or involvement among members; procedures for consultation between group leader(s) and group member(s); fees and time parameters; and potential impacts of group participation.
c. Group Workers obtain the appropriate consent/assent forms for work with minors and other dependent group members.
d. Group Workers define confidentiality and its limits (for example, legal and ethical exceptions and expectations; waivers implicit with treatment plans, documentation and insurance usage). Group Workers have the responsibility to inform all group participants of the need for confidentiality, potential consequences of breaching confidentiality and that legal privilege does not apply to group discussions (unless provided by state statute).

A.8. Professional Development

Group Workers recognize that professional growth is a continuous, ongoing, developmental process throughout their career.

a. Group Workers remain current and increase knowledge and skill competencies through activities such as continuing education, professional supervision, and participation in personal and professional development activities.
b. Group Workers seek consultation and/or supervision regarding ethical concerns that interfere with effective functioning as a group leader. Supervisors have the responsibility to keep abreast of consultation, group theory, process, and adhere to related ethical guidelines.
c. Group Workers seek appropriate professional assistance for their own personal problems or conflicts that are likely to impair their professional judgment or work performance.
d. Group Workers seek consultation and supervision to ensure appropriate practice whenever working with a group for which all knowledge and skill competencies have not been achieved.
e. Group Workers keep abreast of group research and development.

A.9. Trends and Technological Changes

Group Workers are aware of and responsive to technological changes as they affect society, and the profession. These include but are not limited to changes in mental health delivery systems; legislative and insurance industry reforms; shifting population demographics and client needs; and technological advances in Internet and other communication devices and delivery systems. Group Workers adhere to ethical guidelines related to the use of developing technologies.

Section B: Best Practice in Performing

B.1. Self Knowledge

Group Workers are aware of and monitor their strengths and weaknesses and the effects these have on group members. They explore their own cultural identities and how these affect their values and beliefs about group work.

B.2. Group Competencies

Group Workers have a basic knowledge of groups and the principles of group dynamics, and are able to perform the core group competencies, as described in the ASGW Professional Standards for the Training of Group Workers (ASGW, 2000). They gain knowledge, personal, personal awareness, sensitivity, and skills pertinent to working with a diverse client population. Additionally, Group Workers have adequate understanding and skill in any group specialty area chosen for practice (psychotherapy, counseling, task, psychoeducation, as described in the ASGW Training Standards).

B.3. Group Plan Adaptation

a. Group Workers apply and modify knowledge, skills and techniques appropriate to group type and stage, and to the unique needs of various cultural and ethnic groups.
b. Group Workers monitor the group's progress toward the group goals and plan.
c. Group Workers clearly define and maintain ethical, professional, and social relationship boundaries with group members as appropriate to their role in the organization and the type of group being offered.

B.4. Therapeutic Conditions and Dynamics

Group Workers understand and are able to implement appropriate models of group development, process observation and therapeutic conditions. Group Workers manage the flow of communication, addressing safety and pacing of disclosures to protect group members from physical, emotional, or psychological trauma.

B.5. Meaning

Group Workers assist members in generating meaning from the group experience.

B.6. Collaboration

Group Workers assist members in developing individual goals and respect group members as co-equal partners in the group experience.

B.7. Evaluation

Group Workers include evaluation (both formal and informal) between sessions and at the conclusion of the group.

B.8. Diversity

Group Workers practice with broad sensitivity to client differences including but not limited to ethnic, gender, religious, sexual, psychological maturity, economic class, family history, physical characteristics or limitations, and geographic location. Group Workers continuously seek information regarding the cultural issues of the diverse population with whom they are working both by interaction with participants and from using outside resources.

B.9. Ethical Surveillance

Group Workers employ an appropriate ethical decision making model in responding to ethical challenges and issues and in determining courses of action and behavior for self and group members. In addition, Group Workers employ applicable standards as promulgated by ACA, ASGW, or other appropriate professional organizations.

Section C: Best Practice in Group Processing

C.1. Processing Schedule

Group Workers process the workings of the group with themselves, group members, supervisors or other colleagues, as appropriate. This may include assessing progress on group and member goals, leader behaviors and techniques, group dynamics and interventions; developing understanding and acceptance of meaning. Processing may occur both within sessions and before and after each session, at time of termination, and later follow up, as appropriate.

C.2. Reflective Practice

Group Workers attend to opportunities to synthesize theory and practice and to incorporate learning outcomes into ongoing groups. Group Workers attend to session dynamics of members and their interactions and also attend to the relationship between session dynamics and leader values, cognition and affect.

C.3. Evaluation and Follow-Up

a. Group Workers evaluate process and outcomes. Results are used for ongoing program planning, improvement and revisions of current group and/or to contribute to professional research literature. Group Workers follow all applicable policies and standards in using group material for research and reports.
b. Group Workers conduct follow-up contact with group members, as appropriate, to assess outcomes or when requested by a group member(s).

C.4. Consultation and Training with Other Organizations

Group Workers provide consultation and training to organizations in and out of their setting, when appropriate. Group Workers seek out consultation as needed with competent professional persons knowledgeable about group work.

National Organization for Human Services
Council for Standards in Human Service Education
Adopted 1996

Preamble

Human services is a profession developing in response to and in anticipation of the direction of human needs and human problems in the late twentieth century. Characterized particularly by an appreciation of human beings in all of their diversity, human services offers assistance to its clients within the context of their community and environment. Human service professionals and those who educate them, regardless of whether they are students, faculty or practitioners, promote and encourage the unique values and characteristics of human services. In so doing human service professionals and educators uphold the integrity and ethics of the profession, partake in constructive criticism of the profession, promote client and community well-being, and enhance their own professional growth.

The ethical guidelines presented are a set of standards of conduct which the human service professionals and educators consider in ethical and professional decision making. It is hoped that these guidelines will be of assistance when human service professionals and educators are challenged by difficult ethical dilemmas. Although ethical codes are not legal documents, they may be used to assist in the adjudication of issues related to ethical human service behavior.

Section I–Standards for Human Service Professionals

Human service professionals function in many ways and carry out many roles. They enter into professional-client relationships with individuals, families, groups and communities who are all referred to as "clients" in these standards. Among their roles are caregiver, case manager, broker, teacher/educator, behavior changer, consultant, outreach professional, mobilizer, advocate, community planner, community change organizer, evaluator and administrator.[1.] The following standards are written with these multifaceted roles in mind.

The Human Service Professional's Responsibility to Clients

STATEMENT 1

Human service professionals negotiate with clients the purpose, goals, and nature of the helping relationship prior to its onset as well as inform clients of the limitations of the proposed relationship.

STATEMENT 2

Human service professionals respect the integrity and welfare of the client at all times. Each client is treated with respect, acceptance and dignity.

STATEMENT 3

Human service professionals protect the client's right to privacy and confidentiality except when such confidentiality would cause harm to the client or others, when agency guidelines state otherwise, or under other stated conditions (e.g., local, state, or federal laws). Professionals inform clients of the limits of confidentiality prior to the onset of the helping relationship.

STATEMENT 4

If it is suspected that danger or harm may occur to the client or to others as a result of a client's behavior, the human service professional acts in an appropriate and professional manner to protect the safety of those individuals. This may involve seeking consultation, supervision, and/or breaking the confidentiality of the relationship.

STATEMENT 5

Human service professionals protect the integrity, safety, and security of client records. All written client information that is shared with other professionals, except in the course of professional supervision, must have the client's prior written consent.

STATEMENT 6

Human service professionals are aware that in their relationships with clients power and status are unequal. Therefore they recognize that dual or multiple relationships may increase the risk of harm to, or exploitation of, clients, and may impair their professional judgment. However, in some communities and situations it may not be feasible to avoid social or other nonprofessional contact with clients. Human service professionals support the trust implicit in the helping relationship by avoiding dual relationships that may impair professional judgment, increase the risk of harm to clients or lead to exploitation.

STATEMENT 7

Sexual relationships with current clients are not considered to be in the best interest of the client and are prohibited. Sexual relationships with previous clients are considered dual relationships and are addressed in STATEMENT 6 (above).

STATEMENT 8

The client's right to self-determination is protected by human service professionals. They recognize the client's right to receive or refuse services.

STATEMENT 9

Human service professionals recognize and build on client strengths.

The Human Service Professional's Responsibility to the Community and Society

STATEMENT 10

Human service professionals are aware of local, state, and federal laws. They advocate for change in regulations and statutes when such legislation conflicts with ethical guidelines and/or client rights. Where laws are harmful to individuals, groups or communities, human service professionals consider the conflict between the values of obeying the law and the values of serving people and may decide to initiate social action.

STATEMENT 11

Human service professionals keep informed about current social issues as they affect the client and the community. They share that information with clients, groups and community as part of their work.

STATEMENT 12

Human service professionals understand the complex interaction between individuals, their families, the communities in which they live, and society.

STATEMENT 13

Human service professionals act as advocates in addressing unmet client and community needs. Human service professionals provide a mechanism for identifying unmet client needs, calling attention to these needs, and assisting in planning and mobilizing to advocate for those needs at the local community level.

STATEMENT 14

Human service professionals represent their qualifications to the public accurately.

STATEMENT 15

Human service professionals describe the effectiveness of programs, treatments, and/or techniques accurately.

STATEMENT 16

Human service professionals advocate for the rights of all members of society, particularly those who are members of minorities and groups at which discriminatory practices have historically been directed.

STATEMENT 17

Human service professionals provide services without discrimination or preference based on age, ethnicity, culture, race, disability, gender, religion, sexual orientation or socioeconomic status.

STATEMENT 18

Human service professionals are knowledgeable about the cultures and communities within which they practice. They are aware of multiculturalism in society and its impact on the community as well as individuals within the community. They respect individuals and groups, their cultures and beliefs.

STATEMENT 19

Human service professionals are aware of their own cultural backgrounds, beliefs, and values, recognizing the potential for impact on their relationships with others.

STATEMENT 20

Human service professionals are aware of sociopolitical issues that differentially affect clients from diverse backgrounds.

STATEMENT 21

Human service professionals seek the training, experience, education and supervision necessary to ensure their effectiveness in working with culturally diverse client

The Human Service Professional's Responsibility to Colleagues

STATEMENT 22

Human service professionals avoid duplicating another professional's helping relationship with a client They consult with other professionals who are assisting the client in a different type of relationship when it is in the best interest of the client to do so.

STATEMENT 23

When a human service professional has a conflict with a colleague, he or she first seeks out the colleague in an attempt to manage the problem. If necessary, the professional then seeks the assistance of supervisors, consultants or other professionals in efforts to manage the problem.

STATEMENT 24

Human service professionals respond appropriately to unethical behavior of colleagues. Usually this means initially talking directly with the colleague and, if no resolution is forthcoming, reporting the colleague's behavior to supervisory or administrative staff and/or to the Professional organization(s) to which the colleague belongs.

STATEMENT 25

All consultations between human service professionals are kept confidential unless to do so would result in harm to clients or communities.

The Human Service Professional's Responsibility to the Profession

STATEMENT 26

Human service professionals know the limit and scope of their professional knowledge and offer services only within their knowledge and skill base.

STATEMENT 27

Human service professionals seek appropriate consultation and supervision to assist in decision-making when there are legal, ethical or other dilemmas.

STATEMENT 28

Human service professionals act with integrity, honesty, genuineness, and objectivity.

STATEMENT 29

Human service professionals promote cooperation among related disciplines (e.g., psychology, counseling, social work, nursing, family and consumer sciences, medicine, education) to foster professional growth and interests within the various fields.

STATEMENT 30

Human service professionals promote the continuing development of their profession. They encourage membership in professional associations, support research endeavors, foster educational advancement, advocate for appropriate legislative actions, and participate in other related professional activities.

STATEMENT 31

Human service professionals continually seek out new and effective approaches to enhance their professional abilities.

The Human Service Professional's Responsibility to Employers

STATEMENT 32

Human service professionals adhere to commitments made to their employers.

STATEMENT 33

Human service professionals participate in efforts to establish and maintain employment conditions which are conducive to high quality client services. They assist in evaluating the effectiveness of the agency through reliable and valid assessment measures.

STATEMENT 34

When a conflict arises between fulfilling the responsibility to the employer and the responsibility to the client, human service professionals advise both of the conflict and work conjointly with all involved to manage the conflict.

The Human Service Professional's Responsibility to Self

STATEMENT 35

Human service professionals strive to personify those characteristics typically associated with the profession (e.g., accountability, respect for others, genuineness, empathy, pragmatism).

STATEMENT 36

Human service professionals foster self-awareness and personal growth in themselves. They recognize that when professionals are aware of their own values, attitudes, cultural background, and personal needs, the process of helping others is less likely to be negatively impacted by those factors.

STATEMENT 37

Human service professionals recognize a commitment to lifelong learning and continually upgrade knowledge and skills to serve the populations better.

Section II—Standards for Human Service Educators

Human Service educators are familiar with, informed by and accountable to the standards of professional conduct put forth by their institutions of higher learning; their professional disciplines, for example, American Association of University Professors (AAUP), American Counseling Association (ACA), Academy of Criminal Justice (ACJS), American Psychological Association (APA), American Sociological Association (ASA), National Association of Social Workers (NASW), National Board of Certified Counselors (NBCC), National Education Association (NEA); and the National Organization for Human Services (NOHS).

STATEMENT 38

Human service educators uphold the principle of liberal education and embrace the essence of academic freedom, abstaining from inflicting their own personal views/morals on students, and allowing students the freedom to express their views without penalty, censure or ridicule, and to engage in critical thinking.

STATEMENT 39

Human service educators provide students with readily available and explicit program policies and criteria regarding program goals and objectives, recruitment, admission, course requirements, evaluations, retention and dismissal in accordance with due process procedures.

STATEMENT 40

Human service educators demonstrate high standards of scholarship in content areas and of pedagogy by staying current with developments in the field of Human Services and in teaching effectiveness, for example learning styles and teaching styles.

STATEMENT 41

Human service educators monitor students' field experiences to ensure the quality of the placement site, supervisory experience, and learning experience towards the goals of professional identity and skill development.

STATEMENT 42

Human service educators participate actively in the selection of required readings and use them with care, based strictly on the merits of the material's content, and present relevant information accurately, objectively and fully.

STATEMENT 43

Human service educators, at the onset of courses: inform students if sensitive/controversial issues or experiential/affective content or process are part of the course design; ensure that students are offered opportunities to discuss in structured ways their reactions to sensitive or controversial class content; ensure that the presentation of such material is justified on pedagogical grounds directly related to the course; and, differentiate between information based on scientific data, anecdotal data, and personal opinion.

STATEMENT 44

Human service educators develop and demonstrate culturally sensitive knowledge, awareness, and teaching methodology.

STATEMENT 45

Human service educators demonstrate full commitment to their appointed responsibilities, and are enthusiastic about and encouraging of students' learning.

STATEMENT 46

Human service educators model the personal attributes, values and skills of the human service professional, including but not limited to, the willingness to seek and respond to feedback from students.

STATEMENT 47

Human service educators establish and uphold appropriate guidelines concerning self-disclosure or student-disclosure of sensitive/personal information.

STATEMENT 48

Human service educators establish an appropriate and timely process for providing clear and objective feedback to students about their performance on relevant and established course/program academic and personal competence requirements and their suitability for the field.

STATEMENT 49

Human service educators are aware that in their relationships with students, power and status are unequal; therefore, human service educators are responsible to clearly define and maintain ethical and professional relationships with students, and avoid conduct that is demeaning, embarrassing or exploitative of students, and to treat students fairly, equally and without discrimination.

STATEMENT 50

Human service educators recognize and acknowledge the contributions of students to their work, for example in case material, workshops, research, publications.

STATEMENT 51

Human service educators demonstrate professional standards of conduct in managing personal or professional differences with colleagues, for example, not disclosing such differences and/or affirming a student's negative opinion of a faculty/program.

STATEMENT 52

Human service educators ensure that students are familiar with, informed by, and accountable to the ethical standards and policies put forth by their program/department, the course syllabus/instructor, their advisor(s), and the Ethical Standards of Human Service Professionals.

STATEMENT 53

Human service educators are aware of all relevant curriculum standards, including those of the Council for Standards in Human Services Education (CSHSE); the Community Support Skills Standards; and state/local standards, and take them into consideration in designing the curriculum.

STATEMENT 54

Human service educators create a learning context in which students can achieve the knowledge, skills, values and attitudes of the academic program.

American Music Therapy Association (AMTA)
Code of Ethics

Preamble

The members of the American Music Therapy Association, Inc., hereby recognize and publicly accept the proposition that the fundamental purposes of the profession are the progressive development of the use of music to accomplish therapeutic aims and the advancement of training, education, and research in music therapy. Our objectives are to determine and utilize music therapy approaches that effectively aid in the restoration, maintenance, and improvement in mental and physical health. To that end, we believe in the dignity and worth of every person. We promote the use of music in therapy, establish and maintain high standards in public service, and require of ourselves the utmost in ethical conduct.

This Code of Ethics is applicable to all those holding the MT-BC credential or a professional designation of the National Music Therapy Registry and professional membership in the American Music Therapy Association. This Code is also applicable to music therapy students and interns under clinical supervision. We shall not use our professional positions or relationships, nor permit ourselves or our services to be used by others for purposes inconsistent with the principles set forth in this document. Upholding our right to freedom of inquiry and communication, we accept the responsibilities inherent in such freedom: competency, objectivity, consistency, integrity, and continual concern for the best interests of society and our profession. Therefore, we collectively and individually affirm the following declarations of professional conduct.

1.0 Professional Competence and Responsibilities

1.1 The MT will perform only those duties for which he/she has been adequately trained, not engaging outside his/her area of competence.

1.2 The MT will state his/her qualifications, titles, and professional affiliation(s) accurately.

1.3 The MT will participate in continuing education activities to maintain and improve his/her knowledge and skills.

1.4 The MT will assist the public in identifying competent and qualified music therapists and will discourage the misuse and incompetent practice of music therapy.

1.5 The MT is aware of personal limitations, problems, and values that might interfere with his/her professional work and, at an early stage, will take whatever action is necessary (i.e., seeking professional help, limiting or discontinuing work with clients, etc.) to ensure that services to clients are not affected by these limitations and problems.

1.6 The MT respects the rights of others to hold values, attitudes, and opinions that differ from his/her own.

1.7 The MT does not engage in sexual harassment.

1.8 The MT accords sexual harassment grievants and respondents dignity and respect, and does not base decisions solely upon their having made, or having been the subject of, sexual harassment charges.

1.9 The MT practices with integrity, honesty, fairness, and respect for others.

1.10 The MT delegates to his/her employees, students, or co-workers only those responsibilities that such persons can reasonably be expected to perform competently on the basis of their training and experience. The MT takes reasonable steps to see that such persons perform services competently; and, if institutional policies prevent fulfillment of this obligation, the MT attempts to correct the situation to the extent feasible.

2.0 General Standards

2.1 The MT will strive for the highest standards in his/her work, offering the highest quality of services to clients/students.

2.2 The MT will use procedures that conform with his/her interpretation of the Standards of Clinical Practice of the American Music Therapy Association, Inc.

2.3 Moral and Legal Standards
    2.3.1 The MT respects the social and moral expectations of the community in which he/she works. The MT is aware that standards of behavior are a personal matter as they are for other citizens, except as they may concern the fulfillment of professional duties or influence the public attitude and trust towards the profession.
    2.3.2 The MT refuses to participate in activities that are illegal or inhumane, that violate the civil rights of others, or that discriminate against individuals based upon race, ethnicity, language, religion, marital status, gender, gender identity or expression, sexual orientation, age, ability, socioeconomic status, or political affiliation. In addition, the MT works to eliminate the effect of biases based on these factors on his or her work.

3.0 Relationships With Clients/Students/Research Subjects

3.1 The welfare of the client will be of utmost importance to the MT.

3.2 The MT will protect the rights of the individuals with whom he/she works. These rights will include, but are not limited to the following:
- right to safety;
- right to dignity;
- legal and civil rights;
- right to treatment;
- right to self-determination;
- right to respect; and
- right to participate in treatment decisions.

3.3 The MT will not discriminate in relationships with clients/students/research subjects because of race, ethnicity, language, religion, marital status, gender, gender identity or expression, sexual orientation, age, ability, socioeconomic status or political affiliation.

3.4 The MT will not exploit clients/students/research subjects sexually, physically, financially or emotionally.

3.5 The MT will not enter into dual relationships with clients/students/research subjects and will avoid those situations that interfere with professional judgment or objectivity (e.g., those involving competitive and/or conflicting interests) in their relationships.

3.6 The MT will exert caution in predicting the results of services offered, although a reasonable statement of prognosis and/or progress may be made. The MT will make only those claims to clients concerning the efficacy of services that would be willingly submitted for professional scrutiny through peer review, publication in a professional journal, or documentation in the client's record.

3.7 The MT will offer music therapy services only in the context of a professional relationship and in a setting which insures safety and protection for both client and therapist. The MT will avoid deception in representations of music therapy to the public.

3.8 The MT will inform the client and/or guardian as to the purpose, nature, and effects of assessment and treatment.

3.9 The MT will use every available resource to serve the client best.

3.10 The MT will utilize the profession's Standards of Practice as a guideline in accepting or declining referrals or requests for services, as well as in terminating or referring clients when the client no longer benefits from the therapeutic relationship.

3.11 In those emerging areas of practice for which generally recognized standards are not yet defined, the MT will nevertheless utilize cautious judgment and will take reasonable steps to ensure the competence of his/her work, as well as to protect clients, students, and research subjects from harm.

3.12 Confidentiality
   3.12.1 The MT protects the confidentiality of information obtained in the course of practice, supervision, teaching, and/or research.
   3.12.2 In compliance with federal, state and local regulations and organizational policies and procedures, confidential information may be revealed under circumstances which include but are not limited to:
      a. when, under careful deliberation, it is decided that society, the client, or other individuals appear to be in imminent danger. In this situation, information may be shared only with the appropriate authorities, professionals or others. The client is made aware of this when possible and if reasonable.

      b. when other professionals within a facility or agency are directly related with the case or situation.

      c. when the client consents to the releasing of confidential information.

      d. when compelled by a court or administrative order or subpoena, provided such order or subpoena is valid and served in accordance with applicable law.

3.12.3 The MT informs clients of the limits of confidentiality prior to beginning treatment.

3.12.4 The MT disguises the identity of the client in the presentation of case materials for research and teaching. Client or guardian consent is obtained, with full disclosure of the intended use of the material.

3.12.5 All forms of individually identifiable client information, including, but not limited to verbal, written, audio, video and digital will be acquired with the informed client or guardian consent and will be maintained in a confidential manner by the MT. Also, adequate security will be exercised in the preservation and ultimate disposition of these records.

3.12.6 Information obtained in the course of evaluating services, consulting, supervision, peer review, and quality assurance procedures will be kept confidential.

4.0 Relationships With Colleagues

4.1   The MT acts with integrity in regard to colleagues in music therapy and other professions and will cooperate with them whenever appropriate.

4.2   The MT will not offer professional services to a person receiving music therapy from another music therapist except by agreement with that therapist or after termination of the client's relationship with that therapist.

4.3   The MT will attempt to establish harmonious relations with members from other professions and professional organizations and will not damage the professional reputation or practice of others.

4.4   The MT will share with other members of the treatment team information concerning evaluative and therapeutic goals and procedures used.

4.5   The MT will not discriminate in relationships with colleagues because of race, ethnicity, language, religion, marital status, gender, gender identity or expression, sexual orientation, age, ability, socioeconomic status or political affiliation.

5.0 Relationship With Employers

5.1   The MT will observe the regulations, policies, and procedures of employers with the exception of those that are in violation of this code of ethics.

5.2   The MT will inform employers of conditions that may limit the effectiveness of the services being rendered.

5.3   When representing the employer or agency, the MT will differentiate personal views from those of the profession, the employer, and the agency.

5.4   The MT will provide services in an ethical manner and will protect the property, integrity, and reputation of the employing agency.

5.5   The MT will utilize the agency's facilities and resources only as authorized.

5.6   The MT will not use his/her position to obtain clients for private practice, unless authorized to do so by the employing agency.

6.0   Responsibility to Community/Public

6.1   The MT will strive to increase public awareness of music therapy.

6.2   The MT engaged in a private practice or business will abide by federal, state and local regulations relevant to self-employment including but not limited to professional liability, registering and maintaining a business, tax codes and liability, confidentiality and reimbursement.

7.0   Responsibility to the Profession/Association

7.1   The MT respects the rights, rules, and reputation of his/her professional association.

7.2   The MT will distinguish personal from professional views when acting on behalf of his/her association. The MT will represent the association only with appropriate authorization.

7.3   The MT will strive to increase the level of knowledge, skills, and research within the profession.

7.4   The MT will refrain from the misuse of an official position within the association.

7.5   The MT will exercise integrity and confidentiality when carrying out his/her official duties in the association.

8.0   Research

8.1   The MT establishes a precise agreement with research subjects prior to their participation in the study. In this agreement, the responsibilities and rights of all parties are explained, and written consent is obtained. The MT explains all aspects of the research that might influence the subject's willingness to participate, including all possible risks and benefits. The MT will avoid any deception in research.

8.2   Participation of subjects in music therapy research will be voluntary. Appropriate authorization will be obtained from the subjects involved (or specified and/or legal guardians) and the facility. The subject is free to refuse to participate or to withdraw from the research at any time without penalty or loss of services.

8.3 The MT is ultimately responsible for protecting the welfare of the research subjects, both during and after the study, in the event of aftereffects, and will take all precautions to avoid injurious psychological, physical, or social effects to the subjects.

8.4 The MT will store data in a secure location accessible to the researcher. The researcher will determine a set period of time after completion of the study by which all research data must be shredded or erased.

8.5 The MT will be competent in his/her research efforts, being cognizant of his/her limits.

8.6 The MT will present his/her findings without distortion and in a manner that will not be misleading.

8.7 Publication Credit
  8.7.1 Credit is assigned only to those who have contributed to a publication, in proportion to their contribution.
  8.7.2 Major contributions of a professional nature made by several persons to a common project will be recognized by joint authorship.
  8.7.3 Minor contributions such as editing or advising, will be recognized in footnotes or in an introductory statement.
  8.7.4 Acknowledgment through specific citations will be made for unpublished as well as published material that has directly influenced the research or writing.
  8.7.5 The MT who compiles and edits for publication the contribution of others will publish the symposium or report under the title of the committee or symposium, with the therapist's name appearing as chairperson or editor among those of the other contributors or committee members.

9.0 Fees and Commercial Activities

9.1 The MT accepts remuneration only for services actually rendered by himself or herself or under his or her supervision and only in accordance with professional standards that safeguard the best interest of clients and the profession.

9.2 The MT will not take financial advantage of a client. The MT will take into account the client's ability to pay. Financial considerations are secondary to the client's welfare.

9.3 Private fees may not be accepted or charged for services when the MT receives remuneration for these services by the agency.

9.4 No gratuities, gifts or favors should be accepted from clients that could interfere with the MT's decisions or judgments.

9.5 Referral sources may not receive a commission fee, or privilege for making referrals (fee-splitting).

9.6   The MT will not engage in commercial activities that conflict with responsibilities to clients or colleagues.

9.7   The materials or products dispensed to clients should be in the client's best interest, with the client's having the freedom of choice. The MT will not profit from the sale of equipment/materials to clients. Charges for any materials will be separate from the bill for services.

10.0   Announcing Services

10.1   The MT will adhere to professional rather than commercial standards in making known his or her availability for professional services. The MT will offer music therapy services only in a manner that neither discredits the profession nor decreases the trust of the public in the profession.

10.2   The MT will not solicit clients of other MT's.

10.3   The MT will make every effort to ensure that public information materials are accurate and complete in reference to professional services and facilities.

10.4   The MT will avoid the following in announcing services: misleading or deceptive advertising, misrepresentation of specialty, guarantees or false expectations, and the use of the Association's logo.

10.5   The MT will differentiate between private practice and private music studio in announcing services.

10.6   The following materials may be used in announcing services (all of which must be dignified in appearance and content): announcement cards, brochures, letterhead, business cards and the internet. The MT may include the following on these materials: name, title, degrees, schools, dates, certification, location, hours, contact information, and an indication of the nature of the services offered.

10.7   Announcing services through the mail (to other professionals), a listing in the telephone directory, or the internet (i.e., email, website) are acceptable. No advertisement or announcement will be rendered in a manner that will be untruthful and/or deceive the public.

11.0   Education (Teaching, Supervision, Administration)

11.1   The MT involved in teaching establishes a program combining academic, research, clinical, and ethical aspects of practice. The program will include a wide range of methods and exposure to and application of current literature.

11.2   The MT involved in education and/or supervision will use his/her skill to help others acquire the knowledge and skills necessary to perform with high standards of professional competence.

11.3   Theory and methods will be consistent with recent advances in music therapy and related health fields. The MT involved in education will teach new techniques or areas of study only after first undertaking appropriate training, supervision, study, and/or consultation from persons who are competent in those areas or techniques.

11.4   The MT involved in the education of students and internship training will ensure that clinical work performed by students is rendered under adequate supervision by other music therapists, other professionals, and/or the MT educator.

11.5   The MT involved in education and/or supervision will evaluate the competencies of students as required by good educational practices and will identify those students whose limitations impede performance as a competent music therapist. The MT will recommend only those students for internship or membership whom he/she feels will perform as competent music therapists and who meet the academic, clinical, and ethical expectations of the American Music Therapy Association, Inc.

11.6   The MT involved in the education of students and internship training will serve as an exemplary role model in regard to ethical conduct and the enforcement of the Code of Ethics.

11.7   The MT involved in education and training will ensure that students and interns operate under the same ethical standards that govern professionals.

12.0   Implementation

12.1   *Confronting Ethical Issues*
        12.1.1   MT's have an obligation to be familiar with this Code of Ethics.
        12.1.2   When a MT is uncertain whether a particular situation or course of action would violate this Code of Ethics, the MT should consult with a member of the Ethics Board.
        12.1.3   A MT will not disobey this code, even when asked to do so by his/her employer.
        12.1.4   The MT has an obligation to report ethical violations of this Code by other MT's to the Ethics Board.
        12.1.5   The MT does not report or encourage reporting of ethics grievances that are frivolous and are intended to harm the respondent rather than to protect the public and preserve the integrity of the field of music therapy.
        12.1.6   The MT cooperates in ethics investigations, proceedings, and hearings. Failure to cooperate is, itself, an ethics violation.
        12.1.7   Grievances may be reported by any individual or group who has witnessed an apparent ethical violation by a Music Therapist
        12.1.8   Neither the Chair nor any other member of the Ethics Board will take part in the informal or formal resolution procedures if s/he has a conflict of interest.

12.2   *Informal Resolution of Ethical Violations*
        12.2.1   Upon observing or becoming aware of alleged violations of this Code of Ethics by an MT (hereinafter referred to as the respondent), the

observer will consult first with the respondent involved and discuss possible actions to correct the alleged violation when such consultation is appropriate for the resolution of the ethical violation. The MT should document these efforts at informal resolution. In some instances, the individual consultation between the observer and the respondent may be either inappropriate or not feasible. In such instances (which may include, but are not limited to: sexual harassment, fear of physical retaliation, and imminent threats to the observer's employment), the observer should file a formal grievance with an explanation of the reason why individual consultation was not appropriate or feasible.

12.3   *Formal Resolution of Ethical Violations*

     12.3.1   If an apparent ethical violation is not appropriate for informal resolution or is not resolved through consultation, the observer (herein referred to as the grievant) will submit a written report (herein referred to as the grievance) describing the alleged violation(s) to a member of the Ethics Board. The written report will consist of the following: (a) a signed, dated summary, not longer than one page, of the principle allegations (hereinafter referred to as the charge) against the respondent; (b) a thorough explanation of the alleged violation(s); (c) a summary of informal resolution attempts, when such have been made; and (d) collaborative documentation, including signed statements by witnesses, if available.

     12.3.2   The grievance must be made within one year of the last instance of the alleged violation(s) of this code.

     12.3.3   Upon receipt of the grievance by the member of the Ethics, the member in consultation with the Ethics Chairperson and the Executive Director of AMTA will advise the MT respondent, in writing and within 45 days, that an ethics grievance has been made against him/her. Included in this notification will be a copy of the signed charge. The Ethics Board member will invite the respondent to submit a written defense within 60 days, including corroborative documentation and/or signed statements by witnesses, if available.

     12.3.4   The Ethics Chairperson, or his/her designee from the Ethics Board, will conduct an initial inquiry into the grievance to confirm (a) the seriousness of the charge and (b) the possibility of resolution of the issue without a formal hearing.

     12.3.5   After the initial inquiry, the Ethics Chairperson or designee may, at his or her discretion, negotiate a resolution to the grievance that will be presented in writing to the grievant and the respondent. If both parties agree to this resolution, they will sign and abide by the terms therein stated.

     12.3.6   The initial inquiry by the Ethics Chairperson or designee, and negotiated attempts at a resolution, will be conducted within 45 days following receipt of the respondent's defense.

12.3.7 If agreement to a negotiated resolution is not reached, or if 45 days have passed following receipt of the respondent's defense, the Ethics Chairperson will initiate the formal procedure. At that time the Ethics Chairperson will inform in writing the Ethics Board, the Executive Director of AMTA, the President of AMTA, the grievant, and the respondent that the formal hearing procedure has begun and appoint a chair for the hearing panel.

12.4 *Group Grievances*

12.4.1 If the Ethics Chairperson or designee receives more than one grievance related in a substantive way against the same party, the chair or designee may choose to combine the grievances into a single grievance, as long as there is no objection to such combination by the individual grievants. In this instance, the procedure heretofore established will remain the same.

12.4.2 If two or more individuals report a grievance against the same party, they may report a group grievance. This will be handled as a single grievance, following established procedures.

12.4.3 An employing agency may charge a MT with a violation of this Code of Ethics in the same manner as an individual grievant does so. The employing agency will appoint a representative to function in the role of grievant.

12.5 *Corrective Actions*

12.5.1 If the individual takes no corrective action within the designated time-limit, the panel chair will reconvene the hearing panel to determine recommended sanctions to the Executive Board for action. Possible sanctions may include, but are not limited to:

(a) permanent or time-specific withdrawal of an individual's membership in the Association;

(b) rehabilitative activity, such as personal therapy;

(c) a binding agreement by the respondent to conform his/her practice, education/training methods, or research methods to AMTA rules and guidelines;

(d) a written reprimand;

(e) recommendation to the National Music Therapy Registry or the Certification Board for Music Therapists (as appropriate) for the withdrawal of professional designation or credential. The MT may appeal the decision of the Ethics Board to the Judicial Review Board.

Current as of 10/12

American Counseling Association
Code of Ethics

Mission

The mission of the American Counseling Association is to enhance the quality of life in society by promoting the development of professional counselors, advancing the counseling profession, and using the profession and practice of counseling to promote respect for human dignity and diversity.

Preamble

The American Counseling Association is an educational, scientific, and professional organization whose members work in a variety of settings and serve in multiple capacities. ACA members are dedicated to the enhancement of human development throughout the life span. Association members recognize diversity and embrace a cross-cultural approach in support of the worth, dignity, potential, and uniqueness of people within their social and cultural contexts.

Professional values are an important way of living out an ethical commitment. Values inform principles. Inherently held values that guide our behaviors or exceed prescribed behaviors are deeply ingrained in the counselor and developed out of personal dedication, rather than the mandatory requirement of an external organization.

Purpose

The *ACA Code of Ethics* serves five main purposes:
1. The *Code* enables the association to clarify to current and future members, and to those served by members, the nature of the ethical responsibilities held in common by its members.
2. The *Code* helps support the mission of the association.
3. The *Code* establishes principles that define ethical behavior and best practices of association members.
4. The *Code* serves as an ethical guide designed to assist members in constructing a professional course of action that best serves those utilizing counseling services and best promotes the values of the counseling profession.
5. The *Code* serves as the basis for processing of ethical complaints and inquiries initiated against members of the association.

The *ACA Code of Ethics* contains eight main sections that address the following areas:
Section A: The Counseling Relationship
Section B: Confidentiality, Privileged Communication, and Privacy
Section C: Professional Responsibility
Section D: Relationships With Other Professionals
Section E: Evaluation, Assessment, and Interpretation
Section F: Supervision, Training, and Teaching
Section G: Research and Publication
Section H: Resolving Ethical Issues

Each section of the *ACA Code of Ethics* begins with an Introduction. The introductions to each section discuss what counselors should aspire to with regard to ethical behavior and responsibility. The Introduction helps set the tone for that particular section and provides a starting point that invites reflection on the ethical mandates contained in each part of the *ACA Code of Ethics*.

When counselors are faced with ethical dilemmas that are difficult to resolve, they are expected to engage in a carefully considered ethical decision-making process. Reasonable differences of opinion can and do exist among counselors with respect to the ways in which values, ethical principles, and ethical standards would be applied when they conflict. While there is no specific ethical decision-making model that is most effective, counselors are expected to be familiar with a credible model of decision making that can bear public scrutiny and its application.

Through a chosen ethical decision-making process and evaluation of the context of the situation, counselors are empowered to make decisions that help expand the capacity of people to grow and develop.

A brief glossary is given to provide readers with a concise description of some of the terms used in the *ACA Code of Ethics*.

Section A: The Counseling Relationship

Introduction

Counselors encourage client growth and development in ways that foster the interest and welfare of clients and promote formation of healthy relationships. Counselors actively attempt to understand the diverse cultural backgrounds of the clients they serve. Counselors also explore their own cultural identities and how these affect their values and beliefs about the counseling process.

Counselors are encouraged to contribute to society by devoting a portion of their professional activity to services for which there is little or no financial return (pro bono publico).

A.1. Welfare of Those Served by Counselors

A.1.a. Primary Responsibility

The primary responsibility of counselors is to respect the dignity and to promote the welfare of clients.

A.1.b Records

Counselors maintain records necessary for rendering professional services to their clients and as required by laws, regulations, or agency or institution procedures. Counselors include sufficient and timely documentation in their client records to facilitate the delivery and continuity of needed services. Counselors take reasonable steps to ensure that documentation in records accurately reflects client progress and services provided. If errors are made in client records, counselors take steps to properly note the correction of such errors according to agency or institutional policies. *(See A.12.g.7., B.6., B.6.g., G.2.j.)*

A.1.c. Counseling Plans

Counselors and their clients work jointly in devising integrated counseling plans that offer reasonable promise of success and are consistent with abilities and circumstances of clients. Counselors and clients regularly review counseling plans to assess their continued viability and effectiveness, respecting the freedom of choice of clients. *(See A.2.a., A.2.d., A.12.g.)*

A.1.d. Support Network Involvement

Counselors recognize that support networks hold various meanings in the lives of clients and consider enlisting the support, understanding, and involvement of others (e.g., religious/spiritual/community leaders, family members, friends) as positive resources, when appropriate, with client consent.

A.1.e. Employment Needs

Counselors work with their clients considering employment in jobs that are consistent with the overall abilities, vocational limitations, physical restrictions, general temperament, interest and aptitude patterns, social skills, education, general qualifications, and other relevant characteristics and needs of clients. When appropriate, counselors appropriately trained in career development will assist in the placement of clients in positions that are consistent with the interest, culture, and the welfare of clients, employers, and/or the public.

A.2. Informed Consent in the Counseling Relationship

(See A.12.g., B.5., B.6.b., E.3., E.13.b., F.1.c., G.2.a.)

A.2.a. Informed Consent

Clients have the freedom to choose whether to enter into or remain in a counseling relationship and need adequate information about the counseling process and the counselor. Counselors have an obligation to review in writing and verbally with clients the rights and responsibilities of both the counselor and the client. Informed consent is an ongoing part of the counseling process, and counselors appropriately document discussions of informed consent throughout the counseling relationship.

A.2.b. Types of Information Needed

Counselors explicitly explain to clients the nature of all services provided. They inform clients about issues such as, but not limited to, the following: the purposes, goals, techniques, procedures, limitations, potential risks, and benefits of services; the counselor's qualifications, credentials, and relevant experience; continuation of services upon the incapacitation or death of a counselor; and other pertinent information. Counselors take steps to ensure that clients understand the implications of diagnosis, the intended use of tests and reports, fees, and billing arrangements.

Clients have the right to confidentiality and to be provided with an explanation of its limitations (including how supervisors and/or treatment team professionals are involved); to obtain clear information about their records; to participate in the ongoing counseling plans; and to refuse any services or modality change and to be advised of the consequences of such refusal.

A.2.c. Developmental and Cultural Sensitivity

Counselors communicate information in ways that are both developmentally and culturally appropriate. Counselors use clear and understandable language when discussing issues related to informed consent. When clients have difficulty understanding the language used by counselors, they provide necessary services (e.g., arranging for a qualified interpreter or translator) to ensure comprehension by clients. In collaboration with clients, counselors consider cultural implications of informed consent procedures and, where possible, counselors adjust their practices accordingly.

A.2.d. Inability to Give Consent

When counseling minors or persons unable to give voluntary consent, counselors seek the assent of clients to services, and include them in decision making as appropriate. Counselors recognize the need to balance the ethical rights of clients to make choices, their capacity to give consent or assent to receive services, and parental or familial legal rights and responsibilities to protect these clients and make decisions on their behalf.

A.3. Clients Served by Others

When counselors learn that their clients are in a professional relationship with another mental health professional, they request release from clients to inform the other professionals and strive to establish positive and collaborative professional relationships.

A.4. Avoiding Harm and Imposing Values

A.4.a. Avoiding Harm
Counselors act to avoid harming their clients, trainees, and research participants and to minimize or to remedy unavoidable or unanticipated harm.

A.4.b. Personal Values
Counselors are aware of their own values, attitudes, beliefs, and behaviors and avoid imposing values that are inconsistent with counseling goals. Counselors respect the diversity of clients, trainees, and research participants.

A.5. Roles and Relationships With Clients
(See F.3., F.10., G.3.)

A.5.a. Current Clients
Sexual or romantic counselor–client interactions or relationships with current clients, their romantic partners, or their family members are prohibited.

A.5.b. Former Clients
Sexual or romantic counselor–client interactions or relationships with former clients, their romantic partners, or their family members are prohibited for a period of 5 years following the last professional contact. Counselors, before engaging in sexual or romantic interactions or relationships with clients, their romantic partners, or client family members after 5 years following the last professional contact, demonstrate forethought and document (in written form) whether the interactions or relationship can be viewed as exploitive in some way and/or whether there is still potential to harm the former client; in cases of potential exploitation and/or harm, the counselor avoids entering such an interaction or relationship.

A.5.c. Nonprofessional Interactions or Relationships (Other Than Sexual or Romantic Interactions or Relationships)
Counselor–client nonprofessional relationships with clients, former clients, their romantic partners, or their family members should be avoided, except when the inter-action is potentially beneficial to the client. (See A.5.d.)

A.5.d. Potentially Beneficial Interactions
When a counselor–client nonprofessional interaction with a client or former client may be potentially beneficial to the client or former client, the counselor must docu-ment in case records, prior to the interaction (when feasible), the rationale for such an interaction, the potential benefit, and anticipated consequences for the client or former client and other individuals significantly involved with the client or former cli-ent. Such interactions should be initiated with appropriate client consent. Where unintentional harm occurs to the client or former client, or to an individual signifi-cantly involved with the client or former client, due to the nonprofessional interac-tion, the counselor must show evidence of an attempt to remedy such harm. Examples of potentially beneficial interactions include, but are not limited to, attend-ing a formal ceremony (e.g., a wedding/commitment ceremony or graduation); pur-chasing a service or product provided by a client or former client (excepting unrestricted bartering); hospital visits to an ill family member; mutual membership in a professional association, organization, or community. (See A.5.c.)

A.5.e. Role Changes in the Professional Relationship

When a counselor changes a role from the original or most recent contracted relationship, he or she obtains informed consent from the client and explains the right of the client to refuse services related to the change. Examples of role changes include

1. changing from individual to relationship or family counseling, or vice versa;
2. changing from a nonforensic evaluative role to a therapeutic role, or vice versa;
3. changing from a counselor to a researcher role (i.e., enlisting clients as research participants), or vice versa; and
4. changing from a counselor to a mediator role, or vice versa.

Clients must be fully informed of any anticipated consequences (e.g., financial, legal, personal, or therapeutic) of counselor role changes.

A.6. Roles and Relationships at Individual, Group, Institutional, and Societal Levels

A.6.a. Advocacy

When appropriate, counselors advocate at individual, group, institutional, and societal levels to examine potential barriers and obstacles that inhibit access and/or the growth and development of clients.

A.6.b. Confidentiality and Advocacy

Counselors obtain client consent prior to engaging in advocacy efforts on behalf of an identifiable client to improve the provision of services and to work toward removal of systemic barriers or obstacles that inhibit client access, growth, and development.

A.7. Multiple Clients

When a counselor agrees to provide counseling services to two or more persons who have a relationship, the counselor clarifies at the outset which person or persons are clients and the nature of the relationships the counselor will have with each involved person. If it becomes apparent that the counselor may be called upon to perform potentially conflicting roles, the counselor will clarify, adjust, or withdraw from roles appropriately. (See A.8.a., B.4.)

A.8. Group Work

(See B.4.a.)

A.8.a. Screening

Counselors screen prospective group counseling/therapy participants. To the extent possible, counselors select members whose needs and goals are compatible with goals of the group, who will not impede the group process, and whose well-being will not be jeopardized by the group experience.

A.8.b. Protecting Clients

In a group setting, counselors take reasonable precautions to protect clients from physical, emotional, or psychological trauma.

A.9. End-of-Life Care for Terminally Ill Clients

A.9.a. Quality of Care

Counselors strive to take measures that enable clients

1. to obtain high quality end-of-life care for their physical, emotional, social, and spiritual needs;
2. to exercise the highest degree of self-determination possible;
3. to be given every opportunity possible to engage in informed decision making regarding their end-of-life care; and
4. to receive complete and adequate assessment regarding their ability to make competent, rational decisions on their own behalf from a mental health professional who is experienced in end-of-life care practice.

A.9.b. Counselor Competence, Choice, and Referral

Recognizing the personal, moral, and competence issues related to end-of-life decisions, counselors may choose to work or not work with terminally ill clients who wish to explore their end-of-life options. Counselors provide appropriate referral information to ensure that clients receive the necessary help.

A.9.c Confidentiality

Counselors who provide services to terminally ill individuals who are considering hastening their own deaths have the option of breaking or not breaking confidentiality, depending on applicable laws and the specific circumstances of the situation and after seeking consultation or supervision from appropriate professional and legal parties. (See B.5.c., B.7.c.)

A.10. Fees and Bartering

A.10.a. Accepting Fees From Agency Clients

Counselors refuse a private fee or other remuneration for rendering services to persons who are entitled to such services through the counselor's employing agency or institution. The policies of a particular agency may make explicit provisions for agency clients to receive counseling services from members of its staff in private practice. In such instances, the clients must be informed of other options open to them should they seek private counseling services.

A.10.b. Establishing Fees

In establishing fees for professional counseling services, counselors consider the financial status of clients and locality. In the event that the established fee structure is inappropriate for a client, counselors assist clients in attempting to find comparable services of acceptable cost.

A.10.c. Nonpayment of Fees

If counselors intend to use collection agencies or take legal measures to collect fees from clients who do not pay for services as agreed upon, they first inform clients of intended actions and offer clients the opportunity to make payment.

A.10.d. Bartering

Counselors may barter only if the relationship is not exploitive or harmful and does not place the counselor in an unfair advantage, if the client requests it, and if such arrangements are an accepted practice among professionals in the community. Counselors consider the cultural implications of bartering and discuss relevant concerns with clients and document such agreements in a clear written contract.

A.10.e. Receiving Gifts

Counselors understand the challenges of accepting gifts from clients and recognize that in some cultures, small gifts are a token of respect and showing gratitude. When determining whether or not to accept a gift from clients, counselors take into account the therapeutic relationship, the monetary value of the gift, a client's motivation for giving the gift, and the counselor's motivation for wanting or declining the gift.

A.11. Termination and Referral

A.11.a. Abandonment Prohibited

Counselors do not abandon or neglect clients in counseling. Counselors assist in making appropriate arrangements for the continuation of treatment, when necessary, during interruptions such as vacations, illness, and following termination.

A.11.b. Inability to Assist Clients

If counselors determine an inability to be of professional assistance to clients, they avoid entering or continuing counseling relationships. Counselors are knowledgeable about culturally and clinically appropriate referral resources and suggest these alternatives. If clients decline the suggested referrals, counselors should discontinue the relationship.

A.11.c. Appropriate Termination

Counselors terminate a counseling relationship when it becomes reasonably apparent that the client no longer needs assistance, is not likely to benefit, or is being harmed by continued counseling. Counselors may terminate counseling when in jeopardy of harm by the client, or another person with whom the client has a relationship, or when clients do not pay fees as agreed upon. Counselors provide pretermination counseling and recommend other service providers when necessary.

A.11.d. Appropriate Transfer of Services

When counselors transfer or refer clients to other practitioners, they ensure that appropriate clinical and administrative processes are completed and open communication is maintained with both clients and practitioners.

A.12. Technology Applications

A.12.a. Benefits and Limitations

Counselors inform clients of the benefits and limitations of using information technology applications in the counseling process and in business/ billing procedures. Such technologies include but are not limited to computer hardware and software, telephones, the World Wide Web, the Internet, online assessment instruments and other communication devices.

A.12.b. Technology-Assisted Services

When providing technology-assisted distance counseling services, counselors determine that clients are intellectually, emotionally, and physically capable of using the application and that the application is appropriate for the needs of clients.

A.12.c. Inappropriate Services

When technology-assisted distance counseling services are deemed inappropriate by the counselor or client, counselors consider delivering services face to face.

A.12.d. Access

Counselors provide reasonable access to computer applications when providing technology-assisted distance counseling services.

A.12.e. Laws and Statutes
Counselors ensure that the use of technology does not violate the laws of any local, state, national, or international entity and observe all relevant statutes.

A.12.f. Assistance
Counselors seek business, legal, and technical assistance when using technology applications, particularly when the use of such applications crosses state or national boundaries.

A.12.g. Technology and Informed Consent
As part of the process of establishing informed consent, counselors do the following:
1. Address issues related to the difficulty of maintaining the confidentiality of electronically transmitted communications.
2. Inform clients of all colleagues, supervisors, and employees, such as Informational Technology (IT) administrators, who might have authorized or unauthorized access to electronic transmissions.
3. Urge clients to be aware of all authorized or unauthorized users including family members and fellow employees who have access to any technology clients may use in the counseling process.
4. Inform clients of pertinent legal rights and limitations governing the practice of a profession over state lines or international boundaries.
5. Use encrypted Web sites and e-mail communications to help ensure confidentiality when possible.
6. When the use of encryption is not possible, counselors notify clients of this fact and limit electronic transmissions to general communications that are not client specific.
7. Inform clients if and for how long archival storage of transaction records are maintained.
8. Discuss the possibility of technology failure and alternate methods of service delivery.
9. Inform clients of emergency procedures, such as calling 911 or a local crisis hotline, when the counselor is not available.
10. Discuss time zone differences, local customs, and cultural or language differences that might impact service delivery.
11. Inform clients when technology-assisted distance counseling services are not covered by insurance. (See A.2.)

A.12.h. Sites on the World Wide Web
Counselors maintaining sites on the World Wide Web (the Internet) do the following:
1. Regularly check that electronic links are working and professionally appropriate.
2. Establish ways clients can contact the counselor in case of technology failure.
3. Provide electronic links to relevant state licensure and professional certification boards to protect consumer rights and facilitate addressing ethical concerns.
4. Establish a method for verifying client identity.
5. Obtain the written consent of the legal guardian or other authorized legal representative prior to rendering services in the event the client is a minor child, an adult who is legally incompetent, or an adult incapable of giving informed consent.
6. Strive to provide a site that is accessible to persons with disabilities.

7. Strive to provide translation capabilities for clients who have a different primary language while also addressing the imperfect nature of such translations.
8. Assist clients in determining the validity and reliability of information found on the World Wide Web and other technology applications.

Section B: Confidentiality, Privileged Communication, and Privacy

Introduction

Counselors recognize that trust is a cornerstone of the counseling relationship. Counselors aspire to earn the trust of clients by creating an ongoing partnership, establishing and upholding appropriate boundaries, and maintaining confidentiality. Counselors communicate the parameters of confidentiality in a culturally competent manner.

B.1. Respecting Client Rights

B.1.a. Multicultural/Diversity Considerations

Counselors maintain awareness and sensitivity regarding cultural meanings of confidentiality and privacy. Counselors respect differing views toward disclosure of information. Counselors hold ongoing discussions with clients as to how, when, and with whom information is to be shared.

B.1.b. Respect for Privacy

Counselors respect client rights to privacy. Counselors solicit private information from clients only when it is beneficial to the counseling process.

B.1.c. Respect for Confidentiality

Counselors do not share confidential information without client consent or without sound legal or ethical justification.

B.1.d. Explanation of Limitations

At initiation and throughout the counseling process, counselors inform clients of the limitations of confidentiality and seek to identify foreseeable situations in which confidentiality must be breached. (See A.2.b.)

B.2. Exceptions

B.2.a. Danger and Legal Requirements

The general requirement that counselors keep information confidential does not apply when disclosure is required to protect clients or identified others from serious and foreseeable harm or when legal requirements demand that confidential information must be revealed. Counselors consult with other professionals when in doubt as to the validity of an exception. Additional considerations apply when addressing end-of-life issues. (See A.9.c.)

B.2.b. Contagious, Life-Threatening Diseases

When clients disclose that they have a disease commonly known to be both communicable and life threatening, counselors may be justified in disclosing information to identifiable third parties, if they are known to be at demonstrable and high risk of contracting the disease. Prior to making a disclosure, counselors confirm that there is such a diagnosis and assess the intent of clients to inform the third parties about their disease or to engage in any behaviors that may be harmful to an identifiable third party.

B.2.c. Court-Ordered Disclosure

When subpoenaed to release confidential or privileged information without a client's permission, counselors obtain written, informed consent from the client or take steps to prohibit the disclosure or have it limited as narrowly as possible due to potential harm to the client or counseling relationship.

B.2.d. Minimal Disclosure

To the extent possible, clients are informed before confidential information is disclosed and are involved in the disclosure decision-making process. When circumstances require the disclosure of confidential information, only essential information is revealed.

B.3. Information Shared With Others

B.3.a. Subordinates

Counselors make every effort to ensure that privacy and confidentiality of clients are maintained by subordinates, including employees, supervisees, students, clerical assistants, and volunteers. (See F.1.c.)

B.3.b. Treatment Teams

When client treatment involves a continued review or participation by a treatment team, the client will be informed of the team's existence and composition, information being shared, and the purposes of sharing such information.

B.3.c. Confidential Settings

Counselors discuss confidential information only in settings in which they can reasonably ensure client privacy.

B.3.d. Third-Party Payers

Counselors disclose information to third-party payers only when clients have authorized such disclosure.

B.3.e. Transmitting Confidential Information

Counselors take precautions to ensure the confidentiality of information transmitted through the use of computers, electronic mail, facsimile machines, telephones, voicemail, answering machines, and other electronic or computer technology. *(See A.12.g.)*

B.3.f. Deceased Clients

Counselors protect the confidentiality of deceased clients, consistent with legal requirements and agency or setting policies.

B.4. Groups and Families

B.4.a. Group Work

In group work, counselors clearly explain the importance and parameters of confidentiality for the specific group being entered.

B.4.b. Couples and Family Counseling

In couples and family counseling, counselors clearly define who is considered "the client" and discuss expectations and limitations of confidentiality. Counselors seek agreement and document in writing such agreement among all involved parties having capacity to give consent concerning each individual's right to confidentiality and any obligation to preserve the confidentiality of information known.

B.5. Clients Lacking Capacity to Give Informed Consent

B.5.a. Responsibility to Clients

When counseling minor clients or adult clients who lack the capacity to give voluntary, informed consent, counselors protect the confidentiality of information received in the counseling relationship as specified by federal and state laws, written policies, and applicable ethical standards.

B.5.b. Responsibility to Parents and Legal Guardians

Counselors inform parents and legal guardians about the role of counselors and the confidential nature of the counseling relationship. Counselors are sensitive to the cultural diversity of families and respect the inherent rights and responsibilities of parents/guardians over the welfare of their children/charges according to law. Counselors work to establish, as appropriate, collaborative relationships with parents/guardians to best serve clients.

B.5.c. Release of Confidential Information

When counseling minor clients or adult clients who lack the capacity to give voluntary consent to release confidential information, counselors seek permission from an appropriate third party to disclose information. In such instances, counselors inform clients consistent with their level of understanding and take culturally appropriate measures to safeguard client confidentiality.

B.6. Records

B.6.a. Confidentiality of Records

Counselors ensure that records are kept in a secure location and that only authorized persons have access to records.

B.6.b. Permission to Record

Counselors obtain permission from clients prior to recording sessions through electronic or other means.

B.6.c. Permission to Observe

Counselors obtain permission from clients prior to observing counseling sessions, reviewing session transcripts, or viewing recordings of sessions with supervisors, faculty, peers, or others within the training environment.

B.6.d. Client Access

Counselors provide reasonable access to records and copies of records when requested by competent clients. Counselors limit the access of clients to their records, or portions of their records, only when there is compelling evidence that such access would cause harm to the client. Counselors document the request of clients and the rationale for withholding some or all of the record in the files of clients. In situations involving multiple clients, counselors provide individual clients with only those parts of records that related directly to them and do not include confidential information related to any other client.

B.6.e. Assistance With Records

When clients request access to their records, counselors provide assistance and consultation in interpreting counseling records.

B.6.f. Disclosure or Transfer

Unless exceptions to confidentiality exist, counselors obtain written permission from clients to disclose or transfer records to legitimate third parties. Steps are taken to ensure that receivers of counseling records are sensitive to their confidential nature. *(See A.3., E.4.)*

B.6.g. Storage and Disposal After Termination

Counselors store records following termination of services to ensure reasonable future access, maintain records in accordance with state and federal statutes governing records, and dispose of client records and other sensitive materials in a manner that protects client confidentiality. When records are of an artistic nature, counselors obtain client (or guardian) consent with regards to handling of such records or documents. *(See A.1.b.)*

B.6.h. Reasonable Precautions

Counselors take reasonable precautions to protect client confidentiality in the event of the counselor's termination of practice, incapacity, or death. *(See C.2.h.)*

B.7. Research and Training

B.7.a. Institutional Approval

When institutional approval is required, counselors provide accurate information about their research proposals and obtain approval prior to conducting their research. They conduct research in accordance with the approved research protocol.

B.7.b. Adherence to Guidelines

Counselors are responsible for understanding and adhering to state, federal, agency, or institutional policies or applicable guidelines regarding confidentiality in their research practices.

B.7.c. Confidentiality of Information Obtained in Research

Violations of participant privacy and confidentiality are risks of participation in research involving human participants. Investigators maintain all research records in a secure manner. They explain to participants the risks of violations of privacy and confidentiality and disclose to participants any limits of confidentiality that reasonably can be expected. Regardless of the degree to which confidentiality will be maintained, investigators must disclose to participants any limits of confidentiality that reasonably can be expected. *(See G.2.e.)*

B.7.d. Disclosure of Research Information

Counselors do not disclose confidential information that reasonably could lead to the identification of a research participant unless they have obtained the prior consent of the person. Use of data derived from counseling relationships for purposes of training, research, or publication is confined to content that is disguised to ensure the anonymity of the individuals involved. *(See G.2.a., G.2.d.)*

B.7.e. Agreement for Identification

Identification of clients, students, or supervisees in a presentation or publication is permissible only when they have reviewed the material and agreed to its presentation or publication. *(See G.4.d.)*

B.8. Consultation

B.8.a. Agreements

When acting as consultants, counselors seek agreements among all parties involved concerning each individual's rights to confidentiality, the obligation of each individual to preserve confidential information, and the limits of confidentiality of information shared by others.

B.8.b. Respect for Privacy

Information obtained in a consulting relationship is discussed for professional purposes only with persons directly involved with the case. Written and oral reports present only data germane to the purposes of the consultation, and every effort is made to protect client identity and to avoid undue invasion of privacy.

B.8.c. Disclosure of Confidential Information

When consulting with colleagues, counselors do not disclose confidential information that reasonably could lead to the identification of a client or other person or organization with whom they have a confidential relationship unless they have obtained the prior consent of the person or organization or the disclosure cannot be avoided. They disclose information only to the extent necessary to achieve the purposes of the consultation. *(See D.2.d.)*

Section C: Professional Responsibility

Introduction

Counselors aspire to open, honest, and accurate communication in dealing with the public and other professionals. They practice in a non-discriminatory manner within the boundaries of professional and personal competence and have a responsibility to abide by the *ACA Code of Ethics*. Counselors actively participate in local, state, and national associations that foster the development and improvement of counseling. Counselors advocate to promote change at the individual, group, institutional, and societal levels that improve the quality of life for individuals and groups and remove potential barriers to the provision or access of appropriate services being offered. Counselors have a responsibility to the public to engage in counseling practices that are based on rigorous research methodologies. In addition, counselors engage in self-care activities to maintain and promote their emotional, physical, mental, and spiritual well-being to best meet their professional responsibilities.

C.1. Knowledge of Standards

Counselors have a responsibility to read, understand, and follow the *ACA Code of Ethics* and adhere to applicable laws and regulations.

C.2. Professional Competence

C.2.a. Boundaries of Competence

Counselors practice only within the boundaries of their competence, based on their education, training, supervised experience, state and national professional credentials, and appropriate professional experience. Counselors gain knowledge, personal awareness, sensitivity, and skills pertinent to working with a diverse client population. *(See A.9.b., C.4.e., E.2., F.2., F.11.b.)*

C.2.b. New Specialty Areas of Practice

Counselors practice in specialty areas new to them only after appropriate education, training, and supervised experience. While developing skills in new specialty areas, counselors take steps to ensure the competence of their work and to protect others from possible harm. *(See F.6.f.)*

C.2.c. Qualified for Employment

Counselors accept employment only for positions for which they are qualified by education, training, supervised experience, state and national professional credentials, and appropriate professional experience. Counselors hire for professional counseling positions only individuals who are qualified and competent for those positions.

C.2.d. Monitor Effectiveness

Counselors continually monitor their effectiveness as professionals and take steps to improve when necessary. Counselors in private practice take reasonable steps to seek peer supervision as needed to evaluate their efficacy as counselors.

C.2.e. Consultation on Ethical Obligations

Counselors take reasonable steps to consult with other counselors or related professionals when they have questions regarding their ethical obligations or professional practice.

C.2.f. Continuing Education

Counselors recognize the need for continuing education to acquire and maintain a reasonable level of awareness of current scientific and professional information in their fields of activity. They take steps to maintain competence in the skills they use, are open to new procedures, and keep current with the diverse populations and specific populations with whom they work.

C.2.g. Impairment

Counselors are alert to the signs of impairment from their own physical, mental, or emotional problems and refrain from offering or providing professional services when such impairment is likely to harm a client or others. They seek assistance for problems that reach the level of professional impairment, and, if necessary, they limit, suspend, or terminate their professional responsibilities until such time it is determined that they may safely resume their work. Counselors assist colleagues or supervisors in recognizing their own professional impairment and provide consultation and assistance when warranted with colleagues or supervisors showing signs of impairment and intervene as appropriate to prevent imminent harm to clients. *(See A.11.b., F.8.b.)*

C.2.h. Counselor Incapacitation or Termination of Practice

When counselors leave a practice, they follow a prepared plan for transfer of clients and files. Counselors prepare and disseminate to an identified colleague or "records custodian" a plan for the transfer of clients and files in the case of their incapacitation, death, or termination of practice.

C.3. Advertising and Soliciting Clients

C.3.a. Accurate Advertising

When advertising or otherwise representing their services to the public, counselors identify their credentials in an accurate manner that is not false, misleading, deceptive, or fraudulent.

C.3.b. Testimonials

Counselors who use testimonials do not solicit them from current clients nor former clients nor any other persons who may be vulnerable to undue influence.

C.3.c. Statements by Others

Counselors make reasonable efforts to ensure that statements made by others about them or the profession of counseling are accurate.

C.3.d. Recruiting Through Employment

Counselors do not use their places of employment or institutional affiliation to recruit or gain clients, supervisees, or consultees for their private practices.

C.3.e. Products and Training Advertisements

Counselors who develop products related to their profession or conduct workshops or training events ensure that the advertisements concerning these products or events are accurate and disclose adequate information for consumers to make informed choices. *(See C.6.d.)*

C.3.f. Promoting to Those Served

Counselors do not use counseling, teaching, training, or supervisory relationships to promote their products or training events in a manner that is deceptive or would exert undue influence on individuals who may be vulnerable. However, counselor educators may adopt textbooks they have authored for instructional purposes.

C.4. Professional Qualifications

C.4.a. Accurate Representation

Counselors claim or imply only professional qualifications actually completed and correct any known misrepresentations of their qualifications by others. Counselors truthfully represent the qualifications of their professional colleagues. Counselors clearly distinguish between paid and volunteer work experience and accurately describe their continuing education and specialized training. *(See C.2.a.)*

C.4.b. Credentials

Counselors claim only licenses or certifications that are current and in good standing.

C.4.c. Educational Degrees

Counselors clearly differentiate between earned and honorary degrees.

C.4.d. Implying Doctoral-Level Competence

Counselors clearly state their highest earned degree in counseling or closely related field. Counselors do not imply doctoral-level competence when only possessing a master's degree in counseling or a related field by referring to themselves as "Dr." in a counseling context when their doctorate is not in counseling or related field.

C.4.e. Program Accreditation Status

Counselors clearly state the accreditation status of their degree programs at the time the degree was earned.

C.4.f. Professional Membership

Counselors clearly differentiate between current, active memberships and former memberships in associations. Members of the American Counseling Association must clearly differentiate between professional membership, which implies the possession of at least a master's degree in counseling, and regular membership, which is open to individuals whose interests and activities are consistent with those of ACA but are not qualified for professional membership.

C.5. Nondiscrimination

Counselors do not condone or engage in discrimination based on age, culture, disability, ethnicity, race, religion/spirituality, gender, gender identity, sexual orientation, marital status/partnership, language preference, socioeconomic status, or any basis proscribed by law. Counselors do not discriminate against clients, students, employees, supervisees, or research participants in a manner that has a negative impact on these persons.

C.6. Public Responsibility

C.6.a. Sexual Harassment
Counselors do not engage in or condone sexual harassment. Sexual harassment is defined as sexual solicitation, physical advances, or verbal or nonverbal conduct that is sexual in nature, that occurs in connection with professional activities or roles, and that either 1. is unwelcome, is offensive, or creates a hostile workplace or learning environment, and counselors know or are told this; or 2. is sufficiently severe or intense to be perceived as harassment to a reasonable person in the context in which the behavior occurred. Sexual harassment can consist of a single intense or severe act or multiple persistent or pervasive acts.

C.6.b. Reports to Third Parties
Counselors are accurate, honest, and objective in reporting their professional activities and judgments to appropriate third parties, including courts, health insurance companies, those who are the recipients of evaluation reports, and others. *(See B.3., E.4.)*

C.6.c. Media Presentations
When counselors provide advice or comment by means of public lectures, demonstrations, radio or television programs, prerecorded tapes, technology-based applications, printed articles, mailed material, or other media, they take reasonable precautions to ensure that 1. the statements are based on appropriate professional counseling literature and practice, 2. the statements are otherwise consistent with the *ACA Code of Ethics,* and 3. the recipients of the information are not encouraged to infer that a professional counseling relationship has been established.

C.6.d. Exploitation of Others
Counselors do not exploit others in their professional relationships. *(See C.3.e.)*

C.6.e. Scientific Bases for Treatment Modalities
Counselors use techniques/ procedures/modalities that are grounded in. They participate in and contribute to decisions that affect the well-being of clients by drawing on the perspectives, values, and experiences of the counseling profession and those of colleagues from other disciplines. *(See A.1.a.)*

C.7. Responsibility to Other Professionals

C.7.a. Personal Public Statements
When making personal statements in a public context, counselors clarify that they are speaking from their personal perspectives and that they are not speaking on behalf of all counselors or the profession.

Section D: Relationships With Other Professionals

Introduction
Professional counselors recognize that the quality of their interactions with colleagues can influence the quality of services provided to clients. They work to become knowledgeable about colleagues within and outside the field of counseling. Counselors

develop positive working relationships and systems of communication with colleagues to enhance services to clients.

D.1. Relationships With Colleagues, Employers, and Employees

D.1.a. Different Approaches
Counselors are respectful of approaches to counseling services that differ from their own. Counselors are respectful of traditions and practices of other professional groups with which they work.

D.1.b. Forming Relationships
Counselors work to develop and strengthen interdisciplinary relations with colleagues from other disciplines to best serve clients.

D.1.c. Interdisciplinary Teamwork
Counselors who are members of interdisciplinary teams delivering multifaceted services to clients, keep the focus on how to best serve the clients, to expose inappropriate employer policies or practices.

D.1.d. Confidentiality
When counselors are required by law, institutional policy, or extraordinary circumstances to serve in more than one role in judicial or administrative proceedings, they clarify role expectations and the parameters of confidentiality with their colleagues. (See B.1.c., B.1.d., B.2.c., B.2.d., B.3.b.)

D.1.e. Establishing Professional and Ethical Obligations
Counselors who are members of interdisciplinary teams clarify professional and ethical obligations of the team as a whole and of its individual members. When a team decision raises ethical concerns, counselors first attempt to resolve the concern within the team. If they cannot reach resolution among team members, counselors pursue other avenues to address their concerns consistent with client well-being.

D.1.f. Personnel Selection and Assignment
Counselors select competent staff and assign responsibilities compatible with their skills and experiences.

D.1.g. Employer Policies
The acceptance of employment in an agency or institution implies that counselors are in agreement with its general policies and principles. Counselors strive to reach agreement with employers as to acceptable standards of conduct that allow for changes in institutional policy conducive to the growth and development of clients.

D.1.h. Negative Conditions
Counselors alert their employers of inappropriate policies and practices. They attempt to effect changes in such policies or procedures through constructive action within the organization. When such policies are potentially disruptive or damaging to clients or may limit the effectiveness of services provided and change cannot be effected, counselors take appropriate further action. Such action may include referral to appropriate certification, accreditation, or state licensure organizations, or voluntary termination of employment.

D.1.i. Protection From Punitive Action
Counselors take care not to harass or dismiss an employee who has acted in a responsible and ethical manner theory and/or have an empirical or scientific foundation. Counselors who do not must define the techniques/procedures as "unproven" or

"developing" and explain the potential risks and ethical considerations of using such techniques/procedures and take steps to protect clients from possible harm. *(See A.4.a., E.5.c., E.5.d.)*

D.2. Consultation

D.2.a. Consultant Competency
Counselors take reasonable steps to ensure that they have the appropriate resources and competencies when providing consultation services. Counselors provide appropriate referral resources when requested or needed. *(See C.2.a.)*

D.2.b. Understanding Consultees
When providing consultation, counselors attempt to develop with their consultees a clear understanding of problem definition, goals for change, and predicted consequences of interventions selected.

D.2.c. Consultant Goals
The consulting relationship is one in which consultee adaptability and growth toward self-direction are consistently encouraged and cultivated.

D.2.d. Informed Consent in Consultation
When providing consultation, counselors have an obligation to review, in writing and verbally, the rights and responsibilities of both counselors and consultees. Counselors use clear and understandable language to inform all parties involved about the purpose of the services to be provided, relevant costs, potential risks and benefits, and the limits of confidentiality. Working in conjunction with the consultee, counselors attempt to develop a clear definition of the problem, goals for change, and predicted consequences of interventions that are culturally responsive and appropriate to the needs of consultees. *(See A.2.a., A.2.b.)*

Section E: Evaluation, Assessment, and Interpretation

Introduction
Counselors use assessment instruments as one component of the counseling process, taking into account the client personal and cultural context. Counselors promote the well-being of individual clients or groups of clients by developing and using appropriate educational, psychological, and career assessment instruments.

E.1. General

E.1.a. Assessment
The primary purpose of educational, psychological, and career assessment is to provide measurements that are valid and reliable in either comparative or absolute terms. These include, but are not limited to, measurements of ability, personality, interest, intelligence, achievement, and performance. Counselors recognize the need to interpret the statements in this section as applying to both quantitative and qualitative assessments.

E.1.b. Client Welfare
Counselors do not misuse assessment results and interpretations, and they take reasonable steps to prevent others from misusing the information these techniques provide. They respect the client's right to know the results, the interpretations made, and the bases for counselors' conclusions and recommendations.

E.2. Competence to Use and Interpret Assessment Instruments

E.2.a. Limits of Competence

Counselors utilize only those testing and assessment services for which they have been trained and are competent. Counselors using technology assisted test interpretations are trained in the construct being measured and the specific instrument being used prior to using its technology based application. Counselors take reasonable measures to ensure the proper use of psychological and career assessment techniques by persons under their supervision. *(See A.12.)*

E.2.b. Appropriate Use

Counselors are responsible for the appropriate application, scoring, interpretation, and use of assessment instruments relevant to the needs of the client, whether they score and interpret such assessments themselves or use technology or other services.

E.2.c. Decisions Based on Results

Counselors responsible for decisions involving individuals or policies that are based on assessment results have a thorough understanding of educational, psychological, and career measurement, including validation criteria, assessment research, and guidelines for assessment development and use.

E.3. Informed Consent in Assessment

E.3.a. Explanation to Clients

Prior to assessment, counselors explain the nature and purposes of assessment and the specific use of results by potential recipients. The explanation will be given in the language of the client (or other legally authorized person on behalf of the client), unless an explicit exception has been agreed upon in advance. Counselors consider the client's personal or cultural context, the level of the client's understanding of the results, and the impact of the results on the client. *(See A.2., A.12.g., F.1.c.)*

E.3.b. Recipients of Results

Counselors consider the examinee's welfare, explicit understandings, and prior agreements in determining who receives the assessment results. Counselors include accurate and appropriate interpretations with any release of individual or group assessment results. *(See B.2.c., B.5.)*

E.4. Release of Data to Qualified Professionals

Counselors release assessment data in which the client is identified only with the consent of the client or the client's legal representative. Such data are released only to persons recognized by counselors as qualified to interpret the data. *(See B.1., B.3., B.6.b.)*

E.5. Diagnosis of Mental Disorders

E.5.a. Proper Diagnosis

Counselors take special care to provide proper diagnosis of mental disorders. Assessment techniques (including personal interview) used to determine client care (e.g., locus of treatment, type of treatment, or recommended follow-up) are carefully selected and appropriately used.

E.5.b. Cultural Sensitivity

Counselors recognize that culture affects the manner in which clients' problems are defined. Clients' socioeconomic and cultural experiences are considered when diagnosing mental disorders. *(See A.2.c.)*

E.5.c. Historical and Social Prejudices in the Diagnosis of Pathology

Counselors recognize historical and social prejudices in the misdiagnosis and pathologizing of certain individuals and groups and the role of mental health professionals in perpetuating these prejudices through diagnosis and treatment.

E.5.d. Refraining From Diagnosis

Counselors may refrain from making and/or reporting a diagnosis if they believe it would cause harm to the client or others.

E.6. Instrument Selection

E.6.a. Appropriateness of Instruments

Counselors carefully consider the validity, reliability, psychometric limitations, and appropriateness of instruments when selecting assessments.

E.6.b. Referral Information

If a client is referred to a third party for assessment, the counselor provides specific referral questions and sufficient objective data about the client to ensure that appropriate assessment instruments are utilized. *(See A.9.b., B.3.)*

E.6.c. Culturally Diverse Populations

Counselors are cautious when selecting assessments for culturally diverse populations to avoid the use of instruments that lack appropriate psychometric properties for the client population. *(See A.2.c., E.5.b.)*

E.7. Conditions of Assessment Administration *(See A.12.b., A.12.d.)*

E.7.a. Administration Conditions

Counselors administer assessments under the same conditions that were established in their standardization. When assessments are not administered under standard conditions, as may be necessary to accommodate clients with disabilities, or when unusual behavior or irregularities occur during the administration, those conditions are noted in interpretation, and the results may be designated as invalid or of questionable validity.

E.7.b. Technological Administration

Counselors ensure that administration programs function properly and provide clients with accurate results when technological or other electronic methods are used for assessment administration.

E.7.c. Unsupervised Assessments

Unless the assessment instrument is designed, intended, and validated for self-administration and/or scoring, counselors do not permit inadequately supervised use.

E.7.d. Disclosure of Favorable Conditions

Prior to administration of assessments, conditions that produce most favorable assessment results are made known to the examinee.

E.8. Multicultural Issues/Diversity in Assessment

Counselors use with caution assessment techniques that were normed on populations other than that of the client. Counselors recognize the effects of age, color, culture, disability, ethnic group, gender, race, language preference, religion, spirituality, sexual orientation, and socioeconomic status on test administration and interpretation, and place test results in proper perspective with other relevant factors. *(See A.2.c., E.5.b.)*

E.9. Scoring and Interpretation of Assessments

E.9.a. Reporting
In reporting assessment results, counselors indicate reservations that exist regarding validity or reliability due to circumstances of the assessment or the inappropriateness of the norms for the person tested.

E.9.b. Research Instruments
Counselors exercise caution when interpreting the results of research instruments not having sufficient technical data to support respondent results. The specific purposes for the use of such instruments are stated explicitly to the examinee.

E.9.c. Assessment Services
Counselors who provide assessment scoring and interpretation services to support the assessment process confirm the validity of such interpretations. They accurately describe the purpose, norms, validity, reliability, and applications of the procedures and any special qualifications applicable to their use. The public offering of an auto-mated test interpretations service is considered a professional-to-professional consul-tation. The formal responsibility of the consultant is to the consultee, but the ultimate and overriding responsibility is to the client. *(See D.2.)*

E.10. Assessment Security

Counselors maintain the integrity and security of tests and other assessment techni-ques consistent with legal and contractual obligations. Counselors do not appropriate, reproduce, or modify published assessments or parts thereof without acknowledg-ment and permission from the publisher.

E.11. Obsolete Assessments and Outdated Results

Counselors do not use data or results from assessments that are obsolete or outdated for the current purpose. Counselors make every effort to prevent the misuse of obso-lete measures and assessment data by others.

E.12. Assessment Construction

Counselors use established scientific procedures, relevant standards, and current pro-fessional knowledge for assessment design in the development, publication, and utili-zation of educational and psychological assessment techniques.

E.13. Forensic Evaluation: Evaluation for Legal Proceedings

E.13.a. Primary Obligations
When providing forensic evaluations, the primary obligation of counselors is to pro-duce objective findings that can be substantiated based on information and techni-ques appropriate to the evaluation, which may include examination of the individual and/or review of records. Counselors are entitled to form professional opinions based on their professional knowledge and expertise that can be supported by the data

gathered in evaluations. Counselors will define the limits of their reports or testimony, especially when an examination of the individual has not been conducted.

E.13.b. Consent for Evaluation

Individuals being evaluated are informed in writing that the relationship is for the purposes of an evaluation and is not counseling in nature, and entities or individuals who will receive the evaluation report are identified. Written consent to be evaluated is obtained from those being evaluated unless a court orders evaluations to be conducted without the written consent of individuals being evaluated. When children or vulnerable adults are being evaluated, informed written consent is obtained from a parent or guardian.

E.13.c. Client Evaluation Prohibited

Counselors do not evaluate individuals for forensic purposes they currently counsel or individuals they have counseled in the past. Counselors do not accept as counseling clients individuals they are evaluating or individuals they have evaluated in the past for forensic purposes.

E.13.d. Avoid Potentially Harmful Relationships

Counselors who provide forensic evaluations avoid potentially harmful professional or personal relationships with family members, romantic partners, and close friends of individuals they are evaluating or have evaluated in the past.

Section F: Supervision, Training, and Teaching

Introduction

Counselors aspire to foster meaningful and respectful professional relationships and to maintain appropriate boundaries with supervisees and students. Counselors have theoretical and pedagogical foundations for their work and aim to be fair, accurate, and honest in their assessments of counselors-in-training.

F.1. Counselor Supervision and Client Welfare

F.1.a. Client Welfare

A primary obligation of counseling supervisors is to monitor the services provided by other counselors or counselors-in-training. Counseling supervisors monitor client welfare and supervisee clinical performance and professional development. To fulfill these obligations, supervisors meet regularly with supervisees to review case notes, samples of clinical work, or live observations. Supervisees have a responsibility to understand and follow the *ACA Code of Ethics*.

F.1.b. Counselor Credentials

Counseling supervisors work to ensure that clients are aware of the qualifications of the supervisees who render services to the clients. *(See A.2.b.)*

F.1.c. Informed Consent and Client Rights

Supervisors make supervisees aware of client rights including the protection of client privacy and confidentiality in the counseling relationship. Supervisees provide clients with professional disclosure information and inform them of how the supervision process influences the limits of confidentiality. Supervisees make clients aware of who will have access to records of the counseling relationship and how these records will be used. *(See A.2.b., B.1.d.)*

F.2. Counselor Supervision Competence

F.2.a. Supervisor Preparation

Prior to offering clinical supervision services, counselors are trained in supervision methods and techniques. Counselors who offer clinical supervision services regularly pursue continuing education activities including both counseling and supervision topics and skills. *(See C.2.a., C.2.f.)*

F.2.b. Multicultural Issues/Diversity in Supervision

Counseling supervisors are aware of and address the role of multiculturalism/diversity in the supervisory relationship.

F.3. Supervisory Relationships

F.3.a. Relationship Boundaries With Supervisees

Counseling supervisors clearly define and maintain ethical professional, personal, and social relationships with their supervisees. Counseling supervisors avoid nonprofessional relationships with current supervisees. If supervisors must assume other professional roles (e.g., clinical and administrative supervisor, instructor) with supervisees, they work to minimize potential conflicts and explain to supervisees the expectations and responsibilities associated with each role. They do not engage in any form of nonprofessional interaction that may compromise the supervisory relationship.

F.3.b. Sexual Relationships

Sexual or romantic interactions or relationships with current supervisees are prohibited.

F.3.c. Sexual Harassment

Counseling supervisors do not condone or subject supervisees to sexual harassment. *(See C.6.a.)*

F.3.d. Close Relatives and Friends

Counseling supervisors avoid accepting close relatives, romantic partners, or friends as supervisees.

F.3.e. Potentially Beneficial Relationships

Counseling supervisors are aware of the power differential in their relationships with supervisees. If they believe nonprofessional relationships with a supervisee may be potentially beneficial to the supervisee, they take precautions similar to those taken by counselors when working with clients. Examples of potentially beneficial interactions or relationships include attending a formal ceremony; hospital visits; providing support during a stressful event; or mutual membership in a professional association, organization, or community. Counseling supervisors engage in open discussions with supervisees when they consider entering into relationships with them outside of their roles as clinical and/or administrative supervisors. Before engaging in nonprofessional relationships, supervisors discuss with supervisees and document the rationale for such interactions, potential benefits or drawbacks, and anticipated consequences for the supervisee. Supervisors clarify the specific nature and limitations of the additional role(s) they will have with the supervisee.

F.4. Supervisor Responsibilities

F.4.a. Informed Consent for Supervision

Supervisors are responsible for incorporating into their supervision the principles of informed consent and participation. Supervisors inform supervisees of the policies and procedures to which they are to adhere and the mechanisms for due process appeal of individual supervisory actions.

F.4.b. Emergencies and Absences

Supervisors establish and communicate to supervisees procedures for contacting them or, in their absence, alternative on-call supervisors to assist in handling crises.

F.4.c. Standards for Supervisees

Supervisors make their supervisees aware of professional and ethical standards and legal responsibilities. Supervisors of postdegree counselors encourage these counselors to adhere to professional standards of practice. *(See C.1.)*

F.4.d. Termination of the Supervisory Relationship

Supervisors or supervisees have the right to terminate the supervisory relationship with adequate notice. Reasons for withdrawal are provided to the other party. When cultural, clinical, or professional issues are crucial to the viability of the supervisory relationship, both parties make efforts to resolve differences. When termination is warranted, supervisors make appropriate referrals to possible alternative supervisors.

F.5. Counseling Supervision Evaluation, Remediation, and Endorsement

F.5.a. Evaluation

Supervisors document and provide supervisees with ongoing performance appraisal and evaluation feedback and schedule periodic formal evaluative sessions throughout the supervisory relationship.

F.5.b. Limitations

Through ongoing evaluation and appraisal, supervisors are aware of the limitations of supervisees that might impede performance. Supervisors assist supervisees in securing remedial assistance when needed. They recommend dismissal from training programs, applied counseling settings, or state or voluntary professional credentialing processes when those supervisees are unable to provide competent professional services. Supervisors seek consultation and document their decisions to dismiss or refer supervisees for assistance. They ensure that supervisees are aware of options available to them to address such decisions. *(See C.2.g.)*

F.5.c. Counseling for Supervisees

If supervisees request counseling, supervisors provide them with acceptable referrals. Counselors do not provide counseling services to supervisees. Supervisors address interpersonal competencies in terms of the impact of these issues on clients, the supervisory relationship, and professional functioning. *(See F.3.a.)*

F.5.d. Endorsement

Supervisors endorse supervisees for certification, licensure, employment, or completion of an academic or training program only when they believe supervisees are qualified for the endorsement. Regardless of qualifications, supervisors do not endorse supervisees whom they believe to be impaired in any way that would interfere with the performance of the duties associated with the endorsement.

F.6. Responsibilities of Counselor Educators

F.6.a. Counselor Educators

Counselor educators who are responsible for developing, implementing, and supervising educational programs are skilled as teachers and practitioners. They are knowledgeable regarding the ethical, legal, and regulatory aspects of the profession, are skilled in applying that knowledge, and make students and supervisees aware of their responsibilities. Counselor educators conduct counselor education and training programs in an ethical manner and serve as role models for professional behavior. *(See C.1., C.2.a., C.2.c.)*

F.6.b. Infusing Multicultural Issues/Diversity

Counselor educators infuse material related to multiculturalism/diversity into all courses and workshops for the development of professional counselors.

F.6.c. Integration of Study and Practice

Counselor educators establish education and training programs that integrate academic study and supervised practice.

F.6.d. Teaching Ethics

Counselor educators make students and supervisees aware of the ethical responsibilities and standards of the profession and the ethical responsibilities of students to the profession. Counselor educators infuse ethical considerations throughout the curriculum. *(See C.1.)*

F.6.e. Peer Relationships

Counselor educators make every effort to ensure that the rights of peers are not compromised when students or supervisees lead counseling groups or provide clinical supervision. Counselor educators take steps to ensure that students and supervisees understand they have the same ethical obligations as counselor educators, trainers, and supervisors.

F.6.f. Innovative Theories and Techniques

When counselor educators teach counseling techniques/procedures that are innovative, without an empirical foundation, or without a well-grounded theoretical foundation, they define the counseling techniques/procedures as "unproven" or "developing" and explain to students the potential risks and ethical considerations of using such techniques/procedures.

F.6.g. Field Placements

Counselor educators develop clear policies within their training programs regarding field placement and other clinical experiences. Counselor educators provide clearly stated roles and responsibilities for the student or supervisee, the site supervisor, and the program supervisor. They confirm that site supervisors are qualified to provide supervision and inform site supervisors of their professional and ethical responsibilities in this role.

F.6.h. Professional Disclosure

Before initiating counseling services, counselors-in-training disclose their status as students and explain how this status affects the limits of confidentiality. Counselor educators ensure that the clients at field placements are aware of the services rendered and the qualifications of the students and supervisees rendering those services. Students and supervisees obtain client permission before they use any information concerning the counseling relationship in the training process. *(See A.2.b.)*

F.7. Student Welfare

F.7.a. Orientation

Counselor educators recognize that orientation is a developmental process that continues throughout the educational and clinical training of students. Counseling faculty provide prospective students with information about the counselor education program's expectations:

1. the type and level of skill and knowledge acquisition required for successful completion of the training;
2. program training goals, objectives, and mission, and subject matter to be covered;
3. bases for evaluation;
4. training components that encourage self-growth or self-disclosure as part of the training process;
5. the type of supervision settings and requirements of the sites for required clinical field experiences;
6. student and supervisee evaluation and dismissal policies and procedures; and
7. up-to-date employment prospects for graduates.

F.7.b. Self-Growth Experiences

Counselor education programs delineate requirements for self-disclosure or self-growth experiences in their admission and program materials. Counselor educators use professional judgment when designing training experiences they conduct that require student and supervisee selfgrowth or self-disclosure. Students and supervisees are made aware of the ramifications their self-disclosure may have when counselors whose primary role as teacher, trainer, or supervisor requires acting on ethical obligations to the profession. Evaluative components of experiential training experiences explicitly delineate predetermined academic standards that are separate and do not depend on the student's level of selfdisclosure. Counselor educators may require trainees to seek professional help to address any personal concerns that may be affecting their competency.

F.8. Student Responsibilities

F.8.a. Standards for Students

Counselors-in-training have a responsibility to understand and follow the *ACA Code of Ethics* and adhere to applicable laws, regulatory policies, and rules and policies governing professional staff behavior at the agency or placement setting. Students have the same obligation to clients as those required of professional counselors. *(See C.1., H.1.)*

F.8.b. Impairment

Counselors-in-training refrain from offering or providing counseling services when their physical, mental, or emotional problems are likely to harm a client or others. They are alert to the signs of impairment, seek assistance for problems, and notify their program supervisors when they are aware that they are unable to effectively provide services. In addition, they seek appropriate professional services for themselves to remediate the problems that are interfering with their ability to provide services to others. *(See A.1., C.2.d., C.2.g.)*

F.9. Evaluation and Remediation of Students

F.9.a. Evaluation

Counselors clearly state to students, prior to and throughout the training program, the levels of competency expected, appraisal methods, and timing of evaluations for both didactic and clinical competencies. Counselor educators provide students with ongoing performance appraisal and evaluation feedback throughout the training program.

F.9.b. Limitations

Counselor educators, throughout ongoing evaluation and appraisal, are aware of and address the inability of some students to achieve counseling competencies that might impede performance. Counselor educators 1. assist students in securing remedial assistance when needed, 2. seek professional consultation and document their decision to dismiss or refer students for assistance, and 3. ensure that students have recourse in a timely manner to address decisions to require them to seek assistance or to dismiss them and provide students with due process according to institutional policies and procedures. *(See C.2.g.)*

F.9.c. Counseling for Students

If students request counseling or if counseling services are required as part of a remediation process, counselor educators provide acceptable referrals.

F.10. Roles and Relationships Between Counselor

Educators and Students

F.10.a. Sexual or Romantic Relationships

Sexual or romantic interactions or relationships with current students are prohibited.

F.10.b. Sexual Harassment

Counselor educators do not condone or subject students to sexual harassment. *(See C.6.a.)*

F.10.c. Relationships With Former Students

Counselor educators are aware of the power differential in the relationship between faculty and students. Faculty members foster open discussions with former students when considering engaging in a social, sexual, or other intimate relationship. Faculty members discuss with the former student how their former relationship may affect the change in relationship.

F.10.d. Nonprofessional Relationships

Counselor educators avoid nonprofessional or ongoing professional relationships with students in which there is a risk of potential harm to the student or that may compromise the training experience or grades assigned. In addition, counselor educators do not accept any form of professional services, fees, commissions, reimbursement, or remuneration from a site for student or supervisee placement.

F.10.e. Counseling Services

Counselor educators do not serve as counselors to current students unless this is a brief role associated with a training experience.

F.10.f. Potentially Beneficial Relationships

Counselor educators are aware of the power differential in the relationship between faculty and students. If they believe a nonprofessional relationship with a student may be potentially beneficial to the student, they take precautions similar to those taken by counselors when working with clients. Examples of potentially beneficial interactions or relationships include, but are not limited to, attending a formal ceremony; hospital visits; providing support during a stressful event; or mutual membership in a professional association, organization, or community. Counselor educators engage in open discussions with students when they consider entering into relationships with students outside of their roles as teachers and supervisors. They discuss with students the rationale for such interactions, the potential benefits and drawbacks, and the anticipated consequences for the student. Educators clarify the specific nature and limitations of the additional role(s) they will have with the student prior to engaging in a nonprofessional relationship. Nonprofessional relationships with students should be time-limited and initiated with student consent.

F.11. Multicultural/Diversity Competence in Counselor Education and Training Programs

F.11.a. Faculty Diversity
Counselor educators are committed to recruiting and retaining a diverse faculty.

F.11.b. Student Diversity
Counselor educators actively attempt to recruit and retain a diverse student body. Counselor educators demonstrate commitment to multicultural/diversity competence by recognizing and valuing diverse cultures and types of abilities students bring to the training experience. Counselor educators provide appropriate accommodations that enhance and support diverse student well-being and academic performance.

F.11.c. Multicultural/Diversity Competence
Counselor educators actively infuse multicultural/diversity competency in their training and supervision practices. They actively train students to gain awareness, knowledge, and skills in the competencies of multicultural practice. Counselor educators include case examples, role-plays, discussion questions, and other classroom activities that promote and represent various cultural perspectives.

Section G: Research and Publication

Introduction
Counselors who conduct research are encouraged to contribute to the knowledge base of the profession and promote a clearer understanding of the conditions that lead to a healthy and more just society. Counselors support efforts of researchers by participating fully and willingly whenever possible. Counselors minimize bias and respect diversity in designing and implementing research programs.

G.1. Research Responsibilities

G.1.a. Use of Human Research Participants
Counselors plan, design, conduct, and report research in a manner that is consistent with pertinent ethical principles, federal and state laws, host institutional regulations, and scientific standards governing research with human research participants.

G.1.b. Deviation From Standard Practice

Counselors seek consultation and observe stringent safeguards to protect the rights of research participants when a research problem suggests a deviation from standard or acceptable practices.

G.1.c. Independent Researchers

When independent researchers do not have access to an Institutional Review Board (IRB), they should consult with researchers who are familiar with IRB procedures to provide appropriate safeguards.

G.1.d. Precautions to Avoid Injury

Counselors who conduct research with human participants are responsible for the welfare of participants throughout the research process and should take reasonable precautions to avoid causing injurious psychological, emotional, physical, or social effects to participants.

G.1.e. Principal Researcher Responsibility

The ultimate responsibility for ethical research practice lies with the principal researcher. All others involved in the research activities share ethical obligations and responsibility for their own actions.

G.1.f. Minimal Interference

Counselors take reasonable precautions to avoid causing disruptions in the lives of research participants that could be caused by their involvement in research.

G.1.g. Multicultural/Diversity Considerations in Research

When appropriate to research goals, counselors are sensitive to incorporating research procedures that take into account cultural considerations. They seek consultation when appropriate.

G.2. Rights of Research Participants (See A.2, A.7.)

G.2.a. Informed Consent in Research

Individuals have the right to consent to become research participants. In seeking consent, counselors use language that 1. accurately explains the purpose and procedures to be followed, 2. identifies any procedures that are experimental or relatively untried, 3. describes any attendant discomforts and risks, 4. describes any benefits or changes in individuals or organizations that might be reasonably expected, 5. discloses appropriate alternative procedures that would be advantageous for participants, 6. offers to answer any inquiries concerning the procedures, 7. describes any limitations on confidentiality, 8. describes the format and potential target audiences for the dissemination of research findings, and 9. instructs participants that they are free to withdraw their consent and to discontinue participation in the project at any time without penalty.

G.2.b. Deception

Counselors do not conduct research involving deception unless alternative procedures are not feasible and the prospective value of the research justifies the deception. If such deception has the potential to cause physical or emotional harm to research participants, the research is not conducted, regardless of prospective value. When the methodological requirements of a study necessitate concealment or deception, the investigator explains the reasons for this action as soon as possible during the debriefing.

G.2.c. Student/Supervisee Participation

Researchers who involve students or supervisees in research make clear to them that the decision regarding whether or not to participate in research activities does not affect one's academic standing or supervisory relationship. Students or supervisees who choose not to participate in educational research are provided with an appropriate alternative to fulfill their academic or clinical requirements.

G.2.d. Client Participation

Counselors conducting research involving clients make clear in the informed consent process that clients are free to choose whether or not to participate in research activities. Counselors take necessary precautions to protect clients from adverse consequences of declining or withdrawing from participation.

G.2.e. Confidentiality of Information

Information obtained about research participants during the course of an investigation is confidential. When the possibility exists that others may obtain access to such information, ethical research practice requires that the possibility, together with the plans for protecting confidentiality, be explained to participants as a part of the procedure for obtaining informed consent.

G.2.f. Persons Not Capable of Giving Informed Consent

When a person is not capable of giving informed consent, counselors provide an appropriate explanation to, obtain agreement for participation from, and obtain the appropriate consent of a legally authorized person.

G.2.g. Commitments to Participants

Counselors take reasonable measures to honor all commitments to research participants. *(See A.2.c.)*

G.2.h. Explanations After Data Collection

After data are collected, counselors provide participants with full clarification of the nature of the study to remove any misconceptions participants might have regarding the research. Where scientific or human values justify delaying or withholding information, counselors take reasonable measures to avoid causing harm.

G.2.i. Informing Sponsors

Counselors inform sponsors, institutions, and publication channels regarding research procedures and outcomes. Counselors ensure that appropriate bodies and authorities are given pertinent information and acknowledgement.

G.2.j. Disposal of Research Documents and Records

Within a reasonable period of time following the completion of a research project or study, counselors take steps to destroy records or documents (audio, video, digital, and written) containing confidential data or information that identifies research participants. When records are of an artistic nature, researchers obtain participant consent with regard to handling of such records or documents. *(See B.4.a, B.4.g.)*

G.3. Relationships With Research Participants (When Research Involves Intensive or Extended Interactions)

G.3.a. Nonprofessional Relationships

Nonprofessional relationships with research participants should be avoided.

G.3.b. Relationships With Research Participants

Sexual or romantic counselor–research participant interactions or relationships with current research participants are prohibited.

G.3.c. Sexual Harassment and Research Participants

Researchers do not condone or subject research participants to sexual harassment.

G.3.d. Potentially Beneficial Interactions

When a nonprofessional interaction between the researcher and the research participant may be potentially beneficial, the researcher must document, prior to the interaction (when feasible), the rationale for such an interaction, the potential benefit, and anticipated consequences for the research participant. Such interactions should be initiated with appropriate consent of the research participant. Where unintentional harm occurs to the research participant due to the nonprofessional interaction, the researcher must show evidence of an attempt to remedy such harm.

G.4. Reporting Results

G.4.a. Accurate Results

Counselors plan, conduct, and report research accurately. They provide thorough discussions of the limitations of their data and alternative hypotheses. Counselors do not engage in misleading or fraudulent research, distort data, misrepresent data, or deliberately bias their results. They explicitly mention all variables and conditions known to the investigator that may have affected the outcome of a study or the interpretation of data. They describe the extent to which results are applicable for diverse populations.

G.4.b. Obligation to Report Unfavorable Results

Counselors report the results of any research of professional value. Results that reflect unfavorably on institutions, programs, services, prevailing opinions, or vested interests are not withheld.

G.4.c. Reporting Errors

If counselors discover significant errors in their published research, they take reasonable steps to correct such errors in a correction erratum, or through other appropriate publication means.

G.4.d. Identity of Participants

Counselors who supply data, aid in the research of another person, report research results, or make original data available take due care to disguise the identity of respective participants in the absence of specific authorization from the participants to do otherwise. In situations where participants self-identify their involvement in research studies, researchers take active steps to ensure that data is adapted/changed to protect the identity and welfare of all parties and that discussion of results does not cause harm to participants.

G.4.e. Replication Studies

Counselors are obligated to make available sufficient original research data to qualified professionals who may wish to replicate the study.

G.5. Publication

G.5.a. Recognizing Contributions
When conducting and reporting research, counselors are familiar with and give recognition to previous work on the topic, observe copyright laws, and give full credit to those to whom credit is due.

G.5.b. Plagiarism
Counselors do not plagiarize, that is, they do not present another person's work as their own work.

G.5.c. Review/Republication of Data or Ideas
Counselors fully acknowledge and make editorial reviewers aware of prior publication of ideas or data where such ideas or data are submitted for review or publication.

G.5.d. Contributors
Counselors give credit through joint authorship, acknowledgment, footnote statements, or other appropriate means to those who have contributed significantly to research or concept development in accordance with such contributions. The principal contributor is listed first and minor technical or professional contributions are acknowledged in notes or introductory statements.

G.5.e. Agreement of Contributors
Counselors who conduct joint research with colleagues or students/supervisees establish agreements in advance regarding allocation of tasks, publication credit, and types of acknowledgement that will be received.

G.5.f. Student Research
For articles that are substantially based on students course papers, projects, dissertations or theses, and on which students have been the primary contributors, they are listed as principal authors.

G.5.g. Duplicate Submission
Counselors submit manuscripts for consideration to only one journal at a time. Manuscripts that are published in whole or in substantial part in another journal or published work are not submitted for publication without acknowledgment and permission from the previous publication.

G.5.h. Professional Review
Counselors who review material submitted for publication, research, or other scholarly purposes respect the confidentiality and proprietary rights of those who submitted it. Counselors use care to make publication decisions based on valid and defensible standards. Counselors review article submissions in a timely manner and based on their scope and competency in research methodologies. Counselors who serve as reviewers at the request of editors or publishers make every effort to only review materials that are within their scope of competency and use care to avoid personal biases.

Section H: Resolving Ethical Issues

Introduction
Counselors behave in a legal, ethical, and moral manner in the conduct of their professional work. They are aware that client protection and trust in the profession depend on a high level of professional conduct. They hold other counselors to the

same standards and are willing to take appropriate action to ensure that these standards are upheld. Counselors strive to resolve ethical dilemmas with direct and open communication among all parties involved and seek consultation with colleagues and supervisors when necessary. Counselors incorporate ethical practice into their daily professional work. They engage in ongoing professional development regarding current topics in ethical and legal issues in counseling.

H.1. Standards and the Law *(See F.9.a.)*

H.1.a. Knowledge
Counselors understand the *ACA Code of Ethics* and other applicable ethics codes from other professional organizations or from certification and licensure bodies of which they are members. Lack of knowledge or misunderstanding of an ethical responsibility is not a defense against a charge of unethical conduct.

H.1.b. Conflicts Between Ethics and Laws
If ethical responsibilities conflict with law, regulations, or other governing legal authority, counselors make known their commitment to the *ACA Code of Ethics* and take steps to resolve the conflict. If the conflict cannot be resolved by such means, counselors may adhere to the requirements of law, regulations, or other governing legal authority.

H.2. Suspected Violations

H.2.a. Ethical Behavior Expected
Counselors expect colleagues to adhere to the *ACA Code of Ethics*. When counselors possess knowledge that raises doubts as to whether another counselor is acting in an ethical manner, they take appropriate action. *(See H.2.b., H.2.c.)*

H.2.b. Informal Resolution
When counselors have reason to believe that another counselor is violating or has violated an ethical standard, they attempt first to resolve the issue informally with the other counselor if feasible, provided such action does not violate confidentiality rights that may be involved.

H.2.c. Reporting Ethical Violations
If an apparent violation has substantially harmed, or is likely to substantially harm a person or organization and is not appropriate for informal resolution or is not resolved properly, counselors take further action appropriate to the situation. Such action might include referral to state or national committees on professional ethics, voluntary national certification bodies, state licensing boards, or to the appropriate institutional authorities. This standard does not apply when an intervention would violate confidentiality rights or when counselors have been retained to review the work of another counselor whose professional conduct is in question.

H.2.d. Consultation
When uncertain as to whether a particular situation or course of action may be in violation of the *ACA Code of Ethics*, counselors consult with other counselors who are knowledgeable about ethics and the *ACA Code of Ethics*, with colleagues, or with appropriate authorities

H.2.e. Organizational Conflicts

If the demands of an organization with which counselors are affiliated pose a conflict with the *ACA Code of Ethics,* counselors specify the nature of such conflicts and express to their supervisors or other responsible officials their commitment to the *ACA Code of Ethics.* When possible, counselors work toward change within the organization to allow full adherence to the *ACA Code of Ethics.* In doing so, they address any confidentiality issues.

H.2.f. Unwarranted Complaints

Counselors do not initiate, participate in, or encourage the filing of ethics complaints that are made with reckless disregard or willful ignorance of facts that would disprove the allegation.

H.2.g. Unfair Discrimination Against Complainants and Respondents

Counselors do not deny persons employment, advancement, admission to academic or other programs, tenure, or promotion based solely upon their having made or their being the subject of an ethics complaint. This does not preclude taking action based upon the outcome of such proceedings or considering other appropriate information.

H.3. Cooperation With Ethics Committees

Counselors assist in the process of enforcing the *ACA Code of Ethics.* Counselors cooperate with investigations, proceedings, and requirements of the ACA Ethics Committee or ethics committees of other duly constituted associations or boards having jurisdiction over those charged with a violation. Counselors are familiar with the *ACA Policy and Procedures for Processing Complains of Ethical Violations* and use it as a reference for assisting in the enforcement of the *ACA Code of Ethics.*

Glossary of Terms

Advocacy – promotion of the well-being of individuals and groups, and the counseling profession within systems and organizations. Advocacy seeks to remove barriers and obstacles that inhibit access, growth, and development.

Assent – to demonstrate agreement, when a person is otherwise not capable or competent to give formal consent (e.g., informed consent) to a counseling service or plan.

Client – an individual seeking or referred to the professional services of a counselor for help with problem resolution or decision making.

Counselor – a professional (or a student who is a counsel or in-training) engaged in a counseling practice or other counseling-related services. Counselors fulfill many roles and responsibilities such as counselor educators, researchers, supervisors, practitioners, and consultants.

Counselor Educator – a professional counselor engaged primarily in developing, implementing, and supervising the educational preparation of counselors-in-training.

Counselor Supervisor – a professional counselor who engages in a formal relationship with a practicing counselor or counselor-in-training for the purpose of overseeing that individual's counseling work or clinical skill development.

Culture – membership in a socially constructed way of living, which incorporates collective values, beliefs, norms, boundaries, and lifestyles that are cocreated with others who share similar worldviews comprising biological, psychosocial, historical, psychological, and other factors.

Diversity – the similarities and differences that occur within and across cultures, and the intersection of cultural and social identities.

Documents – any written, digital, audio, visual, or artistic recording of the work within the counseling relationship between counselor and client.

Examinee – a recipient of any professional counseling service that includes educational, psychological, and career appraisal utilizing qualitative or quantitative techniques.

Forensic Evaluation – any formal assessment conducted for court or other legal proceedings.

Multicultural/Diversity Competence – a capacity whereby counselors possess cultural and diversity awareness and knowledge about self and others, and how this awareness and knowledge is applied effectively in practice with clients and client groups.

Multicultural/Diversity Counseling – counseling that recognizes diversity and embraces approaches that support the worth, dignity, potential, and uniqueness of individuals within their historical, cultural, economic, political, and psychosocial contexts.

Student – an individual engaged in formal educational preparation as a counselor-in-training.

Supervisee – a professional counselor or counselor-in-training whose counseling work or clinical skill development is being overseen in a formal supervisory relationship by a qualified trained professional.

Supervisor – counselors who are trained to oversee the professional clinical work of counselors and counselors-in-training.

Teaching – all activities engaged in as part of a formal educational program designed to lead to a graduate degree in counseling.

Training – the instruction and practice of skills related to the counseling profession. Training contributes to the ongoing proficiency of students and professional counselors.